HUMAN
SEX-ROLE
BEHAVIOR
(PGPS — 96)

Pergamon Titles of Related Interest

Cook/McHenry SEXUAL ATTRACTION
Cook/Wilson LOVE AND ATTRACTION
Fischer/Gochros HANDBOOK OF BEHAVIOR THERAPY WITH
SEXUAL PROBLEMS
  Volume 1: General Procedures
  Volume 2: Approaches to Specific Problems
Giles/Robinson/Smith SOCIAL PSYCHOLOGY AND LANGUAGE

Related Journals*

BEHAVIORAL ASSESSMENT
BEHAVIOR RESEARCH & THERAPY
CHILD ABUSE & NEGLECT
CHILDREN AND YOUTH SERVICES REVIEW
CLINICAL PSYCHOLOGY REVIEW
INTERNATIONAL JOURNAL OF INTERCULTURAL RELATIONS
JOURNAL OF CHILD PSYCHOLOGY & PSYCHIATRY & ALLIED
DISCIPLINES
JOURNAL OF PSYCHIATRIC TREATMENT & EVALUATION
PERSONALITY AND INDIVIDUAL DIFFERENCES

*Free specimen copies available upon request.

HUMAN SEX-ROLE BEHAVIOR

Alfred B. Heilbrun, Jr.

Emory University

Pergamon Press

New York   Oxford   Toronto   Sydney   Paris   Frankfurt

Pergamon Press Offices:

U.S.A.   Pergamon Press Inc., Maxwell House, Fairview Park,
                Elmsford, New York 10523, U.S.A.

U.K.   Pergamon Press Ltd., Headington Hill Hall,
                Oxford OX3 0BW, England

CANADA   Pergamon Press Canada Ltd., Suite 104, 150 Consumers Road,
                Willowdale, Ontario M2J 1P9, Canada

AUSTRALIA   Pergamon Press (Aust.) Pty. Ltd., P.O. Box 544,
                Potts Point, NSW 2011, Australia

FRANCE   Pergamon Press SARL, 24 rue des Ecoles,
                75240 Paris, Cedex 05, France

FEDERAL REPUBLIC   Pergamon Press GmbH, Hammerweg 6, Postfach 1305,
OF GERMANY   6242 Kronberg/Taunus, Federal Republic of Germany

Library of Congress Cataloging in Publication Data

Heilbrun, Alfred B   1924-
    Human sex-role behavior.

(Pergamon general psychology series ; v. 96)
    Includes bibliographical references.
    1. Sex role. 2. Androgyny (Psychology)
I. Title.
BF692.2.H44   305.3   80-26415
ISBN 0-08-025974-X

Printed in the United States of America

To Marian and our children
Kirk, Lynn, Kim, Leigh, and Mark.

Contents

Preface ix

Chapter

1. The Definition of Sex-Role Behavior   1

2. Myth and Misconception about Sex-Role Behavior 19

3. Measurement of Sex-Role Behavior 38

4. An Empirical Context for Androgyny 64

5. Sex Roles and Personal Competence 86

6. Lifestyle and Cultural Differences in Sex-Role Behavior 114

7. Parent Identification and Sex-Role Behavior of the Child 132

8. Some Reflections on Future Research and Social Applications . . . 167

Appendices 197

Author Index 203

Subject Index 205

About the Author 207

Preface

Few topics of concern to the social scientist present more obstacles to investigation than does human sex-role behavior. We are faced with a situation in which the object of study is difficult to define and even more difficult to effectively reduce to measurement. In themselves these are not unusual challenges for those who investigate the complex social behavior of humans. The most ominous barrier to scientific understanding comes from the involvement of the scientist in the subject matter. Contemporary issues involving women's rights and, to a lesser extent, the rights of men to assume nonstereotypic social roles have aroused broad concern, amid the ranks of social scientists as well as among most other groups.

This combination—an often vague subject matter, imprecise methodology, and issues that touch the value system of the scientist—opens the way for bias that may show up at any stage of the scientific inquiry. The way that one conceptualizes human sex roles, the more specific way they are defined for purposes of study, the procedures used for sex-role measurement, the problem chosen for investigation, the research methodology employed, and the conclusions drawn from the data are all vulnerable to the seepage of values. The extent to which this may have influenced the contributions of social scientists up to this point is impossible to say. This book does not presume to be an exposé of subjective bias in the sex-role literature, since I do not wish to discredit anyone on this score. Indeed, I have been exposed to the same temptations as others, and who knows at what point my own values have been interjected into my research? Forewarned is forearmed: the writing of this book will proceed with the temptations of bias clearly in mind and with its effects minimized or, at least, acknowledged.

There are other ramifications of the current social significance assumed by sex roles. I believe, for example, that strong feelings, pro and con, associated with female and male ''liberation'' have encouraged misconception about sex-role behavior. Objective examination of these popular but misleading assumptions should emphasize the danger of premature conclusions that deter progress at the interface of social science and contemporary society.

This book will not be a comprehensive sourcebook that attempts to review all sex-role research and theory reported in our scientific journals or previously published books. Grambs and Waetjen* estimate that 10,000 research studies bearing on some aspect of sex and sex roles had already appeared in the 1970s by the time the decade reached its halfway mark. By necessity and probably by predilection, I will place major emphasis in this book on my own ideas, measures, and research. Much of my work has been around for several years; some represents recent reanalyses made in the wake of the belated recognition that male and female sex-role behaviors are not mutually exclusive. Still other work reported in this book represents new data generated in order to answer the questions that arose during its writing.

Finally, because I am a clinical psychologist my interests gravitate naturally toward the deviant, ineffective behaviors that mark the maladjusted and the mentally ill in our society. Consistent with those interests, this book will consider the contribution of sex-role failures to human distress. So as not to create a one-sided picture, however, the contribution of sex-role behavior to successful social adaptation also will be examined. In either case, the premise will be a unique one. I assume that no matter what the sex-role outcome of the individual may be, there is a potential for successful or unsuccessful adaptation. This premise, considered at greater length later in the book, led me to consider both the personal problems associated with each type of sex-role outcome and the strengths that may reside in each. If we are going to socially redesign human sex roles, as many would have us do, we might as well be as informed as possible. A catalogue of the assets and liabilities for all sex-role patterns should be helpful even though it can be only sketchy in its details. Even Sears, Roebuck and Company had to start someplace.

*Grambs, J. D., & Waetjen, W. B. *Sex: Does it make a difference?* Belmont, Calif.: Duxbury, 1975.

Chapter 1

The Definition of Sex-Role Behavior

The organization of human social behaviors within an interdependent society must include the assignment of roles that help prescribe the behaviors to be expected of each member. When role markers are clear so that the individual knows what roles are to be assumed and so that behaviors constituting the roles are reasonably well understood, both the individual and society stand to gain. Individuals achieve a clearer idea regarding what is expected of them across a variety of situations, and fulfilling these role demands allows us to avoid the distressing prospect of a continuous stream of decisions throughout our waking day. Society stands to gain by the structure that roles provide for engineering a more effective social system. Roles can be created to complement each other and, thereby, to create mutually satisfying relationships; the parent and child roles are important examples. Other roles allow a society to regulate its continuity. The husband and wife roles created by marriage help to maintain the proper flow of progeny. Sometimes special demands of the society emerge that place a premium upon yet other roles, such as the role of the warrior (soldier) during periods of warfare.

Unfortunately, the role system does not always work. The markers that denote who should assume the adult role and who the child role are blurred for many adolescents and their parents. Neither clearly a child nor an adult, many adolescents can no longer comfortably rely upon child behaviors, nor are they allowed to assume behaviors consistent with being an adult, even if they are capable of doing so.

Sex roles seem to have eroded in effectiveness, in part because a segment of society has challenged the authenticity, legality, and morality of assuming behavioral differences between men and women. Just how much the status of sex roles has been influenced in our society by the feminist movement and other instruments of social change is uncertain, although that question will not be ignored in this book.

This chapter will lay the groundwork for subsequent discussion of sex-role

1

behavior by specifying what is meant by this term and what meaning is not intended. In doing this, I hope to make my job simpler, since the proliferation of similar-sounding terms and careless application of rather straightforward concepts have made communication among social researchers and between the scientific community and the public a sometime thing. Definition will proceed not only on a conceptual level but will include the operations by which the sex roles have been measured in my research.

A DEFINITION OF SEX-ROLE BEHAVIOR

Understanding the meaning of the term *sex-role behavior* as it is to be used in this book requires two levels of definition.

First, *sex role* would be formally defined as those behaviors commonly understood to characterize a person of a given biological sex within a particular society plus those behaviors that appear as correlates of these stereotyped characteristics. Stereotyped and correlated behaviors commonly associated with being a biological male are sex-typed as *masculine;* female-related behaviors are termed *feminine.*

The distinction between stereotyped and correlated behaviors within sex roles is not commonly drawn, yet I believe it to be a meaningful one. For example, later in this chapter we shall see that a list of masculine behaviors will include "cynical" and "vindictive." It is my contention that these behaviors, empirically confirmed as male characteristics, are not part of the primary masculine stereotype passed from one generation to the next but are behaviors made more probable in males because of the masculine stereotyped behaviors that are generationally transmitted (such as aggression). It is difficult for me to picture a father deliberately teaching his son to be cynical or vindictive, but aggressiveness is another matter.

The distinction between stereotyped and correlated sex-typed behaviors is no less important for females. Some of the behaviors that will appear on our femininity list have a neurotic ring to them—"emotional," "excitable," "fearful," "worrying." Is this to be taken to mean that in the rearing of girls, we set out to teach them to be emotionally labile and worrisome? Certainly not, but in the socialization of other stereotyped feminine characteristics, we inadvertently increase the likelihood that these correlates will appear in the behavior of females.

If the distinction between stereotyped and correlated sex-role components is to be a viable one, it should be possible to specify which is which by some clear criterion. The second level of definition required to understand the sex-role behavior of males and females, which specifies orientation, fits this purpose. Parsons and Bales (1955) distinguished between the instrumental qualities of masculinity and the expressive qualities of femininity by the motivation of the instrumental person to pursue goals that transcend the immediate interpersonal situation, to use the interaction as a means to an end, and by his insensitivity to the emotional responses engendered in others by his behavior. An expressive orientation directs the person's concern to the immediate interpersonal situation and to how others are reacting to her and to one another.

The masculine sex role, then, includes those behaviors commonly expected of males, which sustain a goal orientation and reflect interpersonal insensitivity. Femininity refers to behaviors stereotypically expected of females and oriented toward the mutually rewarding qualities of interpersonal relationships. Correlated sex-role behaviors should be the spin-offs of these orientations. We shall examine this assumption further in the next section.

REFINEMENT OF THE SEX-ROLE CONCEPT

Having made an effort to specify what sex-role behavior is, let us now consider some uses of the term that tend to muddy its meaning. One source of confusion can be found in the current controversies involving the issue of women's rights. The emphasis on the generally unfavorable position of women relative to men in most societies is often translated to mean that the "woman's role" is less desirable than the "man's role." This does not accurately convey what the feminist concern is really about. Consider the fact that there are a number of things that distinguish between men and women in our society beyond their biological makeup. We have described two of these discriminanda already as (1) those behaviors stereotypically assigned to foster male instrumentalness and female expressiveness, and (2) those correlated behaviors made more probable by the appearance of these stereotypic behaviors. Both types of behaviors comprise masculine and feminine sex roles as they are defined in this book.

In addition, men and women in a given society usually can be distinguished by the functions or activities normally associated with their gender. Here we refer to such functional divisions as which sex is expected to work on a job outside the home, which to maintain domestic responsibilities in the home, which sex is assigned major responsibilities for child rearing, which the more aggressive aspects of military service. None of these activities refers to behavior as such with any degree of specificity. A man can work by caring for a yard, running a football, flying an airplane, or writing a poem. A woman is assuming the child-rearing function whether she is feeding or bathing her baby, spanking her child, or sharing confidences with her teenage daughter. Whatever current attitudes may be regarding the functional roles of men and women in our society, these attitudes only bear indirectly upon human sex-role behavior, upon masculinity and femininity.

There are also a number of practices that people engage in solely in response to the sex gender of another person, and these too are often mistakenly equated with roles played by men and women. Features of etiquette come to mind; men traditionally are expected to open doors for women, and women, to allow men this opportunity. If one chooses to include door-opening as part of the masculine role, nothing is lost (or gained) by it. A more serious example of sex-gender correlates is job discrimination against women, as when employers pay less salary to and restrict promotions of female employees. Yet whatever injustices have been perpetrated upon women in the past, these grievances do not fit into any meaningful definition of *sex role,* either for the perpetrator or for the victim.

A GLOSSARY OF SIMILAR WORDS

Part of the job of defining *sex-role behavior* is to distinguish the term from others that have similar or related meanings and, unfortunately, have been used interchangeably to some extent in the literature. The glossary presented in table 1.1 may help the reader keep these terms straight, at least within the confines of this book.

Table 1.1. Glossary of Terms

Sex Gender	The biological sex of the individual—male versus female.
Sex role	The psychological sex of the individual—masculine and/or feminine.
Sex-gender identity	The simple discrimination of oneself as a biological male or female.
Sex-role identity	The cognitive representation of one's own sex-typed behavior and functions, often (but not always) culminating in a global judgment of "masculine" or "feminine."
Sex-role stereotype	One's belief about the behaviors and functions characteristic of men and women in a given society, or the consensual belief of that society.
Sex-role behaviors	Manifest behaviors of the individual corresponding to societal stereotypes for men and women or the correlates of these stereotypes.
Sex-role functions	Functional responsibilities within a society distinguishing men from women.
Sex-gender preference	The higher value judgment placed by the individual upon one biological sex on the other.
Sex-role preference	The higher value judgment placed by the individual upon stereotyped/correlated behaviors for one sex or the other.
Sex-gender identification	Vicarious experiencing of reinforcements imposed upon members of the preferred sex gender.
Sex-role correlates	Behaviors that are contingent upon stereotyped behaviors and, therefore, are differentially characteristic of the two sexes.
Sex-gender correlates	Behaviors of other people contingent upon the biological sex of the individual.

This glossary of terms is not as formidable as might first appear. The important things to glean from the list for the time being are really quite few. For one, the term *sex role* encompasses both specific stereotyped and correlated behaviors and broader stereotyped functions, and much confusion can be avoided if it is remembered that a person can accommodate one aspect of a given sex role and not the other. A lot of men with very masculine behavior are terrible fathers!

Another point I would like to emphasize about these terms is that they are more products of common sense than derivatives of rigorous empirical investigation. I look at sex roles this way: the socialization process teaches most of us that stereotypes exist regulating the behavior of males and females, but we accommodate to these expectations to a variable extent, leading to differences in sex-role behavior. We are to some degree aware of our sex-role behaviors, and these cognitive representations provide us a sex-role identity. This identity may be more or less to our liking, so our sex-role preference could be to exchange our identity, relinquish aspects of that identity, or stand pat. Sex-role stereotype, behavior, identity, and preference, taken together, offer a sensible order to this aspect of social role development.

AN OPERATIONAL DEFINITION OF SEX-ROLE BEHAVIOR

The most practical way to explain how this book defines sex roles is to describe in some detail the procedures by which these roles have been defined in my research. Since the material presented here depends to an important extent on findings from studies conducted in my own laboratory, it is crucial that the instrument used to measure sex-role behaviors in this research correspond to the theoretical concept that I have advocated, as well as demonstrate evidence of validity.

The basic instrument used in my laboratory for measuring sex-role status has been the Adjective Check List (ACL) (Gough & Heilbrun, 1965). The ACL poses a deceptively simple task. It includes 300 commonly used behavioral adjectives, originally collected by Gough (1952), and asks the test-taker to select those that are self-characteristic. No time limit for the task is imposed, and the person is free to check as many or as few of these adjectives as desired. The obvious advantages of this psychometric procedure are its ease of administration and the flexible use that can be made of the self-descriptions provided by the test-taker. Ten minutes of time is usually all that is necessary to gain the person's self-description. The ACL is a flexible instrument in that it can be used to identify individual adjectives that characterize particular types of people or things; or responses to the ACL can be scored on scales, a priori clusters of adjectives that measure designated personality variables.

It was stated that the ACL is a deceptively simple instrument. Its effectiveness for research (a bibliography of well over 500 published studies involving its use now exists) may well derive from the fact that the ACL allows the individual to use the natural language of self-evaluation. When we examine our own behavior in day-to-day situations, we very likely will apply adjectival labels to express our judgments. We might consider a past action "intelligent," "careless," or "kind," or anticipate that we better be "cooperative," "tactful," or "honest" in some forthcoming situation. Given our extensive experience in assigning adjectival meanings to our own behavior in day-to-day functioning, a task like the ACL should offer no real obstacles to self-evaluation. Other objective personality assessment techniques, such as true-false, multiple choice, or rating scale approaches, require the person to adopt a less natural approach to self-evaluation and may lose some of their effectiveness as a result.

As we shall see when other objective methods of measuring human sex-role behaviors are considered in Chapter Three, the usual approach to developing sex-role scales is to identify a set of items that elicit somewhat different responses from males and females. The content of the items may vary considerably and may or may not bear relevance to sex-role behavior. Our own approach included a comparison of the responses of college males and females to the ACL, but added one more step. The males who were used had made a primary identification with masculine, instrumental fathers, whereas the girls had made a primary identification with feminine, expressive mothers. The rationale for this added requirement was that we wished to identify the ACL adjectives that distinguished between biological males who were psychologically masculine and biological females who were psychologically feminine. This seemed to offer a more refined procedure for identifying potential sex-role scale items than one that included feminine males and masculine females as sources of error in the comparion of responses, or included behaviors with no apparent relevance to the sex roles.

Conceptual Analysis of the ACL Sex-Role Scales. There are various ways to look at the validity of sex-role scales constructed for the ACL. First, let us examine the actual self-descriptive items that statistical analysis identified as distinguishing masculine males from feminine females. Table 1.2 includes the 53 adjectives that comprise the Masculinity Scale (28 items) and Feminity Scale (25 items); the latter category of behaviors obviously represents those behaviors more characteristic of feminine females.

How well do these scale items satisfy the instrumental and expressive meanings of masculinity and femininity that have been proposed as critical to understanding sex roles? In my opinion at least, the fit between concept and item meaning is impressive. Masculinity as instrumental behavior requires that the person maintain a goal orientation that transcends the immediate interpersonal

Table 1.2. Behaviors Endorsed as Self-Characteristic by Masculine Males and by Feminine Females

Masculinity Scale		Femininity Scale	
Behavior	Sex-Role Rating	Behavior	Sex-Role Rating
aggressive	761	appreciative	317
arrogant	575	considerate	381
assertive	678	contended	428
autocratic	626	cooperative	412
conceited	541	dependent	357
confident	683	emotional	254
cynical	558	excitable	333
deliberate	563	fearful	409
dominant	736	feminine	192
enterprising	645	fickle	344
forceful	723	forgiving	382
foresighted	538	friendly	423
frank	624	frivolous	339
handsome	642	helpful	439
hard-headed	567	modest	411
industrious	605	praising	395
ingenious	527	sensitive	326
inventive	591	sentimental	241
masculine	790	sincere	403
opportunistic	650	submissive	343
outspoken	600	sympathetic	299
self-confident	614	talkative	307
sharp-witted	552	timid	403
shrewd	522	warm	341
stern	622	worrying	428
strong	707		
tough	649		
vindictive	503		

NOTE: Ratings (after Williams & Best, 1977) above 500 represent masculine stereotypes, and below 500 represent feminine stereotypes.

situation, use the interaction as a means to an end, and remain insensitive to the emotional responses his behavior engenders in others. I would expect the instrumental person to be aggressive, arrogant, assertive, autocratic, conceited, confident, cool, cruel, deliberate, dominant, egotistical, enterprising, forceful, foresighted, frank, hardheaded, individualistic, industrious, opportunistic, outspoken, self-confident, sharp-witted, shrewd, strong, and tough. That takes care of the major share of items on the Masculinity Scale.

Expressiveness as the essence of femininity orients the person's concern toward the immediate interpersonal situation and to how people are reacting toward her or toward one another. A substantial number of Femininity Scale items relate to interpersonal sensitivity and the quest for tranquil and rewarding personal relations—appreciative, considerate, contented, cooperative, dependent, emotional, excitable, forgiving, friendly, helpful, praising, sensitive, sentimental, sincere, submissive, sympathetic, talkative, and warm. While there might be debate over an occasional item here and there on either scale, it does seem clear that the Femininity Scale deals largely with behaviors that mediate an expressive orientation and that the Masculinity Scale is made up of instrumental behaviors.

Correspondence of ACL Sex-Role Scales to Stereotype. Another way to examine the validity of the ACL sex-role scales is to compare their behavioral items with the sex-role stereotypes held by comparable people. The work of Williams and Best (1977) at Wake Forest allows us this opportunity. They have derived sex-stereotype index scores for all ACL adjectives based upon the combined ratings of male and female college students who were asked to identify which were more characteristic of men and which of women in our society. Their standard scoring technique assigns scores above 500 when the stereotype is masculine and below 500 when it is feminine. The more deviant the score from 500 in either direction, the greater the masculine or feminine stereotype loading. The Williams and Best stereotype scores for the items on the Masculinity and Femininity Scales are reported on table 1.2. As can be seen, there is perfect agreement between the categorization of scale items and masculine and feminine stereotype scores. (One item, "jolly," was deleted as a feminine item from the original scale when it was discovered that it had received a masculine-stereotyped score of 580 in the Williams and Best system and also was classified as masculine by stereotyping procedures coming out of Janet Spence's laboratories at the University of Texas [personal communication].)

We will have occasion in the next chapter to refer to the sex-role scores of older general population samples of subjects rather than young adults attending college. Accordingly, the fit between our designation of behaviors as masculine or feminine and the sex stereotypes of middle-aged individuals becomes relevant. Zimet and Zimet (1977) obtained sex stereotype ratings for all ACL adjectives from a large sample of white educators, with the average age for both males and females ranging between 42 and 44 years. They required a criterion of 70 percent agreement for judges of both sexes before a behavior would be designated as either masculine or feminine. About 86 percent of the items on the Masculinity Scale achieved this criterion, as did 81 percent of the Femininity Scale items. We can conclude from this that the ACL scales measure sex-role behaviors that conform to not only the stereotypes of young college adults but, less perfectly, to middle-aged stereotypes as well.

To what extent do sex-role stereotypes obtained from college students and from middle-aged educators agree? If we demand of the Williams and Best stereotyping scores a loading that falls at least a half standard deviation in the appropriate direction from the mean as a criterion of masculine (550) and feminine (450), 189 of the ACL items can be assigned to one stereotype or the other. This is very close to the 191 ACL items that achieve a similar stereotyping criterion within the study conducted by the Zimets. There was 80 percent agreement between the stereotype lists provided by Williams and Best and by the Zimets. This can be compared to the 91 percent of the items on the ACL sex-role scales that find representation among the sex-role stereotypes of college students using this more rigorous criterion. Compared in this way, there is better agreement between stereotype and ACL sex-role behavior within college samples than there is agreement on sex-role stereotypes between young and middle-aged adults.

Correspondence of Heilbrun's ACL Sex-Role Scales to Other Similarly Derived Scales. There have been at least three independent efforts to identify sex-differentiated items on the ACL that have depended upon the comparison of the response rates of males and females to an important extent. My approach, already described, compared masculine college males and feminine college females in a type of extreme group analysis. Parker (1969) used over 5,000 college students in his comparison of male and female self-descriptions on the ACL, but allowed masculinity and femininity to vary within the male and female groups. Recently, Gough (personal communication) has derived sets of masculine and feminine adjectives using the same procedure as Parker. His comparisons included close to 10,000 records of males and females (including college students). He also eliminated items from his scales that are less frequently checked by either sex even though they were endorsed to different degrees by females and males.

Although each of these three approaches to constructing sex-role scales from ACL items differed to a degree from the others, some convergence of critical items should be expected, and was found. However, scale differences also were apparent, leaving the question of relative validity an open one. Since I am unaware of any published validity data for the Parker and Gough scales, we shall make the best of what is available. We shall consider how well the three sets of masculine and feminine items generated by these different investigators correspond to the sex-role stereotypes held by other college students, since this offers a way of judging their relative usefulness. The basis for evaluating item agreement among the scales and correspondence to stereotype is found in table 1.3, in which all male /female discriminating items and the Williams and Best stereotype scores are represented.

There are several interesting things to be noted in table 1.3. For one thing, the number of terms that all three investigations designated as masculine or feminine was quite restricted; about 13 percent of all items achieved that high level of concordance. Even when the level of agreement is between but two of the three empirical studies, the figure reaches only about 37 percent. Some of this restricted agreement may be explained in terms of the very large number of items identified as sex-typed by the Parker study, 133 to be exact, and the more conservative numbers culminating from the Gough ($N = 46$) and Heilbrun ($N = 53$) studies. This inevitably restricts the amount of agreement that is possible. However, this explanation goes only so far, since there is not that much more agreement between the conservative Gough and Heilbrun scale items. Only 50 percent of Gough's 20 masculine items appear on Heilbrun's scale, and this agreement figure dwindles to 35 percent for feminine items.

Table 1.3. ACL Items Differentially Endorsed by Males and Females in Three Studies

Males More	Study			Stereo-type Score	Females More	Study			Stereo-type Score
aggressive		H	P	761	affectionate	G		P	270
ambitious	G			702	appreciative	G	H	P	371
argumentative	G		P	553	artistic			P	346
arrogant		H	P	575	attractive	G		P	308
assertive		H		678	bossy			P	498
autocratic		H	P	626	changeable			P	360
calm	G			517	charming			P	373
clear-thinking	G		P	623	cheerful	G		P	343
clever	G		P	506	complicated			P	446
coarse			P	642	confused			P	394
conceited		H		541	coscientious			P	409
confident	G	H	P	683	considerate		H	P	381
cool			P	601	contented		H	P	428
cynical		H		558	conventional			P	530
deliberate	G	H	P	563	cooperative		H	P	412
dissatisfied			P	498	cowardly			P	491
dominant		H		736	dependent		H	P	357
egotistical			P	671	disorderly			P	593
enterprising	G	H	P	645	dreamy			P	322
forceful	G	H	P	723	effeminate			P	397
foresighted	G	H	P	538	efficient	G			460
frank		H		624	emotional	G	H	P	254
handsome		H	P	642	enthusiastic	G		P	429
hard-headed		H		567	excitable		H	P	333
indifferent			P	581	fearful		H	P	409
industrious		H		605	feminine	G	H	P	192
ingenious	G	H	P	527	fickle		H	P	344
inventive	G	H	P	591	flirtatious			P	308
logical	G			661	foolish			P	448

Table 1.3 continued

Males More	Study			Stereo-type Score	Females More	Study			Stereo-type Score
masculine	G	H	P	790	forgiving		H	P	382
opportunistic		H	P	650	friendly		H		423
outspoken		H		600	frivolous		H	P	339
pleasure-seeking			P	608	generous	G		P	466
precise	G			552	gentle			P	312
progressive	G		P	603	headstrong			P	599
rational	G			654	helpful	G	H	P	439
resourceful			P	533	high-strung			P	379
rigid			P	535	hurried			P	446
robust			P	606	idealistic			P	450
self-confident	G	H	P	614	immature			P	487
sharp-witted	G	H	P	552	impulsive			P	392
show-off			P	617	informal			P	576
shrewd		H	P	522	inhibited			P	436
sly			P	523	kind	G		P	374
steady	G			584	loyal	G		P	464
stern		H	P	622	mannerly			P	437
stolid			P	572	meek			P	369
strong		H	P	707	mischievous			P	596
tough		H	P	649	modest		H	P	411
unemotional			P	623	moody			P	407
unexcitable			P	599	nagging			P	348
vindictive		H	P	503	natural	G		P	536
wise			P	584	nervous			P	408
					noisy			P	568
					optimistic			P	447
					outgoing	G		P	543
					patient			P	393
					planful			P	508
					pleasant	G		P	349
					poised			P	356
					praising		H	P	395
					prudish			P	375
					rattlebrained			P	404
					responsible	G		P	508
					selfish			P	556
					sensitive	G	H	P	326
					sentimental	G	H	P	241
					simple			P	466
					sincere	G	H	P	403
					snobbish			P	428
					soft-hearted	G		P	303
					spontaneous	G		P	466

Table 1.3 continued

Males More	Study	Stereo-type Score	Females More	Study			Stereo-type Score
			spunky			P	383
			stubborn			P	599
			submissive		H	P	343
			superstitious			P	425
			sympathetic	G	H	P	299
			talkative		H	P	307
			temperamental			P	416
			tense			P	510
			thoughtful	G		P	419
			timid		H	P	403
			tolerant			P	446
			touchy			P	456
			trusting	G		P	409
			unaffected			P	513
			unassuming			P	476
			understanding	G		P	387
			unrealistic			P	446
			warm	G	H	P	341
			whiny			P	395
			wholesome			P	465
			worrying		H	P	428
			zany			P	455

NOTE: G = Gough, H = Heilbrun, P = Parker. Stereotype score ratings over 500 represent masculine stereotypes, and below 500 represent feminine stereotypes.

There are many possible reasons for the sampling differences in sex-differentiated behaviors on the ACL—diverse methodologies, regional differences in subjects, time differences between studies, and so on. Be that as it may, the important thing for present purposes is to make it clear why the Heilbrun ACL scales, rather than the available alternatives, should be the primary measure of sex-role behavior on which this book depends. One case for this—aside from commitment to my own creation—is found in the greater consistency between scale behaviors and sex-role stereotypes for the Heilbrun items.

The average Williams and Best stereotype values, given in table 1.4, suggest that the Heilbrun sex-role scale items are more in keeping with the concept of masculinity and femininity held by young adults than either the Gough or Parker data. The greater the difference in the mean stereotype score for masculine and feminine items, the more consistent the scales are with sex-role stereotypes. This difference was 265 for the Heilbrun scales, fell to 197 for the Gough scales, and for the Parker scales was only 171.

Table 1.4. Average Stereotype Score

	Masculine Items	Feminine Items
Gough	576	379
Heilbrun	621	356
Parker	583	412

One further comment about stereotyping and the makeup of items on the Heilbrun sex-role scales is in order before continuing, simply because as the central measure discussed in this book they require close scrutiny. These scales included nine items that were not represented among those identified by Parker and Gough. The reader might legitimately question whether these represent questionable choices for the Heilbrun scales. Looking at the stereotype scores for just these items, we find that the eight behaviors that were more characteristic of males only in our scale derivation (assertive, conceited, cynical, dominant, frank, hard-headed, industrious, and outspoken) had an average stereotype score of 614. These are quite masculine items. ''Friendly,'' the ninth item, appears only on our Femininity Scale and has an appropriate stereotype score of 423. Therefore these unshared items are not a matter for concern.

Relations of Heilbrun's ACL Sex-Role Scales to Validity Criteria. The most demanding standard of effectiveness for any psychological test is its ability to predict events that hold some specifiable relation with what the test is presumed to measure. This validational process is hard to accomplish, because there are so few uncontestable criteria available for measures of sex-role behavior. In the case of the ACL Masculinity and Femininity Scales, enough validational evidence has accrued over the past sixteen years to gain the scales some degree of respectability, a second case for their selection as the sex-role measures of choice.

Prior to 1976, validating studies employed the two sex-role scales as a single bipolar scale, subtracting the number of feminine items checked as self-descriptive from the number of masculine items checked. From 1976 on, the two scales were normed separately and recommendations for independent scoring of the Masculinity and the Femininity Scales were made (Heilbrun, 1976). Validity evidence exists based on both methods of using the scales.

For example, Cosentino and Heilbrun (1964) considered the relation between aggression anxiety, a feminine sex-typed trait (Sears, 1961), and scores on the Masculinity-Femininity Scale for college subjects. Significant correlations were found independently for males and females, indicating that more masculine subjects of either sex reported less anxiety over the expression of aggression, as scale validity would require.

Another credible expectation for a measure of sex-role behavior is that it discriminate between heterosexual and homosexual adults. Chang and Block (1960) empirically documented that homosexual males were less masculine and more feminine than heterosexual males; the opposite pattern was found when female homosexuals and heterosexuals were compared. A study of homosexual and heterosexual adults by Thompson, Schwartz, McCandless, and Edwards (1973) confirmed that female homosexuals were more masculine than their heterosexual counterparts and that male homosexuals were more feminine than male heterosexuals. Sex-role status was based on bipolar ACL Masculinity-Femininity Scale sources in the latter study. The Thompson data were subsequently reanalyzed (Heilbrun, 1976) using the separate sex-role scales, with predictable results: heterosexual males were more masculine than homosexual males and differed in degree of femininity in that there were fewer heterosexuals than homosexuals with extremely high Femininity Scale scores. The picture for females was even more striking as far as confirming high masculinity and low femininity within the homosexual group. Evans (1971) has also reported lower masculinity scores on the bipolar ACL scale for homosexual males when compared with heterosexual controls.

Another expectation allowing for scale validation is that there should be a relationship between female sex-role status and female attitudes regarding the woman's role in our society; masculinity should coincide with liberal views, femininity with traditional views (Spence, Helmreich, & Stapp, 1975). The responses of college females to a questionnaire tapping traditional versus liberal attitudes (Fand, 1955) were analyzed in terms of the masculinity and femininity of the respondent (Heilbrun, 1976). As predicted, masculinity in females, as gauged by the ACL Masculinity Scale, was associated with more liberal attitudes. However, degree of femininity made no difference. Earlier examination of the relation between ACL sex-role scores and woman's role attitudes, using the combined Masculinity-Femininity Scale and the Fand questionnaire, presented even clearer evidence of sex-role scale validity (Heilbrun, 1973). Extremes of masculinity and femininity were linked to extremes of liberal and traditional attitudes, respectively, and sex-role scores falling in between coincided with intermediate views. It was not only the case that the ACL predicted liberal and conservative attitudes at the extreme of masculinity *and* femininity, but this was true for both female and male college students.

Career interest development is a behavior that is crucial to the adult male role. Historically, adult males have borne responsibility for achieving a vocation, whether they are married or not. Mature career interests can be thought of as part of an instrumental orientation for the male (or female) within the world of work, as the basis for effective striving toward vocational achievement. Accordingly, the *development* of career interests should bear a positive relation to masculinity in males. Heilbrun (1969) separated college males into more masculine and more feminine groups, based upon the ACL Masculinity-Femininity Scale, and compared the level of maturity of their occupational interests using the Strong Vocational Interest Blank (1959). Masculine males had significantly more career interests than feminine males.

The types of social interaction found to characterize people defined as masculine or feminine on a sex-role scale have obvious relevance to scale validity, since the instrumental and expressive orientations imply distinct styles of social transaction. Wiggins and Holzmuller (1978) reported significant and substantial correlations between several interpersonal scale scores and the separate ACL sex-role scales. Higher scores on the Masculinity Scale indicated interpersonal behaviors categorized as "dominant-ambitious," "arrogant-calculating," and "cold-quarrelsome," and contraindicated "lazy-submissive" and "unassuming-ingenuous." These rather comfortably fit with the social behaviors that might be expected of an instrumental person. Femininity Scale elevations were associated with expressive qualities including "warm-agreeable" and "gregarious-extroverted" dispositions and the absence of "cold-quarrelsome" tendencies. Their findings were based upon combined groups of male and female college subjects.

An earlier investigation by Heilbrun (1968) also provided validity evidence for the measurement of instrumental qualities by the ACL Masculinity-Femininity Scale. The behavior of college females within discussion groups was rated by other group members for instrumental and expressive qualities following several hours of interaction. Girls scoring in the masculine direction were rated by their peers as more instrumental in their conduct within the group than their more feminine counterparts. Interestingly, masculine and feminine females were equally high in expressiveness, an apparent reflection of the androgynous nature of many masculine college women. This gave me the opportunity to anticipate the "discovery" of androgyny by several years, but, unfortunately, I lack even a fundamental grasp of basic Greek.

The ability to assume an analytic (field-independent) approach to problem solution, as opposed to a global (field-dependent) approach, has been frequently reported in the research literature as more characteristic of males than females, especially in the young-adult age range (Bruner, 1977). Field independence, when it does occur in the female, was proposed by Kagan and Kogan (1970) to be linked to a masculine sex-role development. Bruner's (1977) investigation of field dependence-independence in college students failed to find the expected sex difference on this variable, but she did establish a significant positive relation between ACL Masculinity Scale scores and field independence in her female subjects, as the Kagan and Kogan theory would require.

The final bit of data relating to the validity of the ACL sex-role scales has been reserved for last because it seems to punctuate the whole endeavor to measure sex-role behaviors. Kelly, Furman, and Young (1978) selected four current measures of sex-role behavior, each offering independent scales of masculinity and femininity. The common procedure of assigning all subjects (65 males and 65 females) to one of the four sex roles by using a median split of both scales was applied to each sex-role questionnaire. The researchers' interest was in the degree of agreement in assignment to categories among the four popular measures. I took the liberty of abstracting the most general statistic available from their data to report here—the average percentage of agreement between each questionnaire and the remaining three after correction for chance. The results were as follows:

Adjective Check List versus other three:	41.4 percent
Bem Sex-Role Inventory versus other three:	40.0 percent
Personality Research Form ANDRO versus other three:	39.4 percent
Personnel Attributes Questionnaire versus other three:	37.9 percent

The point to be made from these percentages is not that one of them happens to be arithmetically higher than another, but rather that they are all much alike. When corrected for chance sex-role scales in vogue today show agreement with each other, and thus convergent validity, but it is a limited agreement at best. The ACL scales are certainly as good as the other measures in this regard.

SUMMARY AND FURTHER THOUGHTS

In this chapter I have attempted to set the stage for the discussion of sex-role behavior that will follow throughout the remainder of this book. One of the major undertakings was to clearly specify the subject matter. This process first required that the concept of sex-role behavior be defined in the dictionary sense. Combining formal and functional definitions, it was proposed that masculine behaviors are those collectively agreed upon within a particular society as male characteristics, those that facilitate an instrumental (goal-striving) orientation or reflect an interpersonal insensitivity, or that occur more often as correlates of masculine instrumental behaviors. Feminine behaviors, agreed upon as female characteristics, facilitate an expressive orientation that maintains mutually satisfying personal relationships as its goal, or are made more probable by expressive behaviors.

Another definitional task undertaken in this chapter was to demonstrate that the psychological scales of masculinity and femininity, upon which we will depend heavily in this book, actually measure the sex roles as conceptualized. Psychological analysis of scale items, consistency with sex-role stereotypes, and a considerable number of validating studies lead me to conclude that the Masculinity Scale and Femininity Scale taken from responses to the Adjective Check List satisfy this requirement.

Sometime before this first chapter ends, it seems prudent to insert some disclaimer regarding these conceptual and operational definitions of sex roles. Nothing that has been said should be interpreted to mean that this is the only useful way in which the sex roles may be understood. Others may be able to make a case for their definitions with convincing logic. What I would urge, however, is that the reader distinguish between sex-role behaviors, however defined, and the amalgam of propaganda and fact, charges and countercharges, that surround the issue of sexism in contemporary societies. Not that these are unimportant, but they only cloud the work of the scientist concerned with establishing some semblance of social verity.

I also would like to avoid any implication that the ACL sex-role scales are a superior set of psychological instruments without the usual limitations that concern all test developers. The problems of sex-role measurement will be considered in Chapter Three and the ACL will receive its share of attention in this regard. This first chapter was directed to making only one point about the ACL sex-role scales—that their scores should be taken seriously. I have no doubt that the same case should be made for other popular sex-role measure, most notably the Personal Attributes Questionnaire developed by Spence, Helmreich, and Stapp (1975); its parent instrument, the Sex Role Stereotype Questionnaire (Rosenkrantz, Vogel, Bee, Broverman, & Broverman, 1968); the Femininity Scale taken from the California Psychological Inventory (Gough, 1965); and the Bem Sex-Role Inventory (1974). Among the reasons for choosing the ACL here is to take advantage of twenty years of data collection using this instrument, giving a time perspective on human sex-role behavior not possible with the other currently popular measures.

REFERENCES

Bem, S. L. The measurement of psychological androgyny. *Journal of Consulting and Clinical Psychology,* 1974, **42,** 155–62.

Bruner, P. B. The effects of parental nurturance, sex of subject, and practice on Embedded Figures Test performance. Unpublished doctoral dissertation, Emory University, 1977.

Chang, J., & Block, J. A study of identification in male homosexuals. *Journal of Consulting Psychology,* 1960, **24,** 307–10.

Cosentino, F., & Heilbrun, A. B. Anxiety correlates of sex-role identity in college subjects. *Psychological Reports,* 1964, **14,** 729–30.

Evans, R. B. Adjective Check List scores of homosexual men. *Journal of Personality Assessment,* 1971, **35,** 344–49.

Fand, A. B. Sex role and self concept. Unpublished doctoral dissertation, Cornell University, 1955.

Gough, H. G. *Reference handbook for the Gough Adjective Check List.* Berkeley, Calif.: Institute of Personality Assessment and Research, 1952.

Gough, H. G. *Manual for the California Psychological Inventory.* Stanford, Calif.: Consulting Psychologists Press, 1965.

Gough, H. G., & Heilbrun, A. B. *Manual for the Adjective Check List and the Need Scales for the ACL.* Palo Alto, Calif.: Consulting Psychologists Press, 1965.

Heilbrun, A. B. Sex role, instrumental-expressive behavior, and psychopathology in females. *Journal of Abnormal Psychology,* 1968, **73,** 131–36.

Heilbrun, A. B. Parental identification and the patterning of vocational interests in college males and females. *Journal of Counseling Psychology,* 1969, **16,** 342–47.

Heilbrun, A. B. Parent identification and filial sex-role behavior: The importance of biological context. In J. Cole (Ed.), *Nebraska symposium on motivation.* Lincoln: University of Nebraska Press, 1973.

Heilbrun, A. B. Measurement of masculine and feminine sex role identities as independent dimensions. *Journal of Consulting and Clinical Psychology,* 1976, **44,** 183–90.

Kagan, J., & Kogan, N. Individuality and cognitive performance. In P. Mussen (Ed.), *Carmichael's manual of child psychology.* (3rd ed.) New York: Wiley, 1970.

Kelley, J. A., Furman, W., & Young, V. Problems associated with the typological measurement of sex roles and androgyny. *Journal of Consulting and Clinical Psychology,* 1978, **46,** 1574–76.

Parker, G. V. C. Sex differences in self-description on the Adjective Check List. *Educational and Psychological Measurement,* 1969, **29,** 99–113.

Parsons, T., & Bales, R. F. *Family, socialization, and interaction process.* Glencoe, Ill.: Free Press, 1955.

Rosenkrantz, P. S., Vogel, S. R., Bee, H., Broverman, I. K., & Broverman, D. M. Sex role stereotypes and self-concepts in college students. *Journal of Consulting and Clinical Psychology,* 1968, **32,** 287–95.

Sears, R. R. Relation of early socialization experiences to aggression in middle childhood. *Journal of Abnormal and Social Psychology,* 1961, **63,** 466–92.

Spence, J. T., Helmreich, R., & Stapp, J. Ratings of self and peers on sex-role attributes and their relation to self-esteem and conceptions of masculinity and femininity. *Journal of Personality and Social Psychology,* 1975, **32,** 29–39.

Strong, E. K., Jr. *Manual for the Strong Vocational Interest Blank.* Palo Alto, Calif.: Consulting Psychologists Press, 1959.

Thompson, N. L., Jr., Schwartz, D. M., McCandless, B. R., & Edwards, D. A. Parent-child relationships and sexual identity in male and female homosexuals and heterosexuals. *Journal of Consulting and Clinical Psychology,* 1973, **41,** 120–27.

Wiggins, J. S., & Holzmuller, A. Psychological androgyny and interpersonal behavior. *Journal of Consulting and Clinical Psychology,* 1978, **46,** 40–52.

Williams, J. E., & Best, D. L. Sex stereotypes and trait favorability on the Adjective Check List. *Educational and Psychological Measurement,* 1977, **37,** 101–10.

Zimet, S. G., & Zimet, C. N. Teachers view people: Sex-role stereotyping. *Psychological Reports,* 1977, **41,** 583–91.

Chapter 2

Myth and Misconception about Sex-Role Behavior

Vulnerable as the concept of sex role is to different shades of interpretation, it is not surprising that many mistaken ideas have arisen over the years concerning sex-typed behaviors. I choose to believe that such misconceptions have been perpetuated mainly because they were never seriously challenged, at least by scientific data, and that they qualify as true contemporary social myths. Recently scientists and scholars have begun to take a hard look at sex-role behavior without the fetters of past assumptions. While the motivation for doing this has often been as much political as scientific, the important thing is that there has been a breakthrough in our understanding of sex-role behavior. Unfortunately, from a scientific point of view, the scientist's reconceptualization of human sex roles in the 1970s came as a belated recognition of the social ferment and change regarding the status of the sexes that burgeoned in the 1960s and continues to grow today. This has made progress for the social scientist more difficult to attain, since the object of investigation changes as it is being studied. Can you imagine the consternation of the chemist if the chemical composition of sodium chloride shifted in the course of investigating the functional properties of salt?

This chapter will continue consideration of what sex roles mean by examining several popular assumptions regarding these social behaviors. I hope to partially compensate for the shifting subject matter by clearing out a few conceptual cobwebs.

THE FAVORED-ROLE MYTH

It is generally conceded that in our society, in fact in almost all societies, the male role is a more valued one than the female role. By this is usually meant that the male role attracts more rewards and privileges and, perhaps because of this, is accorded greater status by men and women alike than the female role. Transposed strictly into behavioral terms, this assumption would lead us to

19

expect that the behaviors found more prevalently among males that correspond to sex-role stereotype (plus their correlates) will be more highly valued than female sex-role behaviors.

The work of Gough (1955) and Williams and Best (1977) allows us to examine the behaviors included on the ACL Masculinity and Femininity Scales in terms of the social value attributed to them by college students. Gough's original work with the ACL twenty-five years ago included ratings of favorability for each of the 300 adjectives. He categorized those adjectives falling in the upper 25 percent of the ratings as favorable and those falling in the lowest 25 percent as unfavorable. If the number of items on the ACL sex-role scales appearing in each of these quartiles is examined, we find that the Masculinity Scale includes six favorable and four unfavorable behaviors. The Femininity Scale, in turn, features nine favorable and two unfavorable behaviors, according to the Gough categories. Although these proportions do not differ by statistical test, the fact that the Femininity Scale includes a higher ratio of favorable to unfavorable items makes it obvious that the opposite is not true: masculine sex-role behaviors were not attributed more positive social value than feminine behaviors.

One limitation of the Gough data for the present purpose resides in their categorical nature. There are only three possibilities for an adjective; it is either favorable, unfavorable, or neither. Williams and Best obtained favorability ratings from judges of both sexes for all ACL adjectives and converted these ratings into standard scores with a mean of 500 and a standard deviation of 100. Scores above 500 are in the favorable direction and below 500 indicate shades of unfavorability. By using their scores, a specific level of favorability can be assigned to each of the ACL sex-role items, and the limitation of categorical data can be avoided. The average degree of favorability for masculine items on the ACL was 525, slightly above the midpoint of favorability for all adjectives, but the average favorability score for feminine items was 546. Again, statistical tests did not suggest that this difference should be taken seriously but, as before, we can clearly reject any interpretation that higher value is placed upon masculine behaviors.

A by-product of having these two sets of data is the possibility of comparing the value judgments placed upon behavior by students on the campus of a Western university twenty-five years ago and those obtained more recently on a Southern campus. The possibility of finding regional or generational differences in the social values attached to the ACL items cannot be disregarded. Since I intend on subsequent pages to consider ACL records dating back to the 1950s and collected in three regions of the United States, not finding such differences would best serve the clarity of the present exposition. The Gough and the Williams and Best values were compared by determining the overlap between the 25 percent most favorable behaviors from both studies. Sixty-two of Gough's original seventy-five most favorable items were in the upper quartile of the Williams and

Best scores as well; the remaining thirteen Gough items, showing a mean value of 592, were consistently near the quartile cutting point of 600. Thus favorable behaviors then in California are favorable behaviors now in North Carolina. Comparison of the 25 percent most unfavorable items from both studies produced a similar picture. Sixty-five of the seventy-five Gough terms remain among the most unfavorable, and the ten remaining items have clearly negative scores (average = 433) by current standards. Examination of overlap for only the sex-typed items on the ACL presented essentially the same picture. In summary, the qualitative meaning of behavioral terms has remained remarkably stable over time and across geographic locale.

Another way to consider whether masculine or feminine behaviors are held in higher esteem is to note the effects of dissimulation upon self-description. I reported a study (Heilbrun, 1976) in which college subjects were given the ACL under instructions to appear as psychologically healthy as possible ("fake good") and then to simulate a psychologically unhealthy person by their self-description ("fake bad"). The effects of dissimulation upon the ACL sex-role scale scores can tell us something about whether the scale items are viewed positively or negatively. Keep in mind that these scales are normed so that the average score on each is 50 when you consider the means in table 2.1.

Table 2.1. Effect of "Fake Good" and "Fake Bad" Instructions on Masculinity and Femininity Scores

	"Fake Good"		"Fake Bad"	
Scale	Males	Females	Males	Females
Masculinity	56.46	52.68	43.32	51.26
Femininity	46.30	46.42	32.82	19.58

NOTE: These mean scale values should be compared to an expected mean of 50 under standard instructional conditions, and are based on the protocols of 50 males and 19 females.

Looking first at the "fake good" condition, both males and females did much the same thing. They selected sex-role behaviors that made them look slightly more masculine and slightly less feminine than average. At first this sounds like evidence in support of the assumption that masculine behaviors are more highly esteemed than feminine behaviors, but before concluding this, examine the "fake bad" data. In their effort to look as maladjusted as they could, males dropped their Masculinity Scale scores, but females maintained theirs at the same level as in the "fake good" condition. In looking optimally adjusted or looking maladjusted, masculinity was all the same to the female; a loss of masculinity was an important aspect of the male's concept of psychological maladjustment.

By far the most salient effect of the instructions, however, appears in the Femininity Scale changes. Feminine sex-role scores were not high when the subjects were trying to look good (slightly below average for students in general), but they dropped out of sight under "fake bad" instructions. This effect suggests that the presence of strong feminine behaviors is not considered crucial to the stereotype of psychological health by either males or females, but the absence of feminine tendencies is central to the stereotype of poor psychological health held by both sexes.

To summarize this dissimulation study, masculinity assumed very little importance in the female's version of health or illness and femininity was paramount, at least in its absence, in her construction of poor psychological health. For the male, the presence and absence of masculinity was a critical aspect of both adjustment and maladjustment, but restricted femininity was an even more salient feature of maladjustment. Again we seem to find no special status accorded masculine behavior.

THE INFLEXIBLE-ROLE MYTH

Common assumption has it that the male adheres more narrowly to the masculine role than does the female to the feminine role. The reasons for this belief are numerous, although rarely emanating from hard data. I might first mention that this assumption is a natural corollary of the belief just discussed, that the male role is a more valued one in our society: after all, why should men give up a good thing when they have it? Since the belief that male role behavior is more valued has been challenged by the data just presented, we should anticipate some problems with the sex-role flexibility assumption.

There are several other origins for the myth of inflexible sex-typed behavior for men. Studies have confirmed that fathers are more concerned with conformity to stereotypic roles by children of both sexes than are mothers (Block, 1974; Johnson, 1963). Add to this the popular assumption that fathers play the critical socializing role for their sons and that mothers are crucial to their daughters' social development. It would follow logically that the son would be rigidly shaped into the masculine mold by the concerned father while the daughter would be less influenced to adopt a strict feminine orientation by the mother, who maintains a more relaxed attitude toward stereotyping.

The effects of the broader social environment have been thought to enhance the difference in conformity to stereotype between the two sexes by restricting the cross-sex behavior of the male far more than that of the female (Brown, 1958). The most common examples that might be cited of the greater latitude extended to the female than the male in her sex-role development are: (1) the strong sanctions against "sissy" behavior in boys, and the generally mild concern regarding "tomboy" behavior in girls; (2) the acceptance of grooming and clothing styles in the female that are traditionally male (such as short hair and slacks), and the antipathy, ranging from mild to violent, for similar cross-sex choices in males (such as long hair and skirts); and (3) the greater acceptance of a woman who enters the world of work as a full-time commitment than of a man who chooses homemaking as his major function. While some of these examples may be dated (such as longer hair on men), the list could be extended. The greater social problem associated with homosexual choice for the male than for the female is a case in point (Thompson & McCandless, 1976).

Yet another basis for assuming more rigid adherence of the male to stereotypic expectations is the not infrequent complaint of wives that their husbands are derelict in expression of warm and tender emotions, at least toward them. Such observations, commonly voiced in the office of the marriage counselor or in the divorce court, can easily be translated into the inflexibility assumption: husbands in general tend to be so affixed to their masculine role that feminine tenderness displayed toward their wives is next to impossible.

The extent to which any or all of these suppositions regarding inflexible role behavior finds representation in today's males is not at issue here. What does concern us is their convergent contribution to the general assumption that males taken as a whole will be more inflexibly bound to masculine sex-typed behaviors than will females to the feminine role. One way to examine the accuracy of this belief would be to compare the balance of masculine and feminine attributes within the sex-role repertoires of the two sexes. Certainly the person who demonstrates half masculine attributes and half feminine attributes demonstrates more flexibility in the domain of sex-role behavior than others who show all masculine or all feminine attributes.

In order to gather a stable picture of sex-role balance by sex, the ACLs of large samples of male (N = 145) and female (N = 222) college students were drawn from the files, and the numbers of masculine and feminine behaviors endorsed as self-characteristic were determined. These ACLs had been collected in the early 1960s for the females; why these time samples were chosen will be made clear later in this section. The mean number of behaviors checked as characteristic by males from the Masculinity Scale was 9.19, compared to a mean of 10.62 behaviors from the Femininity Scale. Males actually checked more feminine than masculine items, although to me the most salient aspect of these results is the very even balance between masculine and feminine behaviors taken on the average. This is definitely not what would be expected if males were generally restricted to masculine role behavior by sanctions against feminine responses.

The females demonstrated what prior assumption would have led us to expect for males. The average female checked only a relatively few masculine behaviors as self-characteristic, 5.81 to be exact. In contrast, she endorsed 14.48 feminine behaviors as personal attributes. In other words, these data suggest that it is the female and not the male who is more restricted to a stereotyped sex role and who is less inclined to engage in cross-sex behavior.

As a buffer against the possibility that the prevalence of masculine and feminine behaviors reflected in the mean figures above might be outdated and unrepresentative of college students today, smaller samples of ACLs collected in the 1970s were examined in the same way. Again the balance of masculine and feminine behaviors among the 92 males was striking; the mean number of masculine behaviors checked ($\overline{X}$ = 10.08) was close to but less than the mean number of feminine behaviors ($\overline{X}$ = 12.08). The sex-role picture displayed by the 93 females was slightly more masculine than before ($\overline{X}$ = 6.86), though they still showed a preponderance of feminine behaviors ($\overline{X}$ = 14.58). The conclusion that males are more inflexibly committed to stereotyped sex-role behavior than females seems as untrue today as it was fifteen years ago.

There may be some reluctance to relinquish the assumption of more rigid adherence to sex role by the male, even given evidence to the contrary within college samples. College students are, after all, young adults given to experimenting with life styles while still enjoying the sanctuary of the college setting. Or—reasoning from a very different perspective—college students may come from homes that share different values regarding social behavior than those that are to be found in the general population. Either possibility would lend itself to the argument that the data concerning sex-role composition of male and female college students are unrepresentative of the world that fostered the male role-rigidity assumption in the first place.

The best way to deal with skepticism about the representativeness of data collected on college campuses is to take a first-hand look at a broader sample of people and see where that takes us. A sample of 456 ACLs were collected from Midwestern noncampus sources during the early 1960s. (Recall that our primary college samples were gathered during that decade as well.) Included in this total were 286 men and 171 women, all employed on a part-time or full-time basis and a large majority of them married. The average age for the males was about 38 (range 16–69) years, and the somewhat younger female sample averaged about 29 (range 15–73) years of age. Mean educational level for the men was slightly over eleven years, and for women a little over twelve years. Although this total sample would not qualify as a demographer's dream of representativeness for the general population of this country in the 1960s, it nevertheless qualifies as distinct from one marshaled on any college campus.

I shall repeat the figures reported earlier for college subjects and the conclusion drawn from them. Males on the average reported 9.19 (replication = 10.08) masculine behaviors and a balanced 10.62 (replication = 12.08) feminine behaviors. These figures for females were 5.81 (replication = 6.86) masculine and 14.48 (replication = 14.58) feminine behaviors. Conclusion:—males are less restricted to stereotyped masculine behaviors than females are to stereotyped femininity, popular assumption to the contrary. When general population ACLs were examined, the males were found to have endorsed 6.14 masculine behaviors overall and 9.29 feminine behaviors. While both averages are down from those of college males, the differential endorsement of feminine behaviors relative to masculine is even more striking than was the case with our campus data. The female data followed suit. Women on the average identified 4.68 masculine items as self-characteristic compared to 12.51 feminine items. Like the means for general population males, these are down relative to college females. Nevertheless, these figures demonstrate the same tendency among women to adhere to the feminine role as was found on the campus. It seems clear that examination of the sex-role composition of general population males and females offers no more support for the assumption of an inflexible commitment of men to masculinity than had our study of college students.

Averages can be misleading, so there is yet another way to look at the sex-role composition variable that might provide a bridge between the findings just reported and the common assumption that men generally demonstrate a one-sided masculine picture. The general population statistics that were reported represented averages collapsed over a broad span of years. Perhaps something occurs with age that affects the sex-role composition of males in our society, a chronological change that could be overlooked when averaging over ages is done. One might argue that it takes time and experience as an adult to consolidate a strong masculine identity, well beyond the adolescent years that Erik Erikson (1963) describes as the period for establishing a sexual identity. An argument could be waged just as strenuously the other way, of course. Masculinity for men could be viewed as a more critical commodity during the defensive years of adolescence and young adulthood; later, this argument might explain, there is a gradual emergence of the expressive qualities of femininity as marriage and family experiences present themselves and proof of manhood no longer holds urgent priority. Whichever way the argument goes, the presence of a systematic change in the sex-role makeup of men over time would encourage us to believe that male adherence to masculine stereotyped behavior could be demonstrated within a certain age range but not within another; part of the myth might be salvaged.

This interesting possibility was considered by plotting the mean number of masculine and feminine behaviors for the two sexes over decades of life. Figure 2.1 presents the plot of mean masculine and mean feminine behaviors for general-population males and females falling into six decades of life ranging from the teens to the sixties. As it turned out, statistical analysis indicated no effect of age upon sex-role composition for either sex. Males maintained a similar balance of masculine and feminine behaviors from adolescence to the sixties, and females demonstrated a preponderance of feminine behaviors in their self-reported repertoires over the same decades of life.

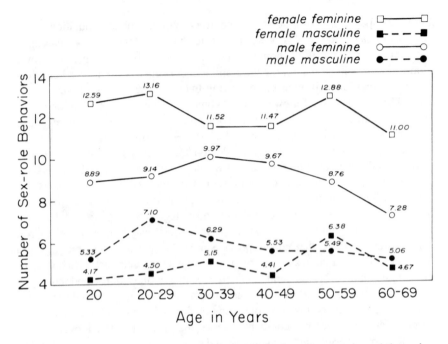

Figure 2.1. Number of masculine and feminine behaviors endorsed by general population males (N = 286) and females (N = 171) at varying ages.

Yet another approach to investigating sex-role flexibility has been used in our program of research. The extent to which males or females are constrained to stereotyped sex-role behavior can be assessed by the shift between masculine and feminine behaviors given different social demands from one type of interpersonal situation to the next. A man strongly committed to masculinity would be expected to demonstrate stereotyped behavior no matter what the interpersonal context might be. Similarly, a highly feminine women should display behavior consistent with this role across a broad interpersonal spectrum.

The basic psychological technique for measuring interpersonal consistency in my research was devised by Block (1961). His intention was to translate part of Erikson's (1963) concept of ego identity into an objective test, that part being the extent to which the individual perceived himself as consistent in his behavior from one interpersonal situation to the next. The technique has been used successfully to support Erikson's contention that higher role consistency would be associated with better psychological adjustment (Block, 1961; Cartwright, 1957, 1961; Heilbrun & Lair, 1964; Meltzer, 1957).

The consistency measure that I have used to look at sex-role behavior was modeled closely after Block's original procedure. Subjects are asked to rate their characteristic behaviors in eight different types of interpersonal transactions, namely, when they are with: (1) someone in whom they are sexually interested, (2) an acquaintance they do not care much about, (3) an employer or someone of similar status, (4) a child, (5) their father (or father figure), (6) their mother (or mother figure), (7) a close same-sex friend, and (8) an acquaintance whom they would like to know better. Ratings are obtained independently for each situation by having the subject rank order a standard list of behaviors from most to least characteristic when relating to that particular type of person.

The major modification of Block's technique introduced for my research was to substitute a new standard list of behavioral adjectives that were to be rated by the subject. The modified list of items were taken from the sex-role scales of the ACL, with ten items from the Masculinity Scale and ten from the Femininity Scale. The specific items differed to some extent between the male and female forms, since I chose to equate the masculine and feminine items in each form for average frequency of endorsement under standard conditions of ACL administration. The masculine and feminine items in both forms represent equally common behaviors whether we are considering college males or females. Although the Williams and Best stereotype and favorability scores were not available to us when the items were selected, we can now report these properties of the sex-role consistency measures as well. (Recall that the average stereotype score is 500, with higher scores indicating masculine loading and lower scores, feminine loading; the average favorability score is 500, with higher scores indicating more favorable attributes and lower scores, less favorable.)

For the male form, the ten masculine behaviors have a stereotype mean of 666, and the ten feminine behaviors average 367. The corresponding values for the female form are 645 and 378. Average favorability of the masculine and feminine items on the male form are 516 and 544, respectively, with these values falling at 524 and 494 on the female form. Descriptively, then, we chose ACL masculine and feminine items for the two sex-role consistency forms that were stereotypically distinct and that overall fell near the midpoint of favorability.

The final thing that the reader may require in order to understand this rather complicated psychometric technique is an explanation of how the rankings are scored so as to come up with a single objective index of sex-role consistency. Once the subject has ranked the twenty sex-role behaviors from most to least characteristic for each of the eight interpersonal situations, a multiple rank-order correlation (w coefficient; Siegel, 1956) is calculated, which may range from .000 to 1.000. A correlation of zero tells us that the pattern of sex-role behaviors described by the individual in any one situation is totally unrelated to the patterns in every other situation. In other words, the person is describing a totally inconsistent pattern of sex-role behaviors across situations. A correlation of

1.000 reflects perfect consistency in the pattern of sex-role behaviors from one situation to the next. Neither extreme score has been achieved by a subject tested in our research, although scores in the .100s and .800s have been observed.

An example of the sex-role consistency measurement technique might be in order before we turn attention to what the measure has disclosed. In this example, instead of using the actual instrument including twenty sex-role behaviors and eight situations, let us assume that only three sex-role behaviors (appreciative, friendly, and dominant) and three interpersonal situations (with your father, best friend, and someone in whom you are sexually interested) were used. The subject's task is to rank the three behaviors from most to least representative of his or her way of relating to each person. If the following ratings were obtained, the subject would be judging his or her own sex-role behavior as totally consistent (W = 1.000) from one personal transaction to the next:

father	*best friend*	*sexual object*
1. friendly	1. friendly	1. friendly
2. appreciative	2. appreciative	2. appreciative
3. dominant	3. dominant	3. dominant

On the other hand, patterns like the following would indicate total inconsistency (W = .000) of sex-role behavior as judged by the individual:

father	*best friend*	*sexual object*
1. appreciative	1. friendly	1. dominant
2. friendly	2. dominant	2. appreciative
3. dominant	3. appreciative	3. friendly

The first probe using the sex-role consistency measure (Heilbrun, 1977) revealed a significantly higher score (p < .05) for the thirty-three college females ($\bar{X}$ = .531) than was found for the forty-two college males ($\bar{X}$ = .391). Males were *more* flexible (less consistent) in their display of masculine and feminine behaviors than females. A second study employing this psychometric instrument (Heilbrun & Pitman, 1979) replicated the significant difference between the sexes. College males averaged .438 and female college subjects, .534; again the men demonstrated less consistency in the masculine/feminine patterning of their sex-role behavior than women (p < .05). As you can see, these consistency results also fail to support the assumption that men adhere more faithfully to masculine stereotyped behavior than do women to femininity. In fact, like the preceding data based on the prevalence of masculine and feminine behaviors within the sex-role repertoire, the consistency results point to the opposite conclusion. Men actually demonstrate a more balanced utilization of masculine and feminine behaviors than do women.

Just to add an empirical postscript to the sex-role consistency discussion, I might point out that the greater consistency found for college women than men does not seem to be true of their social behaviors in general. Prior research (Heilbrun, 1976) has considered the identical Block consistency measure except the twenty behaviors to be rated were not selected with sex roles in mind. Only four of the items on the female form and five on the male form of this earlier version appear on the ACL sex-role scales. Comparison of 104 female college students with 90 male students on this more general role consistency measure revealed only a negligible and nonsignificant difference in means between the females ($\overline{X} = .484$) and the males ($\overline{X} = .461$).

THE MASCULINITY-VERSUS-FEMININITY MYTH

It has been popularly assumed that masculinity and femininity represent mutually exclusive categories of behavior—that the presence of one set of these sex-role attributes meant the relative absence of the other. In other words, we conceptualized people as either masculine or feminine and closed our eyes to exceptions that should have compromised the rule. For example, the older (pre-1970s) sex-role scales were constructed so that masculinity and femininity appeared as extremes on a single bipolar dimension. If high scores meant masculinity, then low scores signified the opposite, feminine, sex-role disposition. It should have bothered test developers (including me) and test users that intermediate scores on such scales were difficult to interpret, being neither high enough nor low enough to warrant a clear interpretation of sex-role status. Furthermore, the balance of masculine and feminine attributes displayed by males, discussed in the previous section, was there to be observed all along.

On the other hand, the assumption that one is masculine or feminine is not without some basis in logic. The nearly perfect discrimination between men and women that is possible based upon biological and anatomical features tempts one to conclude that roles assigned on the basis of these differences should be just as sharply differentiated. Even more sophisticated consideration of the matter in terms of the instrumental and expressive orientations intrinsic to the two sex-roles could lead to the conclusion that some degree of incompatibility must exist between masculinity and femininity: in principle the goal orientation and personal insensitivity of the instrumental orientation does not coordinate very well with the concern for harmonious and rewarding relationships that is the hallmark of the expressive orientation.

Yet in the 1970s we saw the emergence of a new conceptualization of sex-role behavior and a new psychometric technology to accommodate it (Baucom, 1976;

Bem, 1974; Berzins, Welling, & Wetter, 1978; Block, 1974; Carlson, 1971; Constantinople, 1973; Heilbrun, 1976; C. Heilbrun, 1973; Kanner, 1976; Spence, Helmreich, & Stapp, 1975). The realization that potent masculine and feminine attributes could coexist in the same person led to several modifications in the conceptual framework for sex-role research. Psychological androgyny, the presence of masculinity and feminity in one individual, has become the target of inquiry for increasing numbers of studies that have sought to validate this newly discovered phenomenon or to expand our knowledge of its parameters. A somewhat less glamorous product of the new look in sex-role conceptualization is the possibility that humans may develop neither masculine nor feminine attributes, a sex-role outcome that has been designated "undifferentiated" (Spence, Helmreich, & Stapp, 1975). While more controversy surrounds the usefulness of this construct than that of androgyny (discussed in the next chapter, which deals with sex-role measurement issues), in theory the two constructs are equally viable. Both rest on the assumption that sex-role development progresses independently as far as incorporation of masculine traits and feminine traits is concerned; a person may develop variable degrees of masculinity without that having any bearing on the extent to which feminine attributes are learned. If one takes the assumption of noncontingent development seriously, then it is just as reasonable to conclude that some children will show little incorporation of either masculine or feminine behaviors (undifferentiation) as it is to postulate exceptional development of both sex-role potentials (androgyny).

We find emerging from the early stages of reconceptualization of the sex roles, then, either a threefold typology (androgyny—masculine and feminine—masculinity, femininity) or a fourfold typology (androgyny, masculinity, femininity, and undifferentiation—neither masculine nor feminine) to replace the old masculine/feminine dichotomy. The verdict on how well these typologies describe the actual experiences of those in our or similar societies must await considerably more evidence than is presently at hand. However, there is enough evidence available now (see Kelly and Worell, 1977, for review) to require all subsequent sex-role research to avail itself of an instrument capable of separate measurement of masculinity and femininity and an expanded typology of sex-role outcome.

To this point the discussion has been concerned primarily with the role played by the social scientist in reformulating our view of sex-role behavior. Social concerns, especially with regard to the rights of women, have also played a vital role in this reformulation. The concept of androgyny has become a rallying force for many who deplore what they believe to be the dehumanizing effects of stereotyped behavior for either sex, but particularly for women. Sandra Bem concluded a 1974 article describing her new measure of androgyny by saying:

In a society where rigid sex-role differentiation has already outlived its utility, perhaps the androgynous person will come to define a more human standard of psychological health [p. 162].

Janet Spence and her coworkers (Spence, Helmreich, & Stapp, 1975), in a paper describing their own measurement technique, concluded:

Implicit in the masculinity-femininity . . . dichotomy is the assumption that each contributes to personal and social effectiveness. The most desirable state of affairs is androgyny . . . [p. 38].

Following consideration of development influences upon the sex roles, Jeanne Block (1974) contends:

If our social aim can become, both collectively and individually the integration of agency and communion (i.e., androgyny), the behavioral and experiential options of men and women alike will be broadened and enriched and we all can become truly whole, more truly human [p. 526].

Supplementing conclusions drawn by these social researchers, the books of the 1970s voiced similar opinions, although empirical data has usually been scarce. The consensus has been that problems are created by rigid adherence to sex-role stereotypes and that society must create opportunity for androgyny in both sexes. Matteson (1975) emphasizes the problems created by fixed sex roles in the nuclear family, especially as they limit the fulfillment of autonomy and intimacy in both marital partners and discourage androgynous development of the child. A similar thesis is proposed by Oakley (1972), who contended that rigid assignments of role functions by sex stifle the opportunity for men to be more caring and tender and women to be more achievement oriented, indicating that greater androgyny is needed for both sexes. Steinman and Fox (1974) suggest a basic model of health in which masculinity and femininity are not unique to each sex but are shared by both. Human misery due to rigid sex-role expectations concern both Grambs and Waetjen (1975) and Pleck and Sawyer (1974): alcoholism, impotence, heart attacks, and other stress diseases are considered to be the by-products of man's instrumental nature and his suppression of tender feelings, whereas a blurred sense of identity looms as the paramount danger for the woman accepting narrow commitments to marriage and child rearing. Even practical guides to nonsexist child rearing made their appearance (e.g., Greenberg, 1978), representing an attempt to help parents raise their children free of constraining sex stereotypes.

THE ANDROGYNY-WAS-BORN-TODAY MYTH

I trust that sufficient contemporary opinion has been cited regarding stereotyped sex roles to make the point that psychological androgyny is heralded as a solution to many of the social problems of our day. This might lead us to conclude that androgyny is a new phenomenon of the decade just past, growing out of an expanding indictment of stereotyped sex roles by social scientists and advocates of women's and men's liberation. This assumption will be examined now, since it is a matter of interest whether androgyny as a social phenomenon tended to precede or follow the flood of value judgments released during the past decade.

One of the few advantages of aging is that one accrues things that may eventually hold some interest from an historical point of view. My files currently contain samples of ACL self-ratings collected from college students for over twenty years on campuses ranging from the West to the Midwest down to the South. Since these data were collected for a series of independent studies over the years and not with any overall purpose in mind, the total sample includes some flaws that cannot be rectified after the fact. Perhaps the most obvious of these is the confounding of geographic locale and time. For example, it cannot be stated with certainty whether self-report differences between students studied on the University of Iowa campus in 1958 and others assessed in Georgia at Emory University during 1978 are a function of time, place, or a combination of the two. Nevertheless, I am persuaded that the data to be considered next reflect primarily the effects of time, and that campus personality differences contributed little. Reflect on two samples of males collected only two years apart in the mid-1960s, a short enough span that the time difference should mean very little. These samples were obtained at locales as divergent as the large, Far Western, state-supported, presumably liberal University of California at Berkeley, and the small, Southern, private, presumably conservative Emory University. Despite the differences in personality stereotypes that might be anticipated for students on these two campuses, the average sex-role scores of the two male samples were amazingly similar: Masculinity Scale means fell at about 50 and 51, respectively, whereas the mean Femininity Scale scores approximated 46 and 44.

The purpose of considering the ACLs of young men and women over the span of twenty years, 1958 to 1978, is to gain a better appreciation of the effects of our current social climate on sex-role behavior by placing the 1970s in the perspective of prior years. To do this we shall concentrate upon androgyny as a sex-role outcome, since this construct seems to best epitomize the new awareness of the 1970s. Two questions shall interest us. One has to do with the changes in androgyny in college students as this country moved from the tranquil late 1950s (between wars in Korea and Vietnam), through the turbulent years of student unrest in the 1960s and early 1970s, and into the feminist concerns of the early to late 1970s. The other question involves whether the emergence of androgyny in males and females has followed different or similar courses over these years.

Before proceeding further, we should consider how androgyny is to be measured. An index has been devised that reflects both of the necessary attributes of androgyny—extensity and balance of sex-role development (Heilbrun & Pitman, 1979). Stated psychometrically, androgyny would be indicated by elevations on both the Masculinity and Femininity Scales (extensity) and by the similarity of these scores (balance). Both of the sex-role scales are normed so that an average score is set at 50 and the standard deviation at 10, with higher scores indicating greater masculinity (M) or femininity (F). These scores are combined by the androgyny formula,

$$(M + F) - |M - F|;$$

the first term (sum of the two scores) represents extensity and the second term (the absolute difference between the two scores) represents balance.

The use of this formula for combining masculinity and femininity scores in investigating androgyny has both an advantage and a limitation. It considers androgyny as a continuous variable ranging from high to low but existing to some degree in most people. This avoids the problem of unreliability in classifying subjects categorically as androgynous based upon whether they fall above some arbitrary cutting point like the median or mean on independent sex-role scales. As an example, subject X might have scores of 51 and 51 on the Masculinity and Femininity Scales and subject Y might have scores of 50 and 50. Using dichotomous assignment and a cutting score of 51 for "high," subject X would be designated "androgynous" and subject Y "undifferentiated," despite their similarity in score patterns. However, the continuous androgyny score of the first subject would be

$$(51 + 51) - |51 - 51| = (102) - (0) = 102$$

and that of the second a similar

$$(50 + 50) - |50 - 50| = (100) - (0) = 100,$$

and they would be viewed as remarkably similar in androgyny rather than categorically different.

The limitation of the androgyny scoring system for the ACL is that it tells you nothing regarding sex-role status other than degree of androgyny, so it requires a focal interest in that particular variable. This stems from the fact that there is only one way to be androgynous (have high and evenly balanced scores), but three ways of appearing nonandrogynous. Low androgyny can be achieved by those having high masculine–low feminine, low masculine –high feminine, and low masculine–low feminine ACL scores.

Figure 2.2 presents a plot of mean androgyny scores for male and female college samples tested between 1958 and 1978. Inspection of the androgyny trends suggests several things. It can be noted first that the curves assume quite distinct shapes for the two sexes. The ogival curve of the male depicts a drop in androgyny across samples over about the first half of the two-decade period and, with one exception, a steady increase in androgyny over the second half. In contrast, the female samples demonstrated a consistent increase in androgyny during the first half of the period and then a plateau during the second. A second way to look at the two curves by sex is to note that males were considerably more androgynous than females in the late 1950s, females became the more androgynous sex by the late 1960s, and males again demonstrate higher androgyny by the late 1970s.

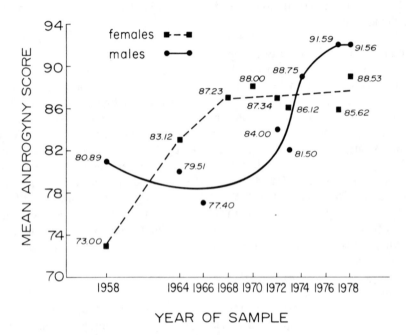

Figure 2.2. Smoothed androgyny curves for samples of college males (N = 408) and females (N = 676) collected between 1958 and 1978.

Drawing even broad social implications from these androgyny data must be done with caution, since the influence of social events can only be inferred by logical conjecture. While awareness of women's rights issues and the rejection of stereotypic guidelines for sex-role behavior may have been social phenomena of the 1970s, their effect on androgyny cannot be observed where it would be expected. The college female did not become systematically more androgynous during the last decade, based upon these samples. It is the male, certainly far less caught up in the sex-role liberation issues than the female, who has demonstrated a remarkable increase in dual sex-role potential during the last decade.

I would also speculate that the period of the 1960s, with its antiestablishment and antiwar protests and its more general concerns about human rights, allowed the college female to expand her sex-role potential, perhaps by creating the opportunity for involvement in instrumental acts such as protest marches and sit-ins that were intended to demonstrate expressive concerns about her fellow humans. Even though many college women did not participate actively in such activities, those who did were there to serve as attractive peer models.

SUMMARY AND FURTHER THOUGHTS

Several shared beliefs about sex-role behavior were considered and found wanting. First among these is the common assumption that higher value is placed upon the male role in our society. This was found not to be true as far as the stereotyped behaviors associated with masculinity and femininity and their correlates are concerned. Neither ratings of favorability nor simulation of psychological health and illness showed masculine behaviors to be more valued than feminine; if anything, the opposite appeared to be the case.

The second assumption that was examined held that males are more inflexibly bound to masculine behaviors than females are to femininity. On the contrary, analysis of the composition of male and female sex-role repertoires found males to be evenly balanced between masculine and feminine behaviors. Females reported disproportionate numbers of feminine behaviors compared to masculine. These data suggest that the male sex-role inflexibility myth actually had the facts turned around. The same results were obtained with noncollege samples and at all adult ages. A different approach to estimating flexibility of sex-role behavior disclosed the same result: women, not men, are less inclined to shift between masculine and feminine behaviors with changing interpersonal situations.

Masculinity and femininity have previously been construed as mutually exclusive categories of behavior. Several authorities have attacked this assumption on conceptual, moral, and empirical grounds, and it is now generally conceded that sex-role behaviors may develop independently. This has opened the way for reconceptualization of sex-role outcomes. Instead of two alternatives as before, masculine or feminine, there are four possibilities: androgyny (both masculine and feminine) and undifferentiation (neither masculine nor feminine) must now be considered as possible outcomes along with masculine and feminine.

Androgyny was identified during the 1970s by scientific study, authors of books, and social action groups as the optimal sex-role outcome for full realization of social effectiveness. It might be assumed that such consensus would facilitate increases in androgynous behavior, especially for the female, who has been most centrally concerned about sex-role limitations. However, a comparison of androgyny scores across a twenty-year period (1958–78) failed to confirm this expectation. Growth of androgyny in college women reached its peak ten years ago and did not increase during the 1970s. The opposite was true for college males. Androgyny showed some decline for college males during the Vietnam War years, but samples of males have registered progressive increases since.

How do beliefs manage to persist when they are at odds with empirical data? Certainly some of it can be explained by the definitional fuzziness that has surrounded sex roles. In Chapter One we identified three distinguishable features of simply being a man or woman: (1) stereotyped and correlated sex-role behaviors, about which this book is primarily concerned; (2) stereotyped sex-role functions; and (3) sex-gender correlates, systematic responses elicited from others because of our sex. I suspect that a great deal of misunderstanding has been generated by the failure to keep these features separated in our thinking. As one example, the idea that the male sex role is more highly valued, a notion central to current feminist concern, could have evolved from the observation that males receive favored treatment in our society. This has little or nothing to do with the male sex role, although it has much to do with prescribed sex-role functions and ubiquitous sex-gender correlates.

A second example of how the failure to keep our terms straight may well account for the persistence of sex-role myths is to be found in the distinction we made between stereotyped behaviors and stereotyped functions. We found that men do not rigidly adhere to expectations regarding masculine sex-role behaviors—far from it. They may be less flexible about exchanging sex-role functions than the female, however, such as assuming the primary domestic and child-rearing responsibilities within the family in exchange for the work role. We have no data at hand to prove this. Whatever answer such data would give us, it still would not bear upon behavior per se, upon masculinity and femininity as we have defined these terms.

REFERENCES

Baucom, D. H. Independent masculinity and femininity scales on the California Psychological Inventory. *Journal of Consulting and Clinical Psychology*, 1976, **44**, 876.

Bem, S. L. The measurement of psychological androgyny. *Journal of Consulting and Clinical Psychology*, 1974, **42**, 155–62.

Berzins, J. I., Welling, M. A., & Wetter, R. E. A new measure of psychological androgyny based upon the Personality Research Form. *Journal of Consulting and Clinical Psychology*, 1978, **46**, 126–38.

Block, J. Ego identity, role variability, and adjustment. *Journal of Consulting Psychology*, 1961, **25**, 392–97.

Block, J. H. Conceptions of sex role: Some cross-cultural and longitudinal perspectives. In R. F. Winch & B. B. Spanier (Eds.), *Selected studies in marriage and the family*. (4th ed.) New York: Holt, Rinehart, and Winston, 1974.

Brown, D. G. Sex-role development in a changing culture. *Psychological Bulletin,* 1958, **55,** 232–42.

Carlson, R. Sex differences in ego functioning. *Journal of Consulting and Clinical Psychology,* 1971, **37,** 267–77.

Cartwright, R. Effects of psychotherapy on self-consistency. *Journal of Counseling Psychology,* 1957, **21,** 15–22.

Cartwright, R. The effects of psychotherapy on self-consistency: A replication and extension. *Journal of Consulting Psychology,* 1961, **25,** 376–83.

Constantinople, A. Masculinity-femininity: An exception to a famous dictum. *Psychological Bulletin,* 1973, **80,** 389-407.

Erikson, E. H. *Childhood and Society.* (2nd ed.) New York: Norton, 1963.

Gough, H. G. *Reference handbook for the Gough Adjective Check List.* Berkeley, Calif.: Institute of Personality Assessment and Research, 1955.

Grambs, J. D., & Waetjen, W. B. *Sex: Does it make a difference?* Belmont, Calif.: Duxbury, 1975.

Greenberg, S. *Right from the start: A guide to nonsexist child rearing.* Boston: Houghton Mifflin, 1978.

Heilbrun, A. B. Measurement of masculine and feminine sex-role identities as independent dimensions. *Journal of Consulting and Clinical Psychology,* 1976, **44,** 183–90.

Heilbrun, A. B. The added dimension of adaptability in male sex-role behavior. Unpublished manuscript, 1977.

Heilbrun, A. B., & Lair, C. V. Decreased role consistency in the aged: Implications for behavioral pathology. *Journal of Gerontology,* 1964, **19,** 325–29.

Heilbrun, A. B., & Pitman, D. Testing some basic assumptions about psychological androgyny. *Journal of Genetic Psychology,* 1979, **135,** 175–188.

Heilbrun, C. *Toward a recognition of androgyny.* New York: Knopf, 1973.

Johnson, M. M. Sex role learning in the nuclear family. *Child Development,* 1963, **34,** 319–33.

Kanner, A. D. Femininity and masculinity: Their relationships to creativity in male architects and their independence from each other. *Journal of Consulting and Clinical Psychology,* 1976, **44,** 802–5.

Kelly, J. A., & Worell, J. New formulations of sex roles and androgyny: A critical review. *Journal of Consulting and Clinical Psychology,* 1977, **45,** 1101-15.

Matteson, D. R. *Adolescence today: Sex roles and the search for identity.* Homewood, Ill.: Dorsey, 1975.

Meltzer, M. L. Role variability as a function of understanding others. Unpublished doctoral dissertation, Catholic University of America, 1957.

Oakley, A. *Sex gender and society.* London: Temple Smith, 1972.

Pleck, J. H., & Sawyer, J. (Eds.) *Men and masculinity.* Englewood Cliffs, N.J.; Prentice-Hall, 1974.

Siegel, S. *Nonparametric statistics for the behavioral sciences.* New York: McGraw-Hill, 1956.

Spence, J. T., Helmreich, R., & Stapp, J. Ratings of self and peers on sex-role attributes and their relation to self-esteem and conceptions of masculinity and femininity. *Journal of Personality and Social Psychology,* 1975, **32,** 29–39.

Steinmann, A., & Fox, D. J. *The male dilemma: How to survive the sexual revolution.* New York: Jason Aronson, 1974.

Thompson, N. L., & McCandless, B. R. The homosexual orientation and its antecedents. In A. Davids (Ed.), *Child personality and psychopathology.* Vol. 3. New York: Wiley, 1976.

Williams, J. E., & Best, D. L. Sex stereotypes and trait favorability on the Adjective Check List. *Educational and Psychological Measurement,* 1977, **37,** 101-10.

Chapter 3

Measurement of Sex-Role Behavior

Generally speaking, discussions of psychological measurement are about as interesting as watching ink dry. Revelations regarding item derivation, reliability, validity, response set, dissimulation, and the like are far less exciting than they are important. In the case of sex-role measures, however, we may have an exception to the rule, since the nebulous qualities of the sex-role concept place special significance on the manner in which sex-role behaviors are reduced to measurement. The elusiveness of the subject matter may tempt the social scientist to substitute procedures by which a yardstick is arbitrarily applied for a definitive specification of that subject matter. Operational definition of sex-role status through test scores replaces conceptual clarity and puts unique demands on the soundness of the measure. Constantinople (1973) makes much the same point in her earlier critique of sex-role measures.

The plan for this chapter will be, first, to consider several issues of special relevance to sex-role measurement. Missing from this discussion will be many of the technical requirements of all psychological tests. Scale validity, reliability, item homogeneity, and effects of response set are routinely considered by those who construct tests, and information relevant to each should be available elsewhere for the psychometric instruments to be discussed later in this chapter. (Validity evidence for the ACL sex-role scales has been reviewed already.) These technical requirements are largely concerned with the meaning that can be inferred from responses made to a questionnaire, and the psychometric issues are much the same whether the object of measurement is sex-role behavior or other psychological variables.

Following the exposition of measurement issues, we will look at some of the better-known sex-role measures, focusing upon those tests that allow for independent scoring of masculinity and femininity and figure prominently in our discussion at one place or another in the book. This progression will allow us to examine each scale in light of the special psychometric issues relevant to sex-role measurement.

ISSUES RELEVANT TO SEX-ROLE MEASUREMENT

Item Form

A personality test, such as a sex-role measure, offers a convenient way of measuring behaviors under standard conditions so that individual differences among individuals along a particular dimension or set of dimensions may be ascertained. While numerous types of responses may be sampled for a personality test, more often than not test developers have chosen to use verbal inquiry to elicit self-report information from the individual.

Self-report personality tests or questionnaires have received their share of criticism but, nevertheless, there are very good reasons why they have maintained their popularity as psychological measures. Alternative approaches to measuring individual regularities in behavior have proven to be neither practical nor effective. For example, direct observation of sex-role behaviors represent a useful research procedure, but logistical problems make this approach too unwieldy for other than special use. Projective approaches, in which subjects are given a vague stimulus and few restrictions are placed upon their responses to the stimulus, are preferred by some. However, I have serious reservations about their potential for sex-role measurement. At least no convincing rationale or body of empirical evidence is apparent that would encourage use of projective tests for this purpose.

Even if we agree that self-administered questionnaires are the most economical way of quantifying sex-role behaviors, there is still considerable latitude in the form chosen for inquiry. Three forms of items will find representation among the sex-role questionnaires to be considered later in this chapter. Ratings have been used to have the individual identify how characteristic an attribute is along a scale from low to high. A true-false option may be offered to the individual regarding whether a given behavior is a stable feature of personality. Similarly, a dichotomous present-absent choice may be required of the individual with regard to a number of potentially characteristic behaviors.

The major a priori difference among these three forms is the apparent advantage of rating scales in that they offer more extensive degrees of choice beyond the simple dichotomy of true-false or present-absent. Some sex-role behaviors may be more salient than others for a given individual, though all of them might be considered "characteristic." Graduated rating scales allow such distinctions to be drawn. The advantage of being able to make more fine-grained judgments regarding sex-role behaviors may be more apparent than real, however. For example, Ruffalo (1971) attempted to improve prediction from the Adjective Check List by introducing a rating-scale format in place of the standard present-absent choice in response to each adjective. More useful self-descriptions were not generated by the ponderous and time-consuming item format. It remains a possibility that even bright, cooperative college subjects can do no better in self-description than make crude present-absent, true-false decisions about their sex-role attributes.

One reason why the opportunity for more refined judgments about personal attributes may contribute little, if anything, to accuracy of sex-role measurement is that we are asking our subjects to abstract their behavioral qualities from a variety of situational contexts, and this places serious limits on what each has to work with. When you ask a person whether he is "dominant" on sex-role inventories, there is little opportunity for him to narrow this decision down to specific situational conditions and to particular reference groups—peers, parents, siblings, strangers, and so forth. Accordingly, he must base his summary judgment of whether he dominates interpersonal relationships on an abstraction distilled from different people and situations, and even from different occasions with a particular person and situation. Allowing the self-rater a seven-point scale for his response may not be much of a favor. The contention that sex-role characteristics (along with other personality attributes) can be only crudely evaluated when there is no clear situational focus is consistent with the growing skepticism about personality prediction without situational reference (Mischel, 1977). In fact, we documented this forcibly in the previous chapter when the Block technique, which combines sex-role self-description and situational context, was discussed. The average consistency of sex-role behavior from one interpersonal context to another was not impressive for either sex, although it was somewhat higher for females.

Unipolar Versus Bipolar Scaling of Sex-Role Behavior

As was noted in Chapter Two, earlier assumptions regarding sex-role behavior held masculinity and femininity to be mutually exclusive both with regard to their development and to their prevalence in the make-up of different individuals. In psychometric terms, masculinity and femininity were previously thought to be on a single bipolar dimension, so that the more you are of one, the less you are of the other. The challenge to this assumption of bipolarity by Constantinople (1973) heralded a reconceptualization of sex roles, leading assessment to be modified to accommodate the notion of the roles' independence of each other.

The issue here is not whether the potentials for masculinity and femininity can coexist within the same individual: the evidence over the past five years shows that they can. What remains in question is what *independent* should be taken to mean. Statistical tradition leads us to define *independence* as "showing a true correlation of zero," and violation of this expectation by any pair of masculine and feminine sex-role scales is currently viewed as reflecting unfavorably upon the construction of the scales. It is presumed that scaling procedures have not captured the true essence of sex-role behavior, which includes the total unrelatedness of its two components.

The major problem with this statistical expectation is that it lacks empirical foundation. The actual relation between masculine and feminine dispositions within the natural social order can only be gauged by using our imperfect measuring devices, including sex-role questionnaires. Current masculinity and femininity scales may have been calibrated in their construction to show as close to zero correlation as possible, but the fact that uncorrelated sex-role scales can be constructed does not confirm the assumption that these behavioral tendencies are uncorrelated to begin with. A certain degree of circularity may be noted.

What is the alternative view? There are really two other positions that could be adopted with regard to the true relation between masculine and feminine dispositions without relinquishing the assumption that these behaviors follow *relatively* independent paths of development. One position would be that a somewhat relaxed version of functional independence is in order; the alternative to being totally mutually exclusive is not necessarily to be totally unrelated. This view would be supported by modest negative (or positive) correlations between masculinity and femininity. A second position, somewhat more complicated, is that mutual exclusiveness may be more the case at certain levels of sex-role behavior than at others. One might look for negative correlations between masculinity and femininity at the extremes of either, but not in a wide middle range. Exceedingly masculine men, for example, may embrace very few feminine qualities so that mutual exclusiveness (and a substantial negative correlation) is the case, but only within a limited and extreme range.

Despite the difficulties in drawing firm conclusions about the true correlation between masculinity and femininity because of imperfections in our measuring instruments, there are ways of looking at relevant data that could shed light on the matter. Since this book will depend primarily upon the ACL sex-role scales for its conclusions, those scales will be used for present purposes. The correlation between the "independent" Masculinity and Femininity Scales of the ACL has been reported to be -.42 for college males and -.24 for college females (Heilbrun, 1976). The 6 percent to 18 percent common variance between the scales, while low, suggests something of the prior notion of mutual exclusivity, in that the negative feature of the relation between masculinity and femininity was retained. In contrast, the Bem Sex-Role Inventory (1974) produced correlations between the two scales hovering around zero in four samples of college males and females ($r = -.14$ to $+.11$). Baucom (1976) reports that none of the four sample correlations between his sex-role scales derived for use with the California Psychological Inventory (Gough, 1957) achieved statistical significance (although we are not told their magnitudes). The sex-role scales for the Personal Attributes Questionnaire (Spence, Helmreich, & Stapp, 1975) were found to diverge most widely of all from prior conceptions of bipolarity for masculine and feminine behaviors. They not only failed to show a high negative correlation but were found to have a low positive correlation ($r = +.14$ for females and $+.47$ for males). Thus, you have a choice regarding the true nature of the relation between masculinity and femininity. If you wish, you can consider these sex-role dispositions to hold a low inverse relation, no relation, or a low positive relation.

Let us pursue the low negative correlations between the ACL Masculinity and Femininity Scales to see what kind of case can be made for their correspondence with the behavioral reality of things. One way to approach this would be to plot the relation for males and females to see whether the covariation is linear or curvilinear (more apparent at the extremes), and whether this holds for both sexes. The relation between degree of masculinity and feminity was considered by determining the mean ACL Femininity Scale score to be found for those within successive half-sigma ranges on the Masculinity Scale. All subjects were college undergraduates and included 471 males and 668 females. The results, plotted in table 3.1, are intriguing. They illustrate the fact that the two scales have a low negative correlation; as the Masculinity Scale score range increases, the Femininity Scale mean tends to drop gradually. However, the curves for the two sexes depart when extremes of masculinity are considered. The female is pictured as showing only a gradual diminishment of femininity even at the extremes of masculinity, whereas males at these extremes demonstrate an abrupt decrement in femininity. The higher negative correlation for males on the ACL is obviously due to a barrenness of femininity in hypermasculine males.

Table 3.1. Variation in Femininity with Changes in Level of Masculinity

Sex	Level of Masculinity								
	<35	35–39	40–44	45–49	50–54	55–59	60–64	65–69	>69
Males									
N	21	40	80	79	96	77	27	29	22
M	55.71	53.60	49.80	49.59	47.47	45.70	46.81	38.34	33.82
Females									
N	52	73	116	94	143	85	43	34	28
M	54.88	52.83	52.87	50.09	48.44	49.34	45.51	45.15	42.89

NOTE: Masculinity and femininity values are based on ACL sex-role scales with a mean of 50 and sigma of 10.

Do these progressions of means, especially the apparent sex difference, make any sense in light of sex-role theory? There is a nucleus of agreement among prominent sex-role researchers (see Bem, 1974; Spence, Helmreich, & Stapp,

1975) that the basic core of masculinity resides in an instrumental orientation, whereas an expressive orientation lies at the heart of femininity. These constructs, initially proposed by Parsons and Bales (1955), refer to the pursuit of personal goals in the former case and a concern with the positive quality of relationships in the latter. If I may return to a point made in the previous chapter, it is commonly overlooked that the instrumental role player, according to this sociological theory, is committed to the achievement of personal goals even at the risk of ignoring or if necessary disrupting personal relationships. It seems to me that the Parsons-Bales theory lends itself to predicting a certain degree of incompatibility between masculine instrumentalness and feminine expressiveness when concern over relationships is at issue. Furthermore, the lack of expressive concern for the quality of personal relationships might be expected to show up only in extreme cases of goal achievement at all cost. As Jeanne Block (1973) has pointed out, femininity as concern with the quality of relationships and with the welfare of others is deeply rooted in the socialization process. Instrumental proclivities would have to be intense indeed to preclude the basic lesson of social concern that receives such emphasis in middle-class society. The question remains whether the ultimate instrumental role player is more likely to be a male than a female. Our data tells us that it is, and such a conclusion seems to have intuitive merit.

This discussion of the issue of independence between the sex roles is not intended to prove to the reader that we have gone too far in dismissing the assumption of an inverse relation between masculine and feminine dispositions. By my own admission, one cannot gain perfect insight into natural social phenomena by using imperfect representations of those phenomena. I have tried to argue persuasively that we should keep our options open regarding this relation until time reveals how much total sex-role independence was a discovery of the 1970s or an invention.

The Measurement of Androgyny

The most important construct to evolve from the new conceptualization of independent masculine and feminine development is that of androgyny, the presence of both dispositions in the same individual. Although the measurement of androgyny has received some attention in an earlier chapter, its importance merits more elaborated comment.

The standard approach to measuring androgyny has been to develop a fourfold table of sex-role outcomes based upon the four possibilities for high-low scores on a masculinity and a femininity scale. With the sample median usually chosen as the midpoint, each person's set of scores may allow for assignment to high masculine–high feminine (androgynous), high masculine–low feminine (masculine), low masculine–high feminine (feminine), or low masculine–low feminine (undifferentiated) categories. This approach to defining androgyny is especially useful when the interest is in comparing the various outcomes to each other.

The problem with the fourfold typology procedure is the unreliability of classification around the midpoints. It was pointed out in the previous chapter that if the median scores for a sample were 50 on both the masculinity and femininity scales, a person scoring 51 on each scale would be defined as androgynous. A person scoring 50 on both scales would be assigned to the undifferentiated category. Yet no one would be surprised if, upon retesting, the two subjects fluctuated enough in their scores so that they exchanged sex roles. One solution to this problem is to exclude subjects for whom either score falls within a certain range on either side of the midpoints. This should result in the elimination of subjects whose borderline scores make categorical assignment a perilous exercise.

A second approach to measuring androgyny treats it as a continuous variable rather than as a discrete category. This offers several advantages and at least one disadvantage. My effort in this regard (Heilbrun & Pitman, 1979) has already been discussed in a previous chapter, but reconsideration at this point will help elaborate the continuous variable approach. Androgyny has two characteristics that define it. First, it requires a potential for masculine and for feminine behavior that exceeds expectation (extensity requirement). Second, it requires a similarity in the strength of both dispositions so that neither will predominate (balance requirement). Given strength and balance of both sex-role dispositions, we have androgyny.

A simple formula that incorporates both the magnitude and balance attributes of androgyny is all that is necessary to represent this construct by a continuous score. The index used in our research is

$$(M + F) - |M - F|$$

where M = masculinity score, F = femininity score, and the terms represent the algebraic sum of the two scores (extensity) minus the absolute difference of the two scores (balance). This is an all-purpose index that can be applied to any pair of sex-role scales as long as they are comparably derived and show similar score ranges. Although more complicated formulas for scoring androgyny could without doubt be derived, the superiority of more impressive-appearing indices should not be taken for granted. As we have said, just so much mathematical refinement is warranted when your raw materials are no more precise than summary behavioral ratings.

The proposed androgyny index, when applied to the ACL sex-role scales, provides a continuous score with a lower limit of 0 and a high score (to date) in our research of about 130. Keep in mind that raw scores on these scales convert to standard scores with a mean of 50 and a standard deviation of 10. Sample androgyny scores have been remarkably stable. An androgyny score median of

92 has been found for most samples that we have inspected thus far, and this has been true for both college males and females. I also have applied this scoring procedure to sex-role scales developed for the California Psychological Inventory and shall describe this effort later in the book. These scales, converted to standard scores with a mean of 50 and sigma of 10, produced average androgyny scores of about 89 for both males and females.

The advantages of treating androgyny as a continuous variable correspond to the disadvantages of defining it in terms of a dichotomous category. Rather than having someone emerge as androgynous on one occasion and as a totally different sex-role type the next, continuous scoring allows for less dramatic shifts in degree of androgyny. Categorical assignment requires that everyone who meets the criteria be considered equally androgynous; continuous scoring offers the opportunity for the researcher to deal with individual differences in androgyny even among those who can be generally so described. Another advantage is that continuous scoring presents the researcher an opportunity to look for curvilinear relations between androgyny and another variable. Such subtleties are likely to be overlooked when a typological approach to sex-role measurement is used.

The one disadvantage that I can see to using an androgyny index is that you lose information about alternative sex-role outcomes. There is only one way to achieve a high androgyny score—demonstrate both extensity and balance in masculinity and femininity scores. However, there are many ways to obtain a low androgyny score—be clearly masculine, feminine, or undifferentiated. If the researcher's interests are served by including the alternative sex-role outcomes, then the typological approach must be used.

Androgynous Self-Description: Articulation or Fluency?

The procedure by which self-descriptions are obtained on the ACL raises an issue that is obscured by other formats used in sex-role assessment. The subject in responding to the ACL is asked to select self-characteristic adjectives among the 300 listed, but is not told how many of these should be selected. Although the average college student tends to endorse about 100 of the behaviors represented on the ACL, the range is considerable. Norms for the many scales that have been developed for the ACL are usually based on the assumption that variability in number of endorsements results largely from differences in fluency, the willingness or ability to represent personal characteristics to the fullest under conditions of assessment. Accordingly, differences in number of endorsements have always been treated as a source of measurement error, and compensated for by comparing each subject's responses to those of similar productivity.

One of the implications of androgyny that has previously not been given much attention is that in theory the androgynous person has a more extensive repertoire of sex-role behaviors than those with stereotyped sex-role makeups, and especially more than the undifferentiated person who is lacking in both masculine and feminine attributes. Presumably, androgyny allows for a highly articulated display of sex-role behaviors; whatever the specific demands of the situation, behaviors are available to meet them. In the case of androgyny, then, it could be argued that the more extensive endorsement of sex-role items is a realistic representation of more articulated behaviors, rather than a more fluent style on the test.

The articulation/fluency issue arose in a recent study (Heilbrun, 1978) that reported extensive differences in mean numbers of endorsements of the ACL for male and female college students defined as androgynous (114, 112), masculine (99, 104), feminine (100, 104), and undifferentiated (79,85). The important finding for our present discussion is that the greater articulation of androgynous subjects (or greater fluency as the case may be) had at least as much to do with their general behavior as with their sex-role behavior; androgynous individuals report a very extensive repertoire of responses available to meet specific situational requirements of all kinds.

The distinction between articulation (the actual number of behavioral characteristics in the individual's repertory) and fluency (the extent to which the individual can or will report behaviors from this actual number) is impossible to make as long as both are being inferred from the same instrument. In order to make this distinction, additional data were collected from 149 college undergraduates (64 males and 85 females) in which fluency and articulation were not confounded. Subjects were asked to rate their own instrumental and expressive qualities on independent ten-point rating scales. The androgyny scoring formula described previously in this chapter was applied to these scores to derive a continuous score that ranged from 6 (low androgyny) to 20 (high androgyny). This distribution of scores was split at its median, separately for each sex, and combined to form high androgynous and low androgynous groups. The same subjects also were asked to describe their own characteristic behaviors by completing the ACL. The number of behaviors checked was also split at the medians (102 endorsements) and chi square procedures were applied. Sixty percent of the high self-rated androgyny subjects also used higher numbers of specific behaviors in self-description, whereas only 38 percent of the low-androgyny subjects surpassed the cutting score. Thus, when androgyny was defined without allowing fluency to lend its influence, the same finding emerged as was reported in the previous study. Androgyny is associated with a more extensive general repertoire of behavior. While confirmation of heightened behavioral articulation in androgyny requires that we go beyond self-report data, it remains my strong conviction that this relation is a real one.

The most important implication of the seeming fact that androgyny is more likely to be found in the highly articulated person has to do with its developmental antecedents, something we shall consider at greater length in the final chapter. As it now stands, the more extended range of sex-role behaviors available to the androgynous person appears to be only part of a more general picture of articulated response dispositions. If so, the focus of our search for antecedents may broaden to include any developmental factor that encourages children and adolescents to differentiate all types of response to finer nuances of situations, and the reward systems that reinforce more varied responses.

An incidental finding concerning these ratings of instrumental and expressive orientations was the frequency with which certain sex types failed to complete them. These two ratings were included among several self-report items, and when subjects were subsequently broken down into sex types based upon the ACL scales, surprising differences emerged. The percentages of males who failed to complete these instrumental and expressive ratings were: androgynous, 6 percent; masculine, 11 percent; feminine, 0 percent; undifferentiated, 19 percent. These percentages for the female groups were: androgynous, 5 percent; masculine, 6 percent; feminine, 28 percent; undifferentiated, 37 percent. The deficit in sex-role development implied by the undifferentiated sex type apparently makes it difficult for the person to gauge these orientations and led many to skip these judgments on the questionnaire.

Independent or Common Norms for the Sexes?

It may come as a surprise that this would be proposed as an issue, since the ACL sex-role scales are normed independently by sex. The question here is whether the strength of masculine or feminine tendencies in the individual should be inferred by comparison of scores with those achieved by his or her own sex or by comparison with the standard of a mixed-sex group. The issue boils down to whether the masculinity or femininity of males should be determined by comparing a subject to other males or to people in general. In the same fashion, should sex-role dispositions in females be gauged relative to only other females?

The usual guidelines for developing test norms would tell us to have separate norms when there are sex differences on the behavior in question, although the decision might await some determination of pragmatic value for independent or mixed norms. Such value, as far as sex-role behavior is concerned, certainly would depend in part how well scales could predict using either type of norm, but this begs the question of what is to be predicted. One underlying consideration is whether people respond to masculine or feminine behaviors in their day-to-day lives on an absolute or relative basis. Do they greet an assertive, goal-directed act by in effect saying, "That's pretty masculine" or "That's pretty masculine *for a woman*"? Is an open show of emotion an occasion for thinking, "How feminine" or "How feminine *for a man*"?

My own impression, for which I cannot provide any solid evidence, is that most people in the American cultural mainstream will demonstrate or respond to masculine and feminine behaviors within a relativistic framework, so that norms separated by sex should be more useful. However, there may be cultural pockets in our own country or cultures outside of the United States in which differential expectations for stereotyped sex-role behaviors are far less powerful, or even nonexistent. In such cases, there would be no need to maintain separate normative standards.

There is one research circumstance in which a common normative standard would be mandatory, even though people respond to masculinity and femininity on a relative basis. Implicit in some feminist social commentary, at least as I interpret it, is the idea that sex-role distinctions should disappear, so that in principle everyone, male or female, can enjoy equal accessibility of masculine and feminine behaviors. If this idea is ever to be seriously investigated, then the extent to which any given person has achieved unisex standards of behavior must be determined by combined norms.

In case anyone is skeptical about whether the use of one or the other normative procedure by the sex-role researcher would make any difference, a simple exercise was performed in which the same college subjects were assigned to the four sex-role types in terms of both. In one case, ACL Masculinity and Femininity Scale responses were scored by reference to separate male and female norms. Median splits were determined for both distributions, and subjects were assigned to the sex-type categories in the usual way. Then the same subjects were combined into a single group, and the masculinity and femininity distributions of the combined group were split at their medians. New assignments to the four sex types were then made. Table 3.2 gives the percentage of agreement between the two sets. As can be seen, the same people form quite different sex-typed groups depending on whether sex-role status is defined on a relative or an absolute basis.

Table 3.2. Agreement between Sex-Typing Assignments Using Separate and Combined Normative References

Sex of Subject	(Percentage of Subjects Appearing in the Same Sex-Role Group)			
	Androgynous	Masculine	Feminine	Undifferentiated
Males	61	64	100	43
Females	41	100	54	40

Social Desirability and Stereotyped Behavior

The position taken by both Bem (1974) and Spence, Helmreich, and Stapp (1975) is that measures of stereotyped sex roles should include only ideal or socially desirable behaviors. I am committed to a somewhat different position, expounded in the first chapter, namely that stereotyped roles have in fact accumulated less positive or even negative correlates in our culture than these other researchers indicate. Obviously, this divergence in opinion lends itself to qualitative differences in the composition of sex-role measures that have evolved out of our respective laboratories. It should be noted that the possible importance of negative sex-typed attributes has not been ignored by the Texas group (Spence & Helmreich, 1978), especially as they contribute to maladjustment, nor by other researchers (Kelly, Caudill, Hathorn, & O'Brien, 1977) as far as qualitative differences in the sex-role composition of the four sex types are concerned.

Persuasion regarding either point of view is not so much at issue here, but rather the psychometric implications of incorporating less socially desirable attributes in a sex-role questionnaire. One danger that occurs to me is that a questionnaire comprised totally of socially desirable items must confound the measurement of androgyny or undifferentiation with self-esteem, thereby limiting the use of the instrument. This follows from the fact that a higher self-rating on any positively valued behavior, masculine or feminine, contributes to eventual classification as androgynous, just as the endorsement of more positively valued behavior also reflects more self-esteem. Conversely, lower ratings on all such items contribute to undifferentiated status and connote less self-esteem. The Spence-Helmreich-Stapp Personal Attributes Questionnaire and the Bem Sex-Role Inventory both seem vulnerable to this limitation. The ACL sex-role scales, which include more favorable than unfavorable attributes, are not above reproach in this regard, although the degree to which androgyny/undifferentiation and self-esteem are confounded should be less. We shall consider ACL data in a moment that will cast some light on this matter.

A second psychometric consideration that could be linked to the type of stereotyped behaviors included in a sex-role inventory is the extent to which response sets may contribute to respondent performance. A response set, for those who missed this tremendously overworked psychometric research issue of the 1960s, is any response disposition that systematically influences performance on a psychological test but is uncorrelated with what the test is trying to predict. Response sets, then, contribute only to measurement error. By far the greatest attention among the many sets thought to be of importance was accorded to "social desirability responding," the tendency to endorse the more socially valued rather than the factually correct response alternative.

My colleague Leonard Goodstein and I were among the few who argued against the emphasis placed upon social desirability as a source of error on questionnaires (Heilbrun, 1964a; Heilbrun & Goodstein, 1961). That our efforts went unnoticed is evident; researchers continue to demonstrate unqualified concern with the extent to which test scores accurately reflect the criterion behavior of the respondent or just a defensive, status-seeking veneer represented by the set to respond in a socially desirable way. Our contention was that the socialization process almost always results in our learning to make positively sanctioned choices, to seek socially valued goals. In short, we are conditioned to behave in socially desirable ways to the extent that the acculturation process is effective. Given this fact, what else could a test respondent do when asked to engage in accurate self-description but to select more socially desirable alternatives? In retrospect, it appears that the notion of a social desirability response set was a grossly overgeneralized version of dissimulation ("faking good") test-taking behavior, in which the individual knowingly lies to establish a more favorable impression.

So much for dated controversies. What is important now is that many still contend that the social desirability of response options is a viable psychometric concern, and therefore this point of view should not be ignored. Its relevance here is that those instruments that include negative stereotyped behaviors, like the ACL, may be more susceptible to defensive sets. (Both the Bem and Spence-Helmreich-Stapp scales have been reported to be uncontaminated by social desirability response set.) One way to establish whether ACL sex-role scores are readily influenced by the subject's attempts to create a favorable impression is to instruct the subject to do just that and see what happens to the scores. Complementing this "fake good" dissimulation condition would be another condition in which subjects would be told to create an unfavorable impression by their choices of characteristic behaviors ("fake bad"). Heilbrun's (1976) study of dissimulation on the ACL has been discussed earlier in this book, regarding how the results reflect upon sex-role stereotypes of psychological health and illness. Our perspective at this juncture has to do with the susceptibility of the sex-role scales to dissimulation.

A summary of the effects of dissimulation on ACL sex-role scales is repeated from Chapter Two in table 3.3 for the convenience of the reader. The most critical aspect of these figures is that the scores do not depart radically from the expected score of 50 even when the subject is trying to depict a totally positive self-image under "fake good" instructions. The 4- to 6-point departure from 50 is little more than would be expected from sampling fluctuations under standard conditions of ACL administration. The "fake bad" instructions had a greater impact upon scores, at least for the Femininity Scale. The college students' version of psychological ill-health resulted in plummeting femininity scores. However, this effect of instructions is not of much consequence in considering the vulnerability of the scales to deception. It would be quite unusual for college students (who make up the bulk of subjects in current sex-role research) to adopt

Table 3.3. Effect of "Fake Good" and "Fake Bad" Instructions on Masculinity and Femininity
Scores

	"Fake Good"		"Fake Bad"	
Scale	Males	Females	Males	Females
Masculinity	56.46	52.68	43.32	51.26
Femininity	46.30	46.42	32.82	19.58

NOTE: These mean scale values should be compared to an expected mean of 50 under standard
instructional conditions, and are based on the protocols of 50 males and 19 females.

this kind of self-derogating set. Unless the draft is reinstituted, there is little
reason to expect these usually candid young men and women to intentionally
portray themselves as psychologically unhealthy.

The implications of including negative sex-role correlates in masculinity and
femininity scales can be considered in yet another way. The ACL Masculinity
and Femininity Scales include both favorable and unfavorable stereotype
qualities, as I have said before. The results of Gough's early work, in which
college students were asked to judge the favorability of ACL behaviors (Gough
& Heilbrun, 1965) allowed him to identify the seventy-five most positive and
seventy-five most negative terms among the 300 on the ACL. Using these
categories as a reference, favorable and unfavorable sex-role subscales were
developed for both the Masculinity and Femininity Scales. The raw score
correlations of these subscales for 145 male and 222 female college students offer
us the opportunity to consider social desirability from a second perspective. If the
endorsement of sex-role traits is to reflect the importance of social desirability as
it has been traditionally understood, we would expect positive correlations
between the number of positive masculine items endorsed and the number of
positive feminine items. This is exactly what was found: $r = .35$ $(p < .01)$ for
males and $r = .27$ $(p < .01)$ for females. There was a low but significant
tendency to subscribe to favorable sex-role attributes of both types. The same
seeming importance of social value as opposed to social reality was observed
when the numbers of negative masculine and feminine items endorsed by the
subjects were correlated. Males who checked more negative masculine items as
characteristic also checked more negative feminine items as characteristic $(r =
.22, p < .01)$. Females followed suit $(r = .15, p < .05)$.

Thus far, it would appear that this correlational analysis portrays the ACL
sex-role scales as vulnerable to some set to describe oneself in favorable or
unfavorable terms. Yet the correlations between scores on favorable and
unfavorable subscales within each sex-role scale are needed to bring the social
desirability question to a convincing conclusion. Negative correlations between

these subscales would mean that the tendency to endorse positive sex-role attributes is associated with the avoidance of negative sex-role attributes in self-description, both sides of the social desirability coin. However, just the opposite was found. Males who selected more positive masculine traits as self-descriptive also selected more negative masculine traits ($r = .71, p < .01$); females also demonstrated the same thing with regard to positive and negative masculine attributes ($r = .47, p < .01$). The correlations between the two qualitative subscales of the Femininity Scale were also positive, indicating that males ($r = .40, p < .01$) and females ($r = .29, p < .01$) who show higher femininity do so in terms of both favorable and unfavorable qualities.

What do these correlations mean? First, they clearly do not support the idea that social desirability is playing a significant role as a response set, whether this is understood in the traditional sense or as positive dissimulation. The correlations between favorable and unfavorable subscales indicate that the same people who endorse more positive behaviors also endorse more negative behaviors. That is not how a social desirability response set is supposed to work. These results do not even fit with our own idea that social desirability responding is important as it reflects the values inculcated by the socialization process. We have reasoned that socially desirable characteristics are learned because we have been reinforced for these behaviors. Thus, when middle-class subjects typically choose desirable response options on personality tests, it can be explained by the fact that these are accurate depictions of how highly socialized people behave in general. It is not easy to explain within this framework why the number of positive and negative sex-role features should covary positively. Reinforcement principles would lead us to expect, for example, that the boy who learns positive masculine attributes because he enjoys the rewards would complement this by not learning unfavorable masculine attributes in order to avoid their aversive consequences. It would appear that explanation may be rooted in the articulation phenomenon, in whatever governs the differences in size of response repertoires available to the individual. The fact that all of the correlations were positive tells us that the larger the number of responses of one type you have, the larger the number of another.

CURRENT SEX-ROLE SCALES

There shall be no attempt here to describe all sex-role measures that have found representation in the research literature over the past several decades. Constantinople (1973) offers such a survey, as well as an important statement regarding the importance of disentangling the measurement of masculine and feminine dispositions. We shall consider only those measures that offer independent sex-role scales in the present survey of tests, and only four of them at that. The choice was guided by several considerations. The four sex-role questionnaires include the two most popular as far as research usage is concerned, the Bem Sex-Role Inventory (1974) and the Spence-Helmreich-Stapp Personal Attributes Questionnaire (1975). Research reported by other investigators commonly involves reference to one or the other of these instruments. The remaining two scales contribute heavily (Heilbrun Masculinity and Femininity Scales; 1976) or more sparingly (Baucom MSC and FMN Scales; 1976) to the data on which the conclusions of this book are based.

As was said at the outset, the "bread and butter" concerns of psychometric instrumentation have not been addressed in this chapter. The fact of the matter is that such test characteristics as validity (whether the test measures what it is alleged to measure) and reliability (whether the test provides stable estimates of whatever it measures) are not issues at all, but obvious psychometric requirements. We have been concerned about these properties in an earlier chapter only in the case of the ACL scales that figure so prominently in this book. References will be cited where such information may be found for the remaining instruments.

Bem Sex-Role Inventory (BSRI)

Bem (1974) traces the evolution of the BSRI back to two basic assumptions: the instrumental/expressive distinction between men and women (Parsons & Bales, 1955); and the positive nature of the traits and behaviors constituting sex-role behaviors. Bem deserves acknowledgement as the first to publish separate masculine and feminine sex-role scales. A large number of personality characteristics were generated judgmentally by Bem and her associates that seemed to be both positive and masculine or feminine in tone. Following this, college undergraduate judges were asked to rate the desirability for men and women of each characteristic along a seven-point scale. The criteria for inclusion in the final scales were independent judgments by male judges and by female judges that a given characteristic was more desirable ($p < .05$) for men than for women or vice versa, and final selection by the test constructor. Twenty items were chosen for the Masculinity Scale and 20 for the Femininity Scale by this progressive series of judgments (see table 3.4). The BSRI also features a social desirability scale, for those committed to the importance of consulting such a feature.

The BSRI requires subjects to indicate how well each of these sex-role characteristics describes their behavior by checking along a seven-point scale ranging from "never or almost never true" to "always or almost always true." The mean self-rating for all masculinity items and for all femininity items can then be used to derive an androgyny score (by subtracting the Masculinity Scale mean from the Femininity Scale mean). When the mean scores depart sufficiently in value from each other, the subject is defined as masculine or feminine depending upon the direction of difference. Similarity in scores denotes androgyny, according to Bem's original scoring system.

Table 3.4. Masculinity and Femininity Scales of the Bem Sex-Role Inventory

Masculinity Scale Items	Femininity Scale Items
Acts as a leader	Affectionate
Aggressive	Cheerful
Ambitious	Childlike
Analytical	Compassionate
Assertive	Does not use hard language
Athletic	Eager to soothe hurt feelings
Competitive	Feminine
Defends own beliefs	Flatterable
Dominant	Gentle
Forceful	Gullible
Has leadership abilities	Loves children
Independent	Loyal
Individualistic	Sensitive to the needs of others
Makes decisions easily	Shy
Masculine	Soft-spoken
Self-reliant	Sympathetic
Self-sufficient	Tender
Strong personality	Understanding
Willing to take a stand	Warm
Willing to take risks	Yielding

A limitation in this original scoring system noted by Spence, Helmreich, and Stapp (1975) is that androgyny scoring involves only the requirement that masculinity and femininity be balanced, and not that they show extensity. The person very low on both sex-role dimensions would have to be considered just as androgynous as the person very high on both. This deficiency was later acknowledged by Bem (1977). If the BSRI scales were used by dichotomizing the sample distribution of each dimension and assigning subjects to one of four high/low sex-role outcomes, the androgyny-scoring problem could be avoided altogether. The formula used to derive a continuous androgyny score for the ACL also could easily be applied to the BSRI with extensity (Femininity Scale mean rating plus Masculinity Scale mean rating) and balance (Femininity Scale mean rating minus Masculinity Scale mean rating) being compared subtractively.

Spence-Helmreich-Stapp Personal Attributes Questionnaire (PAQ)

The other sex-role instrument that has achieved wide usage among researchers is the PAQ developed by Janet Spence and her coworkers, Robert Helmreich and Joy Stapp (1975). Spence and Helmreich (1978) have recently published full information on this and related measures in book form.

The development of the PAQ is traced back to an original pool of items describing characteristics thought by students to differentiate men and women (Rosenkrantz, Vogel, Bee, Broverman, & Broverman, 1968). This pool was exposed to further judgmental scrutiny by the University of Texas group. Additional samples of college undergraduates judged their stereotypic meaning for adult males and females and for male and female college students and considered how well each conformed to the ideal for men and women. Subjects also were asked to describe themselves according to each behavior.

The result of the rational operations was the final selection of fifty-five items that were judged to represent ideal masculine or feminine stereotypic characteristics. Many of these items proved capable of discriminating between college males and females, although the feminine items proved more effective in this regard than the masculine. Since the characteristics represented in all items were deemed socially desirable for both sexes alike, only positive stereotypic features were included. Thus the PAQ and BSRI share two important things in their construction: (1) each was based exclusively on judgments of sex-role stereotypes, and (2) each required that stereotypes represent socially valued behaviors. The forty-one items within the male-valued (masculine) and female-valued (feminine) scales of the PAQ are found in table 3.5; the sex-specific scale need not concern us at this point.

Another important similarity in test development between the PAQ and BSRI rests in the fact that Spence et al. also attribute central importance to the instrumental/expressive distinctions between masculinity and femininity. The aggressive goal orientation of the instrumental orientation is easily inferred from the items making up the PAQ Masculinity Scale, just as expressive concern with human relationships is apparent in the Femininity Scale. However, the range of content within each sex role scale appears to extend far beyond the instrumental/expressive distinction into such dimensions as masculine independence/individualism and feminine emotionality. The same kind of conclusion derives from inspection of ACL sex-role items. It is not surprising, then, that factor analytic studies of the composition of sex-role scales consistently report multifactorial structures with both masculine and feminine items (e.g., Edwards, Van Buren, & Zabriskie, 1978; Edwards, Gaa, & Liberman, 1978). Not that the factorial nomenclatures have proven all that helpful to date, but suggestions for future research that takes multifactorial structure into consideration will be made in the last chapter. At the least, factor analyses serve to remind us that even though instrumental and expressive qualities are important to understanding the sex roles, they are not the whole story by any means.

Table 3.5. Male-Valued and Female-Valued Scales of the Spence-Helmreich-Stapp Personal Attributes Questionnaire

Male-Valued Scale Items	Female-Valued Scale Items
Independent	Emotional
Not easily influenced	Doesn't hide emotions
Good at sports	Considerate
Not excitable in a minor crisis	Grateful
Active	Devotes self to others
Competitive	Tactful
Skilled in business	Strong conscience
Knows way of the world	Gentle
Adventurous	Helpful to others
Outspoken	Kind
Interested in sex	Aware of other's feelings
Makes decisions easily	Neat
Doesn't give up easily	Creative
Outgoing	Understanding
Acts as leader	Warm to others
Intellectual	Likes children
Self-confident	Enjoys art and music
Feels superior	Expresses tender feelings
Takes a stand	
Ambitious	
Stands up under pressure	
Forward	
Not timid	

The item format on the PAQ treats each of the stereotyped characteristics as a bipolar dimension, ranging from strong denial at one end to endorsement in strength at the other end. Five-point rating scales are provided to allow subjects to graduate their responses. Scores are obtained by summing the ratings over all items within the scale of masculinity and the scale of femininity.

With the similarities in test construction between the PAQ and BSRI, one might expect that predictions from the two instruments would be quite comparable. However, correlations between the two sets of sex-role scales (.57–.75) reported by Spence and Helmreich (1978) and agreement percentages in assignment of the same subjects to the four sex-role outcomes (41–52 percent) found by Gaa and Liberman (1978) stand as reminders that limited agreement almost always pertains when different measures of the same personality construct are compared.

Baucom MSC and FMN Scales Scored from the California Psychological Inventory

In contrast to the totally judgmental approaches to item derivation assumed by Bem and the Spence group in constructing their sex-role scales, Baucom (1976) approached the task on a purely empirical basis. The basic pool of items were those included in the California Psychological Inventory (Gough, 1957), a true-false questionnaire measuring a host of normal personality variables (including femininity). The basis for selection was a sex difference in response to a given item by college students. The results of this empirical derivation, summarized in table 3.6, were fifty-four items more frequently endorsed by males (masculinity) and forty-two with higher female endorsement (femininity).

Table 3.6. MSC and FMN Scale Items Scored from the California Psychological Inventory

---

Masculine Items

When answered true
I think I would enjoy having authority over people.
I like adventure stories better than romantic stories.
I prefer a shower to a bathtub.
I have no dread of going into a room by myself where other people have already gathered and are talking.
I do not dread seeing a doctor about a sickness or injury.
If given the chance I would make a good leader of people.
I usually feel that life is worthwhile.
I like science.
I would be willing to describe myself as a pretty "strong" personality.
I think I am usually a leader in my group.
At times I have been so entertained by the cleverness of a crook that I have hoped he would get by with it.

When answered false
When in a group of people I usually do what the others want rather than make suggestions.
I am very slow in making up my mind.
It makes me feel like a failure when I hear of the success of someone I know well.
I think I would like the work of a dress designer.
I doubt whether I would make a good leader.
I become quite irritated when I see someone spit on the sidewalk.
It is hard for me to start a conversation with strangers.
I get very nervous if I think that someone is watching me.
I get very tense and anxious when I think other people are disapproving of me.
I am embarrassed by dirty stories.
Sometimes I cross the street just to avoid meeting someone.
I used to keep a diary.
I often feel as if the world was just passing me by.
I don't like to undertake any project unless I have a pretty good idea as to how it will turn out.

Table 3.6 continued

Sometimes I think of things too bad to talk about.
When in a group of people I have trouble thinking of the right things to talk about.
I am likely not to speak to people until they speak to me.
I am somewhat afraid of the dark.
I have a tendency to give up easily when I meet difficult problems.
I certainly feel useless at times.
I am certainly lacking in self-confidence.
I usually don't like to talk much unless I am with people I know very well.
I am inclined to take things hard.
It is hard for me to find anything to talk about when I meet a new person.
Sometimes I feel that I am about to go to pieces.
Sometimes I just can't seem to get going.
I would like to be a nurse.
I sometimes feel that I am a burden to others.
In school I found it very hard to talk before the class.
I must admit I feel sort of scared when I move to a strange place.
It is hard for me to act natural when I am with new people.
I have never done anything dangerous for the thrill of it.
I am afraid to be alone in the dark.
I have been afraid of things or people that I knew could not hurt me.
I get nervous when I have to ask someone for a job.
I seem to do things that I regret more often than other people do.
I usually have to stop and think before I act even in trifling matters.
I am quite a fast reader.
I am embarrassed with people I do not know well.
I feel like giving up quickly when things go wrong.
Even the idea of giving a talk in public makes me afraid.
I dislike to have to talk in front of a group of people.
I must admit it would bother me to put a worm on a fish hook.

Feminine Items

When answered true

The thought of being in an automobile accident is very frightening to me.
I like poetry.
I would like to wear expensive clothes.
Criticism or scolding makes me very uncomfortable.
I have never been in trouble with the law.
I would rather be a steady and dependable worker than a brilliant but unstable one.
I find that a well-ordered mode of life with regular hours is congenial to my temperament.
I usually try to do what is expected of me, and to avoid criticism.
I'm not the type to be a political leader.

When answered false

I think I would like the work of a building contractor.
It's a good thing to know people in the right places so you can get traffic tags, and such things, taken care of.
I am often said to be hotheaded.
Usually I would prefer to work with women.
When I was going to school I played hooky quite often.

Table 3.6 continued

I must admit that I enjoy playing practical jokes on people.
When someone does me a wrong I feel I should pay him back if I can, just for the principle of the thing.
I think I would like the work of a garage mechanic.
I like adventure stories better than romantic stories.
At times I feel like picking a fist fight with someone.
I don't blame anyone for trying to grab all he can get in this world.
I think I would like to fight in a boxing match sometime.
I very much like hunting.
I have frequently found myself, when alone, pondering such abstract problems as free will, evil, etc.
In school I was sometimes sent to the principal for cutting up.
I like to talk before groups of people.
I like mechanics magazines.
Lawbreakers are almost always caught and punished.
At times I have been very anxious to get away from my family.
I think I would like to belong to a motorcycle club.
I have used alcohol excessively.
I used to steal sometimes when I was a youngster.
My home as a child was less peaceful and quiet than those of most other people.
As a youngster in school I used to give the teachers lots of trouble.
I have more trouble concentrating than others seem to have.
I like to eat my meals quickly and not spend a lot of time at the table visiting and talking.
I must admit that it makes me angry when other people interfere with my daily activity.
If a person doesn't get a few lucky breaks in life it just means that he hasn't been keeping his eyes open.
I sometimes tease animals.
I sweat very easily even on cool days.

The heterogeneous content of the MSC (masculine) and FMN (feminine) items is a hallmark of the empirical approach to scale construction, especially when the basic pool from which the items are derived is itself comprised of a wide range of meanings. Close inspection of the items listed in table 3.6 indicates that masculinity and femininity, as defined by behaviors eliciting differential endorsement by the two sexes, extends well beyond instrumental or expressive sex-role orientations. Accordingly, Baucom's scales appear to be somewhat more general than the Bem and Spence et al. measures, which were rationally derived so as to capture instrumental and expressive attributes.

What do the MSC and FMN items reflect in the way of sex-role distinctions? Almost half the items keyed on the masculinity scale involve the related triad of courage, self-confidence, and willingness to take risks. In addition, a number of other smaller clusters can be identified within the MSC items indicating that males more frequently endorse dominance, self-worth, poise, a sense of optimism, endurance, and a preference for excitement. A number of sex-linked vocational and avocational preferences and a penchant for showers rather than baths pretty well round out the qualities of masculinity represented in the MSC scale.

The feminine items center upon prosocial behaviors including denial of anger and aggression, adherence to the rules, denial of delinquent acts, and aversion to shortcuts in obtaining your goals. Almost half the items equate femininity and socialization. However, a number of other female-endorsed behaviors can be noted, many of them denial of male-endorsed qualities—lack of dominance, a deficit in courage/self-confidence/risk taking, and avoidance of excitement and preference for routine. Add to these some female sex-linked vocational and avocational preferences and a liking for self-adornment and you have the qualities of femininity found on the FMN scale.

Little is known about the Baucom scales except his report of their empirical origins. Since I wish to report data from these scales later in the book, let me note here some additional validity evidence that was collected to increase confidence in their use. The MSC and FMN scale scores for 200 middle-class males and 200 females were generously made available by Drs. Wallace Ford and Harrison Gough from the Institute for Personality Assessment and Research at the University of California at Berkeley. These adults were mostly in their twenties and thirties and college educated, and in many cases were husband and wife. Comparison of the mean scores for these males and females reconfirmed that the MSC ($p < .001$) and FMN ($p < .001$) scales discriminate powerfully between the self-reports of the two sexes.

Heilbrun's Masculinity and Femininity Scales Scored from the Adjective Check List

The ACL Masculinity and Femininity Scales will bear the primary weight of evidence for the conclusions drawn in this treatise. For that reason careful attention already has been directed to the format and validity of these scales in an earlier chapter. What remains to be done is to present a more complete description of scale derivation and item composition.

First, let us consider the construction of the Masculinity and Femininity Scales. As will become evident, these procedures combined the rational and empirical approaches, although they are heavily weighted toward the latter. The criterion groups to be compared for item derivation were defined by two attributes, their sex gender and the masculinity/femininity of their primary parent-identification model. The intention of invoking two criteria was to increase the homogeneity of the two criterion groups, more closely approximating a ''pure'' masculine group (that is, males identified with masculine fathers) and a ''pure'' feminine group (females identified with feminine mothers). The self-descriptions on the ACL of college subjects falling into these homogeneous criterion groups were compared, and those items that elicited differential endorsement rates at a statistically significant level were included in two subscales. Those behaviors selected more frequently by masculine-identified males comprised the masculinity subset, and those behaviors more often endorsed by feminine-identified females were included in the femininity subset. The actual items included in each subset were listed in Chapter Two.

The rational aspects of this item derivation entered in the decision to include the masculinizing and feminizing qualities of parent identification in the definition of the criterion groups. Among other things, this decision ensured that instrumental and expressive qualities would be represented to an appreciable extent in the final scales. The masculinity or femininity of parent models within this approach to measuring parent identification (described in detail elsewhere; see Heilbrun, 1973) is inferred from ratings of parents by the son or daughter on fifteen personality dimensions originally described by Murray (1938). Earlier work (Heilbrun, 1964b) had identified nine of these traits as sex-linked among parents. Four of these traits were predominant among fathers—need for achievement, endurance, dominance, and autonomy. Instrumentalness can be inferred from the priorities assigned to goal attainment and perseverance toward these goals implicit in the first two variables; dominance and independence emerge as complementary masculine attributes represented in almost all masculinity scales. The five traits found to be more prevalent in mothers included nurturance and affiliation—unmistakable hallmarks of expressiveness plus abasement, succorance (emotional dependency), and deference. Instrumental and expressive differences were built into the ACL scales by the decision to require these qualities in the identification models chosen by the criterion groups. Aside from this rational element, the scale construction was an empirical one.

Initial use of the ACL sex-role scales was guided by the assumption, uncontested prior to 1973, that the sex roles were mutually exclusive and should be measured as opposite poles on a single dimension. Accordingly, the two clusters of stereotyped behaviors were included in a single scale and used subtractively to derive a masculinity-femininity score. The Masculinity-Femininity Scale worked satisfactorily despite the conceptual limitation of bipolarity. Twelve years after the scale was initially described in the literature (Cosentino & Heilbrun, 1964), the subscales were separated and their independent usage was discussed and evaluated (Heilbrun, 1976). Our prior review revealed considerable validational support for the scales, and the reliability of each has been reported at about .80 by Wiggins and Holzmuller (1978). College norms for these independent measures of masculinity and femininity are included in Appendices B and C.

The conclusions that I will draw for the ACL sex-role scales apply equally to the other instruments described in this chapter. They all work to some extent and in their own way. Their limitations are the limitations of all personality measures, brought about by the complexity and lack of total consistency found in human social behaviors and the imperfections of our attempts to translate these behaviors into quantifiable psychometric form. Whatever has been accomplished using current sex-role scales has been accomplished *despite* these limitations. Relations reported in the literature, especially those that are replicated across instruments, can be taken as gross underestimates of the power of these effects in the actual social environment.

REFERENCES

Baucom, D. H. Independent masculinity and femininity scales on the California Psychological Inventory. *Journal of Consulting and Clinical Psychology,* 1976, **44,** 876.

Bem, S. L. The measurement of psychological androgyny. *Journal of Consulting and Clinical Psychology,* 1974, **42,** 155-62.

Bem, S. L. On the utility of alternate procedures for assessing psychological androgyny. *Journal of Consulting and Clinical Psychology,* 1977, **45,** 196–205.

Berzins, J. I., Welling, M. A., & Wetter, R. E. A new measure of psychological androgyny based on the Personality Research Form. *Journal of Consulting and Clinical Psychology,* 1978, **46,** 126–38.

Block, J. H. Conceptions of sex role: Some cross-cultural and longitudinal perspectives. *American Psychologist,* 1973, **28,** 512–27.

Constantinople, A. Masculinity-femininity: An exception to a famous dictum. *Psychological Bulletin,* 1973, **80,** 389–407.

Cosentino, F., & Heilbrun, A. B. Anxiety correlates of sex-role identity in college students. *Psychological Reports,* 1964, **14,** 729–30.

Edwards, K. J., Van Buren, J. H., & Zabriskie, F. C. The multidimensional structure of psychological androgyny and relationships to self concept. *Symposium on conceptual and instrumental issues in androgyny.* Meetings of the American Psychological Association, Toronto, Canada, August 1978.

Edwards, T. A., Gaa, J. P., & Liberman, D. A factor analysis of the BSRI and the PAQ *Symposium on conceptual and instrumental issues in androgyny.* Meetings of the American Psychological Association, Toronto, Canada, August 1978.

Gaa, J. P., & Liberman, D. Comparison of categorical assignments of the BSRI and the PAQ. *Symposium on conceptual and instrumental issues in androgyny.* Meetings of the American Psychological Association, Toronto, Canada, August 1978.

Gough, H. G. *Manual for the California Psychological Inventory.* Palo Alto, Calif.: Consulting Psychologists Press, 1957.

Gough, H. G., & Heilbrun, A. B. *Manual for the Adjective Check List and the Need Scales for the ACL.* Palo Alto, Calif.: Consulting Psychologists Press, 1965.

Heilbrun, A. B. Social learning theory, social desirability, and the MMPI. *Psychological Bulletin* 1964, **61,** 377–87. (a)

Heilbrun, A. B. Parent model attributes, nurturant reinforcement and consistency of behavior in adolescents. *Child Development,* 1964, **35,** 151–67. (b)

Heilbrun, A. B. Parent identification and filial sex-role behavior. In J. Cole (Ed.), *Nebraska symposium on motivation.* Lincoln: University of Nebraska Press, 1973.

Heilbrun, A. B. Measurement of masculine and feminine sex role identities as independent dimensions. *Journal of Consulting and Clinical Psychology,* 1976, **44**, 183–90.

Heilbrun, A. B. An exploration of antecedents and attributes of androgynous and undifferentiated sex roles. *Journal of Genetic Psychology,* 1978, **132**, 97–107.

Heilbrun, A. B., & Goodstein, L. D. Social desirability response set: Error or predictor variable? *Journal of Psychology,* 1961, **51**, 321–29.

Heilbrun, A. B., & Pitman, D. Testing some basic assumptions about psychological androgyny. *Journal of Genetic Psychology,* 1979, **135**, 175–88.

Kelly, J. A., Caudill, M. S., Hathorn, S., & O'Brien, C. G. Socially undesirable sex-correlated characteristics: Implications for androgyny and adjustment. *Journal of Consulting and Clinical Psychology,* 1977, **45**, 1185–86.

Mischel, W. On the future of personality measurement. *American Psychologist,* 1977, **32**, 246–54.

Murray, H. A. *Explorations in personality: A clinical and experimental study of fifty men of college age.* Oxford: Oxford University Press, 1938.

Parsons, T., & Bales, R. F. *Family, socialization, and interaction process.* Glencoe, Ill.: Free Press, 1955.

Rosenkrantz, P. S., Vogel, S. R., Bee, H., Broverman, J. K., & Broverman, D. M. Sex-role stereotypes and self concepts in college students. *Journal of Consulting and Clinical Psychology,* 1968, **32**, 287–95.

Ruffalo, C. A rating scale scoring system for the Adjective Check List. Unpublished manuscript, Emory University, 1971.

Spence, J. L., & Helmreich, R. L. *Masculinity and femininity: Their psychological dimensions, correlates, and antecedents.* Austin: University of Texas Press, 1978.

Spence, J. T., Helmreich, R., & Stapp, J. Ratings of self and peers on sex-role attributes and their relation to self-esteem and conceptions of masculinity and femininity. *Journal of Personality and Social Psychology,* 1975, **32**, 29–39.

Wiggins, J. S., & Holzmuller, A. Psychological androgyny and interpersonal behavior. *Journal of Consulting and Clinical Psychology,* 1978, **46**, 40–52.

Chapter 4

An Empirical Context for Androgyny

The reconceptualization of thought about the sex roles in western societies that made its appearance in the literature of the 1970s could not have arrived on the scientific scene under less auspicious circumstances. Androgyny, the major construct to evolve from the proposed independence of masculine and feminine development, was cosponsored from the beginning by social reformers and social scientists, sometimes by individuals attempting to bridge both roles. Androgynous potential was heralded as a panacea for the social ills associated with the limitations of outmoded convention. Emancipation from inflexible sex-role demands could free men to enjoy the emotional rewards of sensitive and intimate interpersonal relationships, and women could be liberated so that they might enter the competitive arena of socially significant achievement and fulfill whatever destinies their competence allows. Taken at face value, the advantages of androgyny are many, and it is not surprising to find it frequently cited in the rhetoric about liberation. Social change is best implemented when its assumptions remain uncomplicated by requirements of logic and proof.

However, the social scientist's situation is not as permissive. We are supposed to keep our values and our work separated, but this has not happened in the study of androgyny. Conclusions about the advantages of androgyny have exceeded the actual data—when data have been considered necessary at all.

Perhaps self-flagellation is the place to start in illustrating these excesses. Many years ago the results of a study conducted at Emory University (Heilbrun, 1968) indicated that college females defined as masculine on a bipolar scale of masculinity-femininity actually appeared to have both instrumental and expressive qualities when peer ratings were obtained. Although I did not use the term *androgyny* to describe this dual potential, it would have been appropriate in light of its subsequent usage. However, I did anticipate the trend of subsequent years by assuming that the inclusion of both instrumental and expressive qualities within the same female would be advantageous:

The greater probability of finding a combination of goal-directedness and interpersonal sensitivity in the masculine girls offers an obvious reason why they should tend to be more effective and thus better adjusted than the feminine girls [p. 134].

In truth, though, I did not consider within the methodology of the study anything that might directly substantiate the assumed benefits of androgyny. For all I knew, these females could have incorporated the worst aspects of instrumental and expressive orientations.

Other psychologists have carried on the tradition of assuming the best when it comes to androgyny despite the sparce evidence in support of this conclusion. Sandra Bem (1974), in the article first describing the psychometric properties of her Sex-Role Inventory, concluded that:

It is hoped that the development of the BSRI will encourage investigators in the areas of sex differences and sex roles to question the traditional assumption that it is the sex-typed individual who typifies mental health and to begin focusing on the behavioral and societal consequences of more flexible sex-role self-concepts. In a society where rigid sex-role differentiation has already outlived its utility, perhaps the androgynous person will come to define a more human standard of psychological health. [p. 161–162].

Since the article included no evidence bearing upon the adaptive consequences of androgyny, it seems obvious that these conclusions expressed Dr. Bem's personal values.

In a more conservative tone, Dr. Janet Spence and her colleagues also reached the conclusion that both masculinity and femininity contribute to personal and social effectiveness and that androgyny thus qualifies as the most desirable sex-role status (Spence, Helmreich, & Stapp, 1975). Evidence was marshaled in that paper to support their conclusion, although self-esteem questionnaire performance does not qualify as hard data concerning personal effectiveness. Furthermore, their self-esteem results pointed toward a far greater contribution of PAQ masculinity to self-esteem scores than PAQ femininity. Correlational analysis showed masculinity to be three to four times more important for male self-esteem than femininity (based on common variance of the two scores), and this figure soars to seven to eight times in the case of females. There is also the problem of using self-esteem scores with the PAQ when the latter instrument includes only socially desirable behaviors. There should be a positive correlation between the endorsement of desirable masculine and feminine attributes and self-esteem scores (Kelly & Worrell, 1977). The case for androgyny was bolstered by reference to life history data showing that androgynous persons receive more honors and awards, dated more, and had a lower incidence of illness, but these effects were confirmed statistically only relative to those having undifferentiated sex-role patterns on the PAQ.

Books published in the 1970s have shown far less restraint in their conclusions than is true of publications in scientific journals. Androgyny, or its conceptual equivalent, liberation from traditional sex-role expectations, has been enthusiastically heralded. Again, hard data to support these conclusions are best noted by their absence. Yorburg (1974) predicted the disappearance of the sex roles in modern society and the liberation of all from restraints upon their temperament and ability. The fulfillment of autonomy and intimacy in both married partners was viewed as the consequence of redefinition of traditional sex roles by Matteson (1975). The unnecessary character of the sex roles was stressed by Oakley (1972), along with the improved quality of living that would accompany androgynization of both men and women. Preconceived gender molds for children were rejected by Steinmann and Foxx (1974), whose suggested child-rearing model is that of simply raising a healthy person. Masculinity and femininity were conceived of as behaviors shared by both sexes within this model. Alcoholism, impotence, heart problems, and yet other stress disorders have been attributed to the inability of males to reach outside the limits of stereotyped masculinity (Grambs & Waetjen, 1975; Pleck & Sawyer, 1974); women's adherence to femininity was thought to result in a blurred sense of identity (Grambs & Waetjen, 1975).

The division of labor within the family that has assigned women the childbearing and child-rearing functions has been considered to be at the heart of female bondage. It has denied her instrumental opportunity or has become the basis for subsequent heterosexual malaise (Firestone, 1970; Whitehurst, 1977). Assuming the virtues of androgyny, child-rearing books firmly counsel parents to raise their children without sex-role boundaries (e.g., Greenberg, 1978).

The point I wish to make here is not that the assertion of adaptiveness for androgyny or for the abolition of sex-role constraints is necessarily wrong. The point is that these conclusions contain to varying but appreciable degrees assumptions based on personal values. The evidence has just begun to be systematically sifted, and it is beginning to look as if androgyny is not an unqualified blessing. The value of androgyny must be considered both in terms of specific correlates (valuable for what?) and particular sex gender (valuable for whom?) (Heilbrun, 1977; Kelly & Worrell, 1977; Wakefield, Sasek, Friedman, & Bowden, 1976).

One of the complications in putting androgyny into clearer perspective is that once independent sex-role measures became available, researchers began immediately to gather ready evidence relevant to the construct without raising some basic questions relating to androgyny. Until these questions are answered research and theory is going to remain diffuse. I shall consider several of these basic questions in this chapter.

SEX DIFFERENCES IN ANDROGYNY

Arguments could be waged either way as to whether males or females, considered as an aggregate, should demonstrate greater androgyny. Brown (1958), in his review of the sex-role literature many years ago, pointed out that males in our culture are exposed to stricter constraints on their sex-role behaviors during development than are females. The boy is given only limited leeway for engaging in the more passive play activities associated with girls or for uncontrolled emotional display of fear, distress, or affection. Obvious and continued violation of these constraints threatens him with the aversive label of "sissy" and ostracism by his peers, and risks the displeasure of his parents, particularly the father. On the other hand, girls were viewed by Brown as experiencing more freedom to cross over stereotypic lines into the active and physical world of play associated with boys; a "tomboy" phase for girls was of less concern. He pointed out that even as adults constraints differed as far as dress and other aspects of grooming were concerned. Females are more likely to offer a "mannish" appearance than males are to display grooming and actions popularly associated with the female sex. If a cross-sex appearance is displayed, it is likely to elicit stronger reactions from others if the unconventional display is by the male. Thompson and McCandless's (1976) review of the homosexual literature points out that male homosexuality is frequently viewed with more concern than is female homosexuality, again suggesting that male deviation from cultural expectation is a more serious matter than is female deviation from convention. The number of male transsexuals far exceeds that of female transsexuals (Green, 1969), as does the number of male as opposed to female requests for such surgery. The prevalent complaint, that the male transsexual feels trapped within the confines of the sex and role assigned at birth, suggests that the male may sense less opportunity for cross-sex-role behavior and seeks more radical means to feminize his identity. These various scraps of evidence suggest that deviation from stereotypic masculine sex-role expectations for the male is a more serious matter in our culture than is female deviation from femininity. If the male is more constrained by stereotyped expectations, androgyny should be a rare commodity. In contrast, the more relaxed attitudes toward female display of masculine appearance and behavior should have the effect of facilitating androgynous development.

Arguments for the opposite expectation—that males as a whole should be more androgynous—are just as readily waged. For example, many believe that boys engage in successive parental identifications in which they make an early identification with the mother followed by a subsequent identification with the father (Lynn, 1969; Sears, 1957). To the extent that this is correct, it should have the effect of laying down both a feminine and a masculine base for the boy. The girl, however, is believed to make successive identifications with the mother, thereby solidifying a singular feminine identity.

A second argument for the greater likelihood of male androgyny has been suggested by Jeanne Block (1973). She pointed out that the socialization process has a way of feminizing children as it inculcates prosocial behavior. Males, particularly those from the middle class (who have been the major source of subjects for sex-role study), are not only encouraged to adopt the masculine role but also to develop prosocial behaviors. These pressures should combine to facilitate their androgynous development. Females, in contrast, are more likely to be reinforced for adopting the feminine role, and the emphasis on socialization only further feminizes them. Block's contention that socialization is related to the adoption of feminine behaviors finds support in the California Psychological Inventory data described in the previous chapter. The MSC and FMN scales developed by Baucom (1976) were checked for item overlap with the Socialization scale, developed as a measure of social maturity and integrity. There were four overlapping items between the MSC and Socialization Scales; three were keyed in opposite directions and only one item (2 percent) was keyed in common. FMN–Socialization Scale overlap involved seven items (17 percent), all keyed in the same direction on both scales.

Of course, the strongest argument favoring enhanced androgyny in the male comes from the data reviewed in Chapter Two concerning sex-role flexibility of the two sexes. The conception of the male as bound to the specific behaviors constituting masculinity was not confirmed. Men more than women appeared flexible in crossing sex-role boundaries and, furthermore, gave evidence of a more balanced repertoire of masculine and feminine attributes.

Androgyny Differences between Males and Females on the ACL. Since the question of whether sex differences in androgyny exist is about as basic as you can get and does lend itself to arguments either way, it seems surprising that no one has bothered to answer it (at least to my knowledge). Bem (1974) as well as Spence and her colleagues (1975) present data relevant to this question as part of the early descriptions of their sex-role instruments, but neither exposed this particular comparison to statistical analysis. However, simply examining the mean BSRI androgyny scores reported by Bem for male and female college students suggests no difference between the sexes, although these means were based on an early formulation of androgyny that considered balance in masculinity and femininity scores but not their extensity. Sex differences in androgyny as gauged by the PAQ also appear to be negligible. The percentages of college males and females defined as androgynous were not dissimilar when subjects were assigned to a fourfold sex-role typology table using common cutting scores on the scales of masculinity and femininity. There remains some doubt whether the BSRI is appropriate for examining sex differences in androgyny, since it was developed on the premise that only socially desirable sex-role behavior should be considered. This may serve to diminish differences in behavioral endorsement between males and females. The PAQ is clearly inappropriate for such a purpose, because the items represent stereotyped behaviors deemed socially desirable for both sexes.

There has been ample evidence collected in my laboratory to answer the question before us, at least in terms of androgyny as estimated from ACL sex-role scales (Heilbrun & Schwartz, in press). In fact, it may appear that the question has already been considered back in Chapter Two when the "growth curve" for androgyny was plotted over a twenty-year span, 1958–78. The curves representing androgyny levels for the two sexes at various points over these two decades cannot be considered for our present purpose, however, since they are based on relative scores generated from independent norms for each sex. Thus, a score of 60 on the Masculinity Scale for a male has a different meaning (that is, is more masculine in an absolute sense) than a score of 60 on this scale for a female. The curves presented in Chapter Two depict changes in androgyny over the years for males *relative to college males in general* and for females *relative only to their female college peers*.

What is required if sex differences in androgyny are to be directly examined in terms of ACL scores is that the data be pooled for the two sexes. We accomplished this by the simple expedient of using raw scores on the Masculinity and Femininity Scales to infer the strength of sex-role dispositions, rather than transforming them into standard scores independently by sex. These raw scores represent the number of masculine stereotyped behaviors out of the total twenty-eight and the number of feminine stereotyped behaviors out of the total twenty-five that were endorsed by the subject. The same index for measuring androgyny can be applied to these raw scores as was applied previously to standard scores in Chapter Two, except that straightforward frequency counts of masculine and feminine behaviors are introduced into the $(M + F) - |M - F|$ formula. The primary requirement for the use of this formula, an approximately equal number range of scores in both scales, is satisfied in both the standard score and raw score applications.

A new sample of college undergraduates (not included in the twenty-year profiles) was asked to complete the ACL in the fall of 1978. The sample of 105 females and 69 males turned out to be very representative for our program of research as far as their average age (between 18 and 19 years) and their sex-role scores were concerned. Their combined median T-scores on the Masculinity and Femininity Scales were 51 and 50, respectively, with an expected median of 50 based on our college norms developed independently by sex. The raw androgyny score for the females proved to be 12.11 compared to 18.55 for the males, a highly significant difference ($p < .0001$). The males in this 1978 sample demonstrated a substantially higher level of androgyny than did the females.

Other direct comparisons between males and females using the androgyny formula with ACL sex-role raw scores were conducted in order to confirm the sex difference and shed light on its generality. I shall now describe a number of subsequent analyses that will serve this purpose. One question to be answered is whether higher male androgyny would be found in other recent samples of Emory undergraduates. A second question concerns whether the androgyny sex difference can be generalized to college students in regions outside the South and to periods other than the 1970s. (The possible effects of locale and period on results has already been discussed in Chapter Two.) Table 4.1 summarizes the raw score androgyny index means for additional college samples varying in region and time. The conclusion to be drawn from these comparisions of male and female college samples seems unequivocal. Males emerge as more androgynous than females whether we look at self-descriptions of the 1950s, 1960s, or 1970s or whether these were collected in the Southern, Far Western, or Midwestern United States.

Table 4.1. Androgyny of College Males and Females (Based on Pooled Raw Sex-Role Score Formula)

Location and Time of Sample	Males		Females		Significance Level
	N	M	N	M	
Emory University (1976–77)	93	16.67	93	13.29	<.02
University of California at Berkeley (1963–64)	94	14.26	57	10.46	<.01
University of Iowa (1958)	56	15.27	44	8.11	<.0001

Generalization of androgyny differences found between the sexes on college campuses also may be limited by other known attributes of college students— their youth, intelligence, educational attainment, and the prevalence of middle-class backgrounds. Social idealism and high career ambitions are probably safely added to the college stereotype. Available samples of ACLs do not allow anything approaching a thorough and systematic analysis of all of these possible parameters of androgyny, but we can at least consider the age and education variables by examining androgyny in older samples collected in the community rather than on campuses. Two sources of data are available for this purpose. Thompson obtained ACLs from heterosexual males and females as a control group for his doctoral research into homosexuality. Sex-role results of this study were originally reported in terms of the bipolar ACL Masculinity-Femininity Scale (Thompson, Schwartz, McCandless, & Edwards, 1973) and were subsequently reanalyzed and reported in terms of the independent sex-role scales (Heilbrun & Thompson, 1977). The Thompson sample of heterosexuals differs from our undergraduate samples in being older (averaging about 28 years of age), being married in a substantial proportion of cases, and being screened for sexual orientation. They were college graduates for the most part. The second noncampus sample was obtained during 1961 and 1962 and was comprised of job-holders within a small urban area surrounding the University of Iowa. The demographic features of this sample, described in Chapter Two, portray this sample of 289 men and 134 women as considerably older than the subjects in the Thompson study; their educational attainment was less and their predominantly married status was about the same. Raw score androgyny means for these community samples are reported in table 4.2.

Table 4.2. Androgyny of Community Males and Females (Based on Pooled Raw Sex-Role Score Formula)

Location and Time of Sample	Males		Females		Significance Level
	N	M	N	M	
Iowa (1961–62)	289	11.16	134	9.00	<.01
Georgia, with some Far West representation (early 1970s)	106	16.39	89	13.28	<.05

The obvious conclusion, based on the extension of androgyny differences to the older samples described in table 4.2 as well as the campus samples represented in table 4.1, would be that males are generally more androgynous than females and that this has been true for two decades. I also would conclude, although with far less confidence, that the disparity in androgyny between the sexes decreases with age and social-economic status. At least we observe a shrinkage in mean androgyny score differences from 6 to 7 for late adolescents on the campus to about 3 for young adults in the community, down to approximately 2 for a sample in which over 50 percent of the subjects were 35 years of age or older.

Psychometric Evidence of Sex Differences in Sex-Role Flexibility. The most critical and prevalent assumption held about androgyny is that it allows the person to lead a more effective life because of the greater flexibility it provides in situations where either masculine or feminine dispositions would be more appropriate (Bem, 1974). Those who have achieved stereotype masculine or feminine identities are commonly described in terms of constraint and inflexibility when situational options present themselves. The assumption of androgynous flexibility has the weight of logic on its side. Certainly those who incorporate both masculine and feminine dispositions should be in a position to display more variety in their choice of sex-role behaviors. While an alternative to increased flexibility within the androgynous condition will be explored in the section to follow, it seems safe enough to consider this to be *one possible consequence* of dual sex-role potential. By doing so, we can examine sex-role flexibility in males and females as another way of comparing the androgynous quality of the two sexes. In fact, this already has been accomplished in an earlier chapter, when the assumption of sex-role commitment in the male was evaluated in terms of the Block role consistency measure (1961) applied to sex-role attributes.

There were two samples of sex-role consistency data that were reported. One sample retrieved from our data bank included thirty-three college females and forty-two college males (Heilbrun, 1977). The female average (.531) and male average (.391) were discrepant ($p < .01$) and suggested more flexible sex-role behaviors across interpersonal situations for men. The second sample (Heilbrun & Pitman, 1979) included twenty-one college subjects of each sex; their sex-role consistency scores once again depicted men ($M = .438$) as more flexible than women ($M = .534$), with the difference achieving statistical reliability ($p < .05$). Accordingly, males not only appear more androgynous than females in light of self-reported sex-role attributes, but they also describe themselves as more flexible in their display of masculine and feminine behaviors across interpersonal situations, an assumed correlate of androgyny.

Before leaving this application of the Block rating technique behind us, a brief historical comment is in order. I find it interesting that the Block procedure has survived a complete turnabout in the assumptions regarding healthy psychological development in the thirty years since Erikson's (1950) influential treatise on human developmental stages. Erikson proposed that the psychological health of the adolescent depended on establishing a stable sense of identity based in part on a view of self as essentially the same from one personal situation to the next. Stability of interpersonal behaviors would seem to represent the sine qua non of psychological health for the adolescent, in Erikson's theory. Current androgyny literature more frequently conveys the opposite view, at least as far as sex-role behaviors are concerned—that situational variability is the more promising commodity. Depending which way you wish to argue, you can choose ''flexibility'' if you wish to describe a virtue, ''instability'' if the same characteristic is to be considered a liability. Similarly, your point of view may lead you to describe the same level of consistency as ''stable'' if you are an Eriksonian, ''inflexible'' if contemporary sex-role assumptions are more compelling.

Laboratory Investigation of Androgyny Sex Differences. The evidence regarding sex differences in androgyny considered so far—in fact almost all the evidence concerning sex roles presented in this book—is based on self-report. While the use of subjects' appraisals of their own behaviors is commonplace in sex-role research, there may be some skepticism regarding the accuracy of self-reporting. Sometimes such concern is answered by emphasizing the self-conceptual nature of the responses. No matter how inaccurate self-reports may be, this reasoning goes, they still can be of functional significance to the extent that the individual believes them to be true. This somewhat apologetic contention seems to be implicit in the conceptual distinction between sex-role identity and sex-role behavior emphasized by some. I have a somewhat higher regard for behavioral self-description, if reasonable questions are asked of psychologically sound individuals who have no compelling reason to be deceptive. Even so, it must be acknowledged that there are inaccuracies in self-evaluations of this sort that may be traced to subject and instrument limitations. For this reason, a study was devised in our laboratory (Heilbrun & Schwartz, in press) that considered the question of sex differences in androgyny without depending upon self-report. This study will allow us to consider the androgynous character of behavior from the viewpoint of an observer.

College subjects were assigned in pairs to the laboratory session after initial group testing. Overall there were seven pairs of males, thirteen pairs of females, and five male-female pairs; generally speaking, the couples were unfamiliar with one another prior to the session. The session was explained to the subjects as a contest in which one pair would win a cash prize at the experiment's end. They were told that three controversial issues would be presented to them and that they would have a period of time to discuss each and reach agreement on how they felt. More specifically, the experimenter's instructions went like this:

This study will involve a consideration of several current issues. Your job will be to discuss these issues with one another and come to some conclusion that you both can agree upon. If perfect agreement isn't possible, at least you should agree upon some compromise conclusion. There will be three issues to discuss, and you will have exactly 15 minutes to conclude your assignment. The issues are described on this form . . .

Notice that the three issues described on the form are the value of maintaining traditional sex-role distinctions, legalizing the possession and use of marijuana, and premarital sex. For each of these, your joint conclusion is to be recorded on a rating scale from 1 to 10. You can check any point along this 10-point scale. I'd recommend that you use the entire 15 minutes to come to your conclusions or about 5 minutes for each issue.

The award of a cash prize and how the winning team is to be determined is then discussed. After the fifteen-minute period elapsed, the experimenter reentered the room and collected the decisions recorded by the pairs of subjects. Then the subjects were asked to privately rate the partner along two independent seven-point rating scales, describing various levels of instrumental and expressive behaviors observed during the preceding fifteen minutes. These were the critical data of the study.

The contest conditions of the laboratory procedure represented cover for the intended purpose of forcing the kind of interaction between two people in which goal behavior (instrumentality) as well as concern for the quality of relationship (expressiveness) would be expected behaviors.

The instrumental and expressive behavioral ratings from 1 to 7 were converted to androgyny scores by using the generalized formula based upon magnitude and balance: $(I + E) - |I - E|$. This created a potential arithmetic range of androgyny scores from 2 to 14. Female subjects achieved an average rated androgyny score of 6.00 compared to the males' mean of 8.53. Male subjects were viewed as more androgynous than females by partners of both sexes following the fifteen-minute laboratory interaction ($p < .01$). The finding of greater male androgyny that emerged from sample after sample of self-reported behaviors was replicated in this study when outside observers were used, at least as far as the instrumental and expressive qualities of the sex roles are concerned.

Implications. A couple of conclusions surface in the wake of an empirical verdict that males hold more androgynous potential than females. Considering the surge of sex-role studies that can be observed over the past few years, perhaps it is appropriate that research implications be considered first. The more highly developed androgyny found in males makes it imperative that researchers be more cognizant of the relative-absolute measurement distinction in future empirical comparisons involving the two sexes. This should hold true whether direct comparisons are contemplated within a study or whether generalization from a study of one sex alone is being considered. Our data now suggest that androgynous males and females identified by psychometric operations, while they can be made to look comparable in a relative sense, do not display the same degree of androgyny in an absolute sense. It is just as though we were concerned with the size of human beings, defined by height and weight, and had to face up to the fact that "large" (taller and heavier) men are not the same as "large" women.

That researchers should begin to concern themselves with the conditions under which absolute differences in androgyny make a difference also holds true for studies that investigate the correlates of androgyny. The literature describing the correlates of androgyny is replete with sex differences (Heilbrun & Pitman, 1979; Kelly & Worrell, 1977; Wakefield, Sasek, Friedman, & Bowden, 1976), almost to the point that this is the rule rather than the exception. The extent to which these inconsistencies can be attributed to absolute differences in androgyny between males and females should be ascertained.

The importance of the relative-absolute distinction in sex-role research is not to be decided, in the final analysis, by considerations of scientific elegance. The real test of importance resides in the natural world of social behavior to which our research is presumably addressed. It is a matter of some significance for us to know whether the natural social consequences of our sex-role behaviors are more likely to be evaluated within a relative or absolute perspective. For example, are expectations for stereotyped sex-role responses so geared to the sex that performs them that different levels are mandated for males and females? Will forcefully dominating behaviors prove more effective if they are demonstrated by males than by females, and will the same level of emotionality be tolerated in males as in females? I believe that a cultural relativism does exist regarding sex-role behaviors, so that the reception accorded to them is to some extent predicated on separate sex standards. You might try a test of this on yourself. Think about some feature of your own sex-role makeup and place a label from strong to weak on it. Now examine the context for your judgement. Was it the degree to which this behavior is shown by others of the same sex, or of the opposite sex, or by people in general? My guess would be that you used your own sex as a reference.

If the impact of sex-role behaviors is contingent on the sex of the person demonstrating them, then researchers are fully justified in maintaining independent standards for these behaviors in their research. Ideally the solution should involve the selection of a relative (separately by sex) or an absolute (combined over sex) basis for inference for a sex-role measure based upon our knowledge of the situation toward which we wish to make some prediction.

The final implication of finding a sex-gender difference in androgyny concerns the practically unchallenged assumption among social activists that androgyny promises a happier and more effective life. This is not the place to consider these claims; Chapters Five and Six will allow a more fully informed consideration of this point. What we can note at this point is that efforts toward "male liberation" have to be taken with a grain of salt, since men are found to be the more androgynous sex. To the extent that androgyny proves to be advantageous, females represent a far more convincing target for sex-role renovation than do males. We shall concern ourselves in the next chapter with the contribution of androgyny and other sex roles to self-esteem and other criteria of behavioral effectiveness. The value of androgyny for males and for females will be one of our prime interests.

HOW ANDROGYNY WORKS

Given the ease of explaining androgyny in the simplest terms possible, it is not difficult to understand the excitement the concept has generated. Not that everyone would agree how androgyny works, even in uncomplicated terms, but the following might represent how thinking tends to go. The androgynous person has gone beyond the expectation that his or her sex-role behavior will conform to cultural stereotype by demonstrating potential for both masculine and feminine behaviors. Consistent with the terminology of this book, we would refer to these as sex-role repertoires. It could be said of the androgynous person, then, that substantial masculine and feminine repertoires are available. Such individuals enjoy the advantage of having more options open to them in situations calling for sex-typed behaviors, rather than being inflexibly bound to a single repertoire of stereotyped responses. Given this extended range of options, the androgynous person will select the more effective and rewarding alternative, depending upon whether instrumental or expressive qualities will prove more advantageous.

There are two problems with this somewhat oversimplied analysis. Is it profitable to think of androgyny as involving dual repertoires of sex-role behaviors available on call, or does the androgynous person tend to combine masculine and feminine behaviors into some unique blend? In other words, the androgynous person may not have increased repertoires of sex-role behaviors, but only a different repertoire in which pure instrumental or expressive acts are integrated into unique blends. The second bit of presumption that accompanies the simple version of how androgyny works is that if an androgynous individual does have a greater number of sex-role options, he or she will exercise this capability judiciously. What is there to keep the individual from opting to go masculine when feminine qualities would prove more effective and rewarding, and vice versa? The argument certainly cannot be that people should be expected to make wise choices when given the opportunity to choose. Some do and some do not, and one person does sometimes and does not other times. It is only when the halo effect already extended to androgyny is stretched to include the assumption of wisdom that androgyny's advantages seem so obvious. As the next two chapters will make clear, androgyny is a mixed bag as far as personal success is concerned. The remainder of this chapter is concerned with the blending issue and evidence relevant to it. The chapters following will contend with the adaptive value of androgyny.

Sex-Role Blending: A Theoretical Background. Our introductory comments regarding the oversimplified assumptions underlying androgyny should not be taken to mean that others have not confronted the question of whether androgynous sex-role behaviors are likely to appear in blended or relatively pure forms. Bem (1978), for example, has suggested that masculine and feminine behaviors may be blended by the androgynous individual of either sex. I reached this conclusion earlier (Heilbrun & Pitman, 1979), but identified blending as being more likely in the androgynous female than the male. This conclusion was based on the correlations between self-reported sex-role variability and level of androgyny. For females the correlation ($r = -.31$) suggested that more androgynous individuals were actually less flexible in the patterns of sex-role behavior displayed across interpersonal situations. This finding, while not proof of the thesis that androgynous females blend sex-role behaviors, was at least consistent with that view. The negative correlation seems to suggest that androgynous females mix both masculine and feminine qualities into more or less stable patterns. In contrast, androgynous males demonstrated the opposite type of correlation ($r = .72$); the greater androgyny, the greater the variability in self-reported sex-role behaviors from one situation to the next. This kind of variable display of masculine and feminine behaviors could be explained in terms of the use of sex-role behaviors as strategies for obtaining social reinforcement by the androgynous male. The use of such strategems by males but not by females had been proposed by Kelly, Caudill, Hathorn, and O'Brien (1977).

There is an obvious need for empirical data that will begin to fill gaps in our understanding of androgyny, such as the form in which androgynous sex-role behaviors manifest themselves and whether this depends on the sex of the individual. The problem is that data are hard to come by, or, at least, I have found them to be so. While psychometric measures of sex-role blending appear to be relevant, these instruments also appear to be lacking in power. When behavior observations have been collected in the laboratory, relevance to blending was open to question. I have attemped to resolve this dilemma by presenting three types of data that were collected to help clear up the questions about sex-role blending in androgyny. If there are consistencies across independent bodies of data, we should be able to generate confidence in these findings despite the known methodological limitations.

Sex-Role Blending: The Data. The first body of data that can be used to consider whether the sex roles are blended or retained as more or less discrete repertoires in androgyny came from a study that was described earlier in this chapter (Heilbrun & Schwartz, in press). Recall the laboratory investigation that entailed a fifteen-minute interaction between pairs of college subjects. Each pair had the assignment of reaching decisions concerning several contemporary issues, but it was required that these goals be achieved by consensus following consideration of both viewpoints. The purpose of this methodology was to facilitate both instrumental (goal-oriented) and expressive (relationship-oriented) behaviors. Scale ratings of both qualities were obtained from the subjects on their laboratory partners when the task was completed, and the instrumental/ expressive values for each subject were converted into an androgyny score using our generalized index. A generally higher androgyny rating for males relative to females was found.

The same laboratory results could be construed as relevant to our current discussion if it were assumed that blending instrumental and expressive behaviors tended to obscure both dispositions for the observer. Androgyny that takes a blended form is more likely to assume a more subtle character than androgyny involving an alteration of more pure instrumental and expressive behaviors. This could have a ceiling effect on the rated magnitudes of the two dispositions and systematically lower the androgyny score. This highly speculative conclusion is not subject to verification within the data of the laboratory study, although one unreported analysis is suggestive. ACLs given to all subjects allow us to scale androgyny based upon self-reported Masculinity and Femininity Scale T-scores. Comparison of how observers viewed females and female self-report can be used to infer how difficult it is to evaluate instrumental and expressive tendencies in women. As it turned out, women who were rated by their partners as less androgynous had a higher average androgyny score (96.57) than women who were rated as more androgynous (90.94). This was not true of men; those rated as less androgynous by others were less androgynous in their own eyes (75.71) than those rated as more androgynous (88.67). Women and observers did not agree about sex-role orientations, whereas men and observers did.

A second source of evidence bearing on the tendencies to blend masculine and feminine behaviors by the two sexes requires that we again consider the role consistency measure developed by Block and modified for use with sex roles. That measure, as you may remember, allowed us to gauge the degree to which the individual reported variations in masculine and feminine sex-role behaviors displayed in different interpersonal situations. Males reported greater variation in this regard than females; as a sex, males demonstrated greater sex-role flexibility, perhaps the cardinal attribute of androgyny. The same instrument, looked at in a different way, offers a means of considering whether males and females differ in the extent to which they blend their sex-role behaviors. What is necessary, of course, is to find a way of disentangling intersituational flexibility and intrasituational blending. Instead of analyzing the ranks across situations to establish degree of correspondence, attention can be directed to the ranks within situations to establish the extent to which the masculine and feminine behaviors are interspersed or clustered. The former should approximate the effects of blending masculine and feminine behaviors within a given personal transaction, and the latter would represent the emergence of stereotypic response in pure form.

Examples of stereotypically blended or pure types of self-description might be useful. The same six-item, three-situation miniature measure used earlier in the book will serve our purpose. A person who blends her masculine and feminine sex-role behaviors might give us a set of rankings like those depicted in the top half of table 4.3. The alternation of masculine and feminine attributes as one proceeds down the ranks within each column suggests that the person has no clearly masculine or feminine style of transaction in any of these situations, consistent with the concept of blending.

The contrasting case of a female who perceives herself as behaving in an unadulteratedly masculine or feminine way within each situation would present the pattern of rankings like those found in the bottom half of table 4.3. It can be

noted that the three masculine or feminine items are clustered though not
necessarily in the same ranks across situations. This subject describes herself as
predominantly feminine with someone in whom she is sexually interested and
with her mother, but as predominantly masculine with an employer.

Table 4.3 Hypothetical Blended and Pure Sex-Role Rankings on the Role Consistency Measure

	Interpersonal Context		
Rank	Sexual Object	Mother	Employer
1	self-confident	modest	aggressive
2	considerate	frank	modest
3	frank	considerate	frank
4	modest	self-confident	submissive
5	aggressive	submissive	self-confident
6	submissive	aggressive	considerate
1	considerate	considerate	frank
2	modest	submissive	aggressive
3	submissive	modest	self-confident
4	frank	self-confident	modest
5	self-confident	aggressive	considerate
6	aggressive	frank	submissive

A blending score can be readily obtained from the sex-role consistency
measure by summing the ranks assigned to all masculine items and to all
feminine items in a given situation and then obtaining the absolute difference
between these sums. The more the two sex-typed behaviors are intermixed within
the rankings, the less the absolute difference. To illustrate this, go back to the
column in table 4.3 headed "Sexual Object" for the female who blended her
sex-role behaviors in the first example (top half of the table). The column
blending score would be given by the absolute difference between the masculine
rank values ($1 + 3 + 5 = 9$) and the feminine rank values ($2 + 4 + 6 = 12$), a
low score of 3. The second hypothetical subject who presented her rankings in
more clustered stereotypic form would be assigned a high score of 9 for this
column, based on the difference between a masculine rank total of $4 + 5 + 6 =
15$ and a feminine rank total of $1 + 2 + 3 = 6$. A total blending score would be
obtained for the entire sex-role consistency measure by summing the column
blending scores across the eight situations.

The blending scores for sixty-seven college males and sixty college females
were obtained by combining all of the sex-role consistency measures that had
accumulated in our files. The average blending score for females (keeping in
mind that twenty ranks are involved in each of eight situations) was lower (M =

261.28) than the average for the males (M = 294.66). This difference, which proved to be significant ($p < .05$), indicates that females blend masculine and feminine behaviors in their interpersonal dealings more than is the case for males. Thus, the implication we drew from the laboratory study—that females may have looked less androgynous than males in part because they blend their masculine and feminine behavior—has psychometric support.

It is also worth noting that the same protocols, analyzed in terms of sex-role flexibility, had demonstrated females to be more stable across interpersonal situations than males. The fact that the same test responses found females to be both more stable in their sex-role behavior across situations and more inclined to blend masculine and feminine within situations suggests that androgyny when it occurs in women may be more subtle than that in men, for two reasons. It may not only appear in more blended form, but will not show the contrast in interpersonal style from one personal transaction to the next that is evident in men.

The final set of data bearing on the form of sex-role behavior was designed to bring us as close as psychometrics allow to the question at hand: does androgyny in females result in the blending of masculine and feminine behaviors to a greater extent than is true for males? Thus far the data reported on this issue have been rather inferential. This time 103 females and 69 males from our campus completed the ACL, as well as two rating scales in which they were asked to judge the degree to which they blended instrumental (goal-oriented) and expressive (relationship-oriented) behaviors. These ratings should prove enlightening for two reasons. For one, they will allow us an absolute basis for gauging whether blending really does occur in the two sexes and to what degree, at least for these two aspects of masculine and feminine behavior. For the other, these data will allow us to look directly at the relation between androgyny and blending in males and females.

The instructions to the subjects covering the two ratings went to great lengths to make the concepts of instrumental and expressive blending understandable to the subjects. I shall quote these parts of the instructions, since it may serve to clear up lingering questions in the mind of the reader.

> While it is true that people differ considerably with regard to the priorities placed upon a goal orientation and a relationship orientation, it is also true that almost everyone will actively seek to achieve some goal or actively concern themselves with the quality of a personal relationship at one time or another. It is possible that when either of these happen, whether it is seldom or frequently, that the person may blend the two orientations into one.
>
> On the one hand, the person who is pursuing a goal (such as doing well in college, seeking a status position in an organization, or achieving in an athletic contest) may do so with varying degrees of concern about how his or her efforts will affect relationships with others. One extreme would be the person who goes after the goal with the singular purpose of achieving it and is not concerned about those who may be after the same goals or how others will feel about his or her determined efforts. The other extremes would be those who in seeking after their own

goals make as certain as possible that in doing so no one else is adversely affected or that their personal relationships are not diminished.

Consider your own style of goal striving when it occurs and rate the extent to which it is blended with relationship concerns on the 10-point scale below . . .

The second possibility is that a relationship orientation may or may not be blended with a goal orientation. At the one extreme, the person may value positive relationships but as a means to an end such as being able to take advantage of being popular to achieve other goals like election to office, to have people you can count on in an emergency, or to gain self-esteem by having many friends. At the other extreme, the person may value positive relationships as an end in itself; having a good relationship simply makes you and someone else happy and that's enough. Consider your own style of relationship orientation and rate the extent to which it is blended with a goal orientation on the 10-point scale below . . .

The first question to be asked of these ratings is the extent to which the phenomenon of sex-role blending exists among college students. The ten-point rating scales for goal blending (expressive concerns blended into instrumental acts) and relationship blending (instrumental concerns within expressive acts) were constructed so that ratings in the upper reaches of the scales (points 7–10) represent some degree of endorsement of blending, ratings low in the scales (points 1–4) represent some degree of denial, and those in the middle (points 5–6) indicate equivocation. Percentages of subjects falling in each of these ranges should tell us something about the base rates of blending (table 4.4). As can be seen, goal blending is not only amply represented in the ratings, but some degree of expressive concern within instrumental acts is the rule rather than the exception. Instrumental expressiveness was substantially less endorsed, although some degree of relationship blending still appeared in about a third of the subjects. Perhaps these figures prove the intuitively obvious; instrumental and expressive orientations do not simply manifest themselves in unadulterated form.

Table 4.4. Prevalence of Instrumental and Expressive Blending Endorsed by College Students

Type of Blending	Level of Endorsement		
	Endorsement of Blending	Equivocal about Blending	Denial of Blending
Goal			
Males (N = 69)	57	27	16
Females (N = 103)	69	22	9
Relationship			
Males (N = 69)	35	27	38
Females (N = 103)	29	21	50

NOTE: Goal = expressive concerns blended into instrumental activities. Relationship = instrumental concerns blended into expressive activities.

They also suggest that blending tends to be higher when the basic mode not conventionally assigned to a given sex is considered. Females in general are far more likely to temper goal seeking with expressive concern than not (69 percent versus 9 percent); this is true to a lesser extent for males (57 percent versus 16 percent). On the other hand, males as a whole were about equally likely to introduce an instrumental quality into their personal relationships as not (35 percent versus 38 percent), whereas females were less inclined to do so than not (29 percent versus 50 percent). Neither trend was significant when tested by nonparametric analysis, however.

Comparison of the average blending scores achieved by males and females followed suit. The mean goal blending score of the males (6.70) did not differ reliably from that achieved by the females (7.17). Similarly, the relationship blending means for males (5.13) and females (4.80) were not different by statistical standards. To this point, the expectation that females would demonstrate more blending than males was not confirmed. Yet it should be kept in mind that this expectation originated in the behavior hypothesized for the androgynous person, and these data give us the opportunity to consider blending as a function of both sex and androgyny.

Level of androgyny was determined by the androgyny formula applied to the ACL sex-role scale T-scores with independent median splits determined separately for males (> 88) and females (> 92). Level of goal blending was defined in the same fashion; the median for both sexes fell near eight. Table 4.5 presents the frequency data that reflect the contingency between androgyny and goal blending for the two sexes. Chi-square analysis of these frequency data revealed no special tendency for androgynous males to blend expressive and instrumental qualities. However, the androgynous female group did include a higher proportion of goal blenders than their nonandrogynous counterparts ($p < .05$). The expectation that blending would be observed in androgynous females but not in androgynous males found support in these goal-orientation results.

Table 4.5. Goal Blending and Androgyny

| | Level of Androgyny | | | |
| | High | | Low | |
Sex	Number of High Goal Blenders	Number of Low Goal Blenders	Number of High Goal Blenders	Number of Low Goal Blenders
Males	15	13	17	24
Females	29	19	22	33

Identical procedures were used to consider relationship blending. The numbers of androgynous and nonandrogynous subjects rating themselves as high (> 5) and low blenders for the males and high (> 4) and low blenders among the females are reported in table 4.6. No relation between this form of blending and androgyny was evident for either sex.

Table 4.6. Relationship Blending and Androgyny

| | Level of Androgyny | | | |
| | High | | Low | |
Sex	Number of High Relationship Blenders	Number of Low Relationship Blenders	Number of High Relationship Blenders	Number of Low Relationship Blenders
Males	11	18	21	20
Females	23	25	28	26

Inspection of the distributions of relationship-blending scores suggested a curvilinear relation for the females, so a supplementary analysis of the scores was conducted using two levels of androgyny and three levels of goal blending rather than the previous two. Frequencies, given a tripartite division of relationship blending, are presented in table 4.7. The apparent curvilinarity of the con-

Table 4.7. Androgyny and Three Levels of Goal Blending

| | Level of Androgyny | | | | | |
| | High | | | Low | | |
Sex	Number of High Relationship Blenders	Number of Equivocal Relationship Blenders	Number of Low Relationship Blenders	Number of High Relationship Blenders	Number of Equivocal Relationship Blenders	Number of Low Relationship Blenders
Males	7	10	12	16	15	10
Females	16	9	23	14	24	16

NOTE: Relationship-blending score ranges for tripartite divisioning of each distribution was the same for each sex: 1–3 = low level blending, 4–6 = equivocal level of blending, 7–10 = high level of blending.

tingency between androgyny and relationship blending for females proved to be statistically significant ($p < .05$). The more highly androgynous females tended to be represented at either extreme, to be either high or low blenders. Low-androgynous females appeared in the intermediate range more often and less frequently at either extreme. In other words, androgyny in females was associated with clear-cut manifestations of instrumental expressiveness or pure expressiveness. Male frequencies in the same table suggest a linear relation between relationship blending and androgyny in which greater androgyny in males is associated with low blending. Although the differences for males failed to achieve statistical significance, their direction certainly argues against an assumption of blending as a correlate of male androgyny.

Taking all of the blending evidence available to us at this time into account, two conclusions can be drawn. Males, at least those on the Emory campus, tend to keep the masculine and feminine behaviors maintained within their sex-role repertoire as relatively distinct dispositions. Even when males at a higher level of androgyny were considered, the same differentiation of instrumental and expressive behaviors was observed. This conclusion concerning males is consistent with those reached following earlier work in our laboratory (Heilbrun & Pitman, 1979). The extent to which the clearer discrimination of masculine and feminine behaviors can be explained by the androgynous male's search for social reinforcements contingent upon specific situational choices is still a matter of opinion. However I find this explanation intuitively appealing, since I believe that males are governed by a pervasive instrumental orientation that permeates all of their activities with goal achievement. Social reinforcement is a readily available goal. Why females tend to blend the instrumental and, to a lesser extent, the expressive components of androgyny, as our evidence suggests that they do, does not seem so readily explained.

REFERENCES

Baucom, D. H. Independent masculinity and femininity scales on the California Psychological Inventory. *Journal of Consulting and Clinical Psychology,* 1976, **44**, 876.

Bem, S. L. The measurement of psychological androgyny. *Journal of Consulting and Clinical Psychology,* 1974, **42**, 155–62.

Bem, S. L. Beyond androgyny: Some presumptious prescriptions for a liberated sexual identity. In J. Sherman & F. Denmark (Eds.), *Psychology of women: Future directions and research.* New York: Psychological Dimensions, 1978.

Block, J. Ego identity, role variability, and adjustment. *Journal of Consulting Psychology,* 1961, **25**, 392–97.

Block, J. H. Conceptions of sex-role: Some cross-cultural and longitudinal perspectives. *American Psychologist,* 1973, **28**, 512–26.

Brown, D. G. Sex-role development in a changing culture. *Psychological Bulletin,* 1958, **55**, 232–42.

Erickson, E. H. *Childhood and society*. New York: Norton, 1950.

Firestone, S. *The dialectic of sex*. New York: William Morrow, 1970.

Grambs, J. D., & Waetjen, W. B. *Sex: Does it make a difference?* Belmont, Calif.: Duxbury, 1975

Green, R. Childhood cross-gender identification. In R. Green & J. Money (Eds.), *Transsexualism and sex reassignment*. Baltimore: Johns Hopkins Press, 1969.

Greenberg, S. *Right from the start: A guide to nonsexist child rearing*. Boston: Houghton Mifflin, 1978.

Heilbrun, A. B. Sex role, instrumental-expressive behavior, and psychopathology in females. *Journal of Abnormal Psychology*, 1968, **73**, 131–36.

Heilbrun, A. B. The added dimension of adaptability in male sex-role behavior. Unpublished manuscript, 1977.

Heilbrun, A. B., & Pitman, D. Testing some basic assumptions about psychological androgyny. *Journal of Genetic Psychology*, 1979, **135**, 175–88.

Heilbrun, A. B., & Schwartz, H. Sex-gender differences in level of androgyny. *Sex Roles: A Journal of Research*, in press.

Heilbrun, A. B., & Thompson, N. L., Jr. Sex-role identity and male and female homosexuality. *Sex Roles: A Journal of Research*, 1977, **3**, 65–79.

Kelly, J. A., Caudill, M. S., Hathorn, S. & O'Brien, C. G. Socially undesirable sex-correlated characteristics: Implications for androgyny and adjustment. *Journal of Consulting and Clinical Psychology*, 1977, **45**, 1185–86.

Kelly, J. A., & Worrell, J. New formulations of sex roles and androgyny: A critical review. *Journal of Consulting and Clinical Psychology*, 1977, **45**, 1101–15.

Lynn, D. B. *Parent and sex-role identification: A theoretical formulation*. Berkeley, Calif.: McCutchan, 1969.

Matteson, D. R. *Adolescence today: Sex roles and the search for identity*. Homewood, Ill.: Dorsey, 1975.

Oakley, A. *Sex gender and society*. London: Temple Smith, 1972

Pleck, J. H., & Sawyer, J. (Eds.) *Men and masculinity*. Englewood Cliffs, N. J.: Prentice-Hall, 1974.

Sears, R. R. Identification as a form of behavioral development. In D. B. Harris (Eds.), *The concept of development*. Minneapolis: University of Minnesota Press, 1957.

Spence, J. T., Helmreich, R., & Stapp, J. Ratings of self and peers on sex-role attributes and their relation to self-esteem and conceptions of masculinity and femininity. *Journal of Personality and Social Psychology*, 1975, **32**, 29-39.

Steinmann, A., & Fox, D. J. *The male dilemma: How to survive the sexual revolution*. New York: Jason Aronson, 1974.

Thompson, N. L., & McCandless, B. R. The homosexual orientation and its antecedents. In A. Davids (Ed.), *Child personality and psychopathology: Current topics*. Vol. 3. New York: Wiley, 1976.

Thompson, N. J., Jr., Schwartz, D. M., McCandless, B. R., & Edwards, D. A. Parent-child relationships and sexual identity in male and female homosexuals and heterosexuals. *Journal of Consulting and Clinical Psychology*, 1973, **41**, 120–27.

Wakefield, J. A., Jr., Sasek, J., Friedman, A. F., & Bowden, J. D. Androgyny and other measures of masculinity-femininity. *Journal of Consulting and Clinical Psychology*, 1976, **44**, 766–70.

Whitehurst, C. A. *Women in America: The oppressed majority*. Santa Monica, Calif.: Goodyear, 1977.

Yorburg, B. *Sexual identity: Sex roles and social change*. New York: Wiley, 1974.

Chapter 5

Sex Roles and Personal Competence

Questions and answers arising from the revitalized interest in sex-role behavior since 1973 are of scientific importance insofar as they extend our knowledge of contemporary social behavior. However, to many the importance of studying sex roles has a much more pragmatic ring to it. Only one question really matters: do sex roles make a difference when the concerns of the individual and society are considered? I have weighed this pragmatic issue from a number of perspectives that will be presented in this chapter—self-esteem, the attributes of distinction, homosexual versus heterosexual orientation, client maladjustment, and criminal behavior—and I have concluded, as many have before, that sex-role status does matter. However, the evidence has led me to elaborate on this conclusion, and a statement of this altered perspective might prove helpful in setting the stage for presentation of the data. Sex-role status consistently assumed some importance when the various types of evidence of social competence were examined, but I became encouraged to view the sex roles as contributing to social adaptation in only a narrow sense. That is, a particular sex-role status can be adaptive when considered from one social perspective, but the same role might prove a social liability when considered from another vantage point.

Prior research into the adaptive value of sex-role behavior, not even to mention more popular writing without data base, has not encouraged the kind of conservatism suggested by these introductory comments, at least when masculinity and femininity have been considered as independent and androgyny as a viable construct. Kelly and Worrell's 1977 review of sex-role research had prepared me to some extent when it concluded that high self-esteem is related primarily to the presence of masculine-type behavior and minimally to the presence of feminine-type behavior. This, as they pointed out, leaves unanswered the question of how the feminine component of androgyny contributes to feelings of self-worth. Their findings also challenge the contention that androgyny represents the most promising sex-role contribution to effective behavior and, presumably, to high self-esteem. Kelly and Worrell also qualified their conclusions about the value of androgyny by suggesting that the same sex-role behavior might have different social consequences depending on whether it was displayed by a male or female. The possibility that androgyny might be more profitable for females than males was suggested in my own research by the finding that androgynous females were underrepresented within the population of clients seeking assistance for personal problems on a college campus and undifferentiated females were overrepresented (Heilbrun, 1976). The same trend was observed in comparable male client data, but failed to achieve statistical significance.

A more recent report (Jones, Chernovetz, & Hansson, 1978) of a program of studies testing the proposition that psychological androgyny lends itself to better adjustment reaffirmed the greater value of masculine sex-role behavior than androgyny. These researchers, however, concluded that this held true for both males and females. It is worth noting that the failure for evidence to support the early enthusiastic contention that androgyny was a social panacea for the ills of stereotyped role conformity does not mean that androgyny has been shown to have harmful effects. Feminine and undifferentiated sex-role behaviors have most often achieved that dubious distinction in studies bearing on personal effectiveness. My own preference at this point, as I have said, is to approach the question of the relationship between sex role and competence from a perspective assuming no absolutes—that any given outcome should not be expected to be adaptive under all circumstances or for both sexes. This complicates our thinking, requiring as it does that we seek moderating variables that may influence adaptive value for the various sex roles. The evidence we are about to consider will, I hope, convince you that this is a profitable view.

SEX ROLES AND SELF-ESTEEM

Perhaps the simplest place to start weighing the evidence regarding sex role and competence is to consider the individual's appraisal of his own personal effectiveness. Many will prefer a term such as *self-esteem* to describe such data, in that it suggests a more conservative posture with regard to how factual the appraisal is expected to be.

One pressing concern in researching self-esteem was the selection of reference points in the person's life that would serve most meaningfully as the basis for personal judgments of competence. As it turned out, the responsibility for assigning importance to each category of experience was shared with the individual subject. I selected what I believed to be important aspects of college student life, but self-raters were given the opportunity to assign their own weights of importance as well.

The second consideration that influenced the selection of competence areas was the limiting interest in how sex-role development contributes to personal effectiveness. Presumably, the sex roles should have their major impact upon sense of competence in domains of behavior most closely linked to instrumental and expressive concerns, and that is where we chose to concentrate our efforts. Instrumental competence was gauged by rated achievement in pursuit of widely recognized goals, presumably central to masculine role development; expressive competence was considered in terms of successful personal relationships, assumed to be the special province of femininity (Bakan, 1966; Bem, 1975; Parsons & Bales, 1955; Spence, Helmreich, & Stapp, 1975). Data concerning the relations between sex-role behavior and instrumental and expressive self-esteem were collected in the fall of 1978 from 105 female and 69 male Emory College students. The ACL was administered along with a self-esteem questionnaire devised especially for the study. Order of administration involved initial self-descriptions on the ACL, forming the basis for inferring sex role, and then self-ratings on the questionnaire.

The competence measure began with the following instructions to the subject:

> There are several aspects of middle-class life that are generally considered to be important indicators of being a successful person at college age. Please think about how satisfied you are with yourself as far as the following are concerned. Rate each along the 10-point scale and the relative importance of this aspect of your life.

Each dimension of competence was anchored at point 1 by "highly unsatisfied with myself" and at point 10 by "highly satisfied with myself." Importance was rated as 2, 1, or 0 depending on whether the person considered the particular aspect quite important, fairly important, or not important.

Instrumental self-esteem was based upon ratings of satisfaction and importance for (1) academic achievement and (2) career progress. Expressive self-esteem was based upon ratings concerning (1) peer relationships (friendships), (2) heterosexual relationships (dating), and (3) family relationships. Finally, as a set of control dimensions chosen as irrelevant to sex-role status, nonspecific self-esteem included ratings of satisfaction/importance for (1) extracurricular activities, (2) physical appearance, and (3) personal values.

The score for each self-esteem category was the sum of the satisfaction ratings weighted (multiplied) by the importance assigned to each dimension of self-esteem within that category by the subject. For example, consider the following set of ratings for expressive competence:

Dimension	Satisfaction		Importance	
Peer relationships	7	×	1	= 7
Heterosexual relationships	6	×	0	= 0
Family relationships	4	×	2	= 8

Sum score = 15

The subject would be assigned a score of 15, which is on the low side considering the total possible score of 60. Median-split procedures were used to define high/low dichotomies on the ACL Masculinity and Femininity Scales independently by sex. Subjects were assigned to one of the four resultant sex-role outcomes.

Table 5.1 includes the total self-esteem scores as well as the component instrumental, expressive, and nonspecific self-esteem scores for each of the sex-role groups. Total scores, which were not our central interest, did accommodate well to the most consistent result reported by self-esteem researchers, according to the review by Kelly and Worrell (1977). High masculine males and females (Columns 1–4) achieved higher overall self-esteem scores ($p < .05$) than their low masculine counterparts (Columns 5–8). Androgynous subjects of both sexes emerged as most competent, although only the androgynous females differed significantly from the remaining sex-role groups combined ($p < .05$).

Table 5.1. Sex Role and Self-Esteem in College Males and Females

	Sex Role							
	High Masculine– High Feminine (Androgynous)		High Masculine– Low Feminine (Masculine)		Low Masculine– High Feminine (Feminine)		Low Masculine– Low Feminine (Undifferentiated)	
Aspect of Competence	Males (N=16)	Females (N=19)	Males (N=19)	Females (N=35)	Males (N=18)	Females (N=32)	Males (N=16)	Females (N=19)
Instrumental	21.25	26.68	23.53	24.11	19.00	19.06	21.69	24.05
Expressive	40.44	45.82	36.53	42.86	42.44	41.81	32.38	41.42
Nonspecific	33.19	31.58	32.26	33.19	30.72	31.72	29.31	31.79
Total	94.88	104.08	92.32	100.16	92.16	92.59	83.38	97.26

If we examine self-esteem at a somewhat more specific level, that of instrumental and expressive self-esteem combined, we can see from table 5.1 that androgynous females are uniquely high (72.50) relative to females of masculine (66.97), feminine (60.87), and undifferentiated (65.47) sex-role status. While standard analysis of variance revealed no significant effects of sex role, comparison of the androgynous females to all other groups combined verified the significance of their elevated instrumental/expressive self-esteem scores ($p < .01$). The same androgynous females did not display higher self-esteem, however, when aspects of their lives unrelated to sex-role behavior were considered. Androgynous (61.69), masculine (60.06), and feminine (61.44) males looked very much alike on combined instrumental/expressive self-esteem, and it was the undifferentiated male who emerged as deviant (54.07). However, no statistical comparisons achieved significance.

The androgyny index applied to the ACL Masculinity and Femininity Scale T-scores gives us another way of considering sex role and combined instrumental/expressive self-esteem. The distributions of androgyny scores were cut at the respective medians for each sex and mean instrumental/expressive self-esteem scores were found for high and low androgynous subjects. This mode of analysis affirmed the value of androgyny for both sexes, rather than just for females as was the case in the prior analysis using the fourfold typology. Androgynous males had higher self-esteem scores (64.28) than low androgynous males (55.06). Females defined as high and low androgynous presented the same pattern of means (68.40 versus 63.07). The significant effect for level of androgyny within the analysis of variance ($p < .01$) allows us to say with some confidence that androgyny in either sex is accompanied by higher self-esteem in both the instrumental and expressive domains.

Self-esteem scores were next analyzed at their most specific levels, at least for our purposes. Consideration of the instrumental and expressive self-esteem scores separately produced results for which I was not prepared by previous studies of sex role and adjustment. Masculinity proved to be positively related to instrumental self-esteem for the female ($p < .05$), but a significant interaction ($p < .05$) isolated this effect within only two of the groups. Androgynous women subscribed to much higher instrumental self-esteem (26.68) than feminine women (19.00); masculine women were nearly identical in this regard (24.11) to undifferentiated women (24.05). No significant differences nor suggestive trends were found among the women's sex-role groups in expressive self-esteem, traditionally associated with the female sex role.

A complementary pattern of findings emerged for males. No self-esteem differences were found among the four male sex-role groups for goal-oriented activities (academic and career achievement) traditionally associated with men. However, femininity in males was associated with higher expressive self-esteem ($p < .05$). This represents a very unusual finding in sex-role research—that is, that femininity in men has any kind of positive behavioral connotation. Evidently, by being selective about the type of experience in question, we were able to identify a rare adaptive value of femininity in men.

Finally, nonspecific competence scores failed to relate to sex role for either sex. While negative results must always be conservatively interpreted, I am encouraged to believe that this supports an important thesis. Sex roles, no matter what their advantages or disadvantages, should not be expected to extend their effects into all aspects of peoples' lives.

SEX ROLES AND LEVELS OF PERSONAL EFFECTIVENESS DEFINED BY CRITERION GROUPS

We now shift from self-esteem to considering the relations of sex roles to a very different criterion of personal effectiveness. The general approach to doing this will involve sex-role comparisons among groups of college students that fall at distinctly different points along a continuum of personal effectiveness. This reverses the process of analysis discussed in the previous section. Instead of categorizing the subjects by sex role and then considering continuous self-esteem variables, subjects will be categorized by level of personal competence and sex-role scores will become our continuous variables for purpose of analysis.

Selection of groups on the Emory campus for which there might be consensual agreement regarding adjustment differences was not difficult, up to a point. The poorly adjusted group, as in a plethora of studies reported in the journals, was comprised of students applying for services of a personal nature at the college mental health agency. Application for psychotherapeutic service does not necessarily mean that the person will demonstrate deficits in instrumental/ expressive competence as considered in the previous section, but experience has taught me that soliciting such help offers excellent odds for evidence of both. The thirty-nine males and seventy-three females included in the least effective group represent an unsystematic sample of personal clients (almost exclusively under-graduate) contacting the agency between September 1977 and June 1979.

Another common procedure for constituting groups at varying points on the adjustment continuum is to use more or less random samples of college students as a standard against which maladjusted client samples can be compared. This is a defensible procedure, although the researcher must acknowledge the heterogeneous character of such samples. There will be some subjects included in this kind of random college sample that are just as maladjusted as the clients. However, the danger of this kind of error is not likely to be excessive unless the prevalence of psychological disturbance is quite high on the campus or some inadvertent bias has crept into the sampling procedure. Neither is true for this intermediate effectiveness group, as far as I can tell. The 69 males and 105 females (who provided the self-esteem data in the previous section) came from a large undergraduate class that I taught in the fall of 1978. Except for the few who sat in the back row and maintained rigid disattention to the realities of the classroom, these students did not appear to be extraordinary.

Just as one depends on a low campus base rate for personal maladjustment in representing a random sample of students as having achieved a satisfactory level of personal effectiveness, it is equally true that the low base rate for personal excellence on a campus does not allow one to describe a random sample as representative of extraordinary effectiveness. For that reason, a special effort was made to identify students on the Emory campus who were recognized as combining exceptional personal and academic accomplishment by their peers and by representatives of the university administration. Two campus organizations were recommended by the personnel deans as including only students who met these criteria, and membership lists were obtained with their generous assistance. Letters were dispatched requesting that each exceptional student complete and return the enclosed ACL anonymously. About 60 percent of those contacted were willing to do so, and the self-descriptions of these thirty males and twenty females allow us to examine sex-role behaviors in those students deemed to be of superior personal effectiveness. Members of the two campus organizations from which the sample was drawn are predominantly upperclass college students.

Inclusion of a distinguished student group permits us to examine the relation between sex role and behavioral effectiveness using three points on the latter dimension rather than the usual two. This could assume importance, since it allows an estimate of whether any given relation is linear or curvilinear. For example, it is possible that androgyny may be a correlate of personal effectiveness only when one extreme or the other of personal competence is examined. We shall find, in fact, a version of this to in fact be the case.

Let us consider first the question of whether students at these varying levels of effectiveness differ in masculinity and femininity from one another. Table 5.2 includes the mean ACL scale scores that formed the basis for our analysis. Analysis of variance applied to the masculinity scores disclosed one significant effect: both males and females demonstrated a monotonic increase in masculinity with increments in personal competence ($p < .025$). Similar analysis of femininity scores indicated that the differences observed in the means could be attributed to chance.

Table 5.2.   Masculinity and Femininity Scores and Competence

Levels of Competence	Masculinity			Femininity	
	Males	Females		Males	Females
Low	46.54	50.30		44.21	44.85
Intermediate	49.81	52.28		45.86	49.91
High	52.97	56.95		48.10	45.40

These results are consistent with the overall self-esteem findings reported earlier. For the college female, greater masculinity is accompanied by higher self-esteem and with greater actual personal effectiveness as judged by comparison of criterion groups. Masculinity in college males also was found to be a positive correlate of both overall self-esteem and personal competence defined by criterion groups. The prevailing importance of masculinity in facilitating effectiveness for both males and females on a college campus places our results in the mainstream of prior findings cited at the beginning of this chapter (Jones, Chernovetz, & Hansson, 1978; Kelly & Worell, 1977).

What about androgyny and the belief shared by many that expanded sex-role potential would contribute to more effective lifestyles? To consider this question, the androgyny index was applied to the ACL sex-role scores for the three adjustment groups. The raw score formula will be reported so that direct comparison between the sexes will be more meaningful. I reported on previous pages that males consistently achieve a higher level of androgyny than females when sheer number of masculine and feminine behaviors are considered without being obliterated by independent norming procedures.

Raw score androgyny levels for the groups representing three tiers of adjustment (table 5.3) offer striking testimony to the assumption that androgyny mediates more effective behavior. Analysis of variance identified two general effects. More competent people of either sex are more androgynous than less competent people ($p < .001$), and (as we knew) males are more androgynous than females ($p < .01$). Another interesting effect emerged in the form of an interaction between competence level and sex ($p < .05$). This means that the relations between androgyny and level of effectiveness were different for males and females, even though both were positive. If you refer to table 5.3 you will

Table 5.3.   Level of Androgyny at Different Personal Competence Levels

	Level of Competence		
Sex	Low	Intermediate	High
Male	11.13	18.55	21.00
Female	11.97	12.11	17.20

NOTE: Figures represent mean raw androgyny index scores.

note that neither the progression of androgyny means for males nor that for females appears to be linear; that is, neither shows a steady increase over the three competence levels starting with the low group (clinic clients). It was the male with personal problems who provided the divergent (low) level of androgyny relative to the others; males from the general sample and from the sample of distinguished students were higher in androgyny and rather similar to each other in this regard. In contrast, female clients and those from the general sample were comparable to one another, both being markedly lower in androgyny than the distinguished females.

These distinct patterns for the two sexes make rather good sense when considered in light of the ubiquitous finding of an overall sex difference in androgyny. Males may have less to gain in competence from excessive androgynous potential than to lose from a deficit; this presupposes a point of diminishing returns for increasing male androgyny. On the other hand, females are generally lower in androgyny, so that increments may stand a better chance of making a positive adaptive contribution than lower reaches of androgyny have of proving a handicap—a point of diminishing costs to the female.

The apparent difference in curvilinear functions for males and females between level of personal effectiveness and androgyny suggested by the table 5.3 means redirected our attention back to the self-esteem data presented in the previous section. If there is merit in the contention that a sex-linked difference in function exists, it might be possible to pick this up using the self-esteem variable. The instrumental/expressive self-esteem scores were calculated by quartiles of scores on the androgyny index. These mean figures (table 5.4) offer at least partial support for my proposal. Men in the lowest quartile of androgyny scores demonstrate the most deviant self-esteem score of the four groups; androgyny renders its most remarkable effect for males by its relative absence.

Table 5.4 tells a different story for women. A deficit in androgyny seems to make little difference in self-esteem, as evidenced by the comparable means for the first and second quartiles; whatever modest effect can be noted is observed in the higher reaches of androgyny represented in the third and fourth quartiles. High androgyny contributes to self-esteem for females, but lower androgyny seems to make no difference. By the way, the interaction effect within this analysis of variance achieved significance ($p < .05$), so the difference in sex-linked functions for androgyny and self-esteem was statistically confirmed just as it was for androgyny and personal competence.

Table 5.4.   Self-Rated Instrumental/Expressive Competence and Androgyny

| Sex of Subject | Level of Androgyny | | | |
	First Quartile (Lowest)	Second Quartile	Third Quartile	Fourth Quartile (Highest)
Male	47.24	61.84	60.69	68.53
Female	63.96	63.42	65.70	67.75

ADAPTIVE VALUE OF SPECIFIC SEX-ROLE BEHAVIORS

The sex-role self-descriptions for subjects at the three competence levels described in the previous section offer us the opportunity to examine the base rates of endorsement for each of the ACL masculine and feminine behaviors at each of these levels. The intermediate and low-effectiveness groups were bolstered in number to 145 males and 193 females and 160 males and 107 females, respectively, for purposes of nonparametric analysis. There was nothing that we could do to bolster the size of the high-effectiveness samples. This more refined analysis of sex-role behavior and personal effectiveness takes cognizance of the fact that masculinity and femininity represent heterogeneous types of behavior, and it is very possible that some aspects of each sex role are related to competence and some are not. Furthermore, even if related, some may show linear and others curvilinear trends across these levels of competence.

Tables 5.5 and 5.6 present the male and female base rates of endorsement for the fifty-three masculine and feminine behaviors across the three competence groups, as well as a statistical indication of which of these triads involved significantly different endorsement rates.

Table 5.5.   Male Endorsement Base Rates of Specific Sex-Role Behaviors at Three Levels of Competence

Masculine	High Competence (%)	Intermediate Competence (%)	Low Competence (%)	Probability
aggressive	53	37	28	.05
arrogant	17	8	18	.05
assertive	70	35	31	.001
autocratic	33	12	15	.05
conceited	20	11	23	.05
confident	83	58	39	.001
cynical	30	34	45	
deliberate	30	34	34	
dominant	50	36	20	.001
enterprising	57	43	29	.01
forceful	20	24	19	
foresighted	57	41	41	
frank	73	58	67	
handsome	60	35	27	.01
hard-headed	30	30	38	
industrious	67	43	38	.05
ingenious	17	23	23	
inventive	43	37	24	.01
masculine	53	58	66	
opportunistic	57	28	18	.001
outspoken	37	25	24	
self-confident	83	49	40	.001
sharp-witted	33	33	37	
shrewd	30	22	20	
stern	17	12	14	

Table 5.5 continued

Masculine	High Competence (%)	Intermediate Competence (%)	Low Competence (%)	Probability
strong	67	43	36	.05
tough	27	20	19	
vindictive	7	6	12	

Feminine				
appreciative	83	75	71	
considerate	93	84	78	
contented	47	29	21	.05
cooperative	87	71	74	
dependent	7	25	41	.001
emotional	53	57	60	
excitable	43	47	50	
fearful	3	8	29	.001
feminine	0	1	0	
fickle	13	6	13	
forgiving	70	68	70	
friendly	97	79	81	
frivolous	0	4	9	
helpful	87	58	65	.01
modest	47	45	48	
praising	37	27	30	
sensitive	90	67	75	.05
sentimental	77	54	56	
sincere	93	63	78	.001
submissive	0	10	22	.001
sympathetic	87	52	67	.001
talkative	33	34	31	
timid	7	12	25	.01
warm	70	59	56	
worrying	30	21	62	.001

One of the most striking features of these two tables is the comparable numbers of masculine and feminine attributes that vary significantly in endorsement across personal competence levels. Furthermore, the comparability in significant items holds true for both males and females, although the specific attributes agree in only twelve of thirty-three cases. Men varying in personal effectiveness, for example, demonstrated base rate differences on fourteen of the twenty-eight (50 percent) masculine attributes but also on ten of the twenty-five (40 percent) feminine behaviors. Base rate differences for women appeared for eleven of twenty-eight (39 percent) masculine and ten of twenty-five (40 percent) feminine terms.

These results appear to be inconsistent with those reported previously (see table 5.2) that reflected significant increments in Masculinity Scale scores for both sexes with increasing competence, but no comparable effect for femininity scores. Thus, the earlier results suggest that masculine behaviors contribute systematically to personal competence and feminine behaviors do not when considered by scales; present results indicate the comparable importance of masculinity and femininity when analysis is based on the items constituting the scales. Since the intermediate and low competence groups used in the two analyses were overlapping but not identical, disparate conclusions about the adaptive value of sex-role attributes could be explained in terms of sampling fluctuation. However, the same criteria for assignment of new subjects to the

Table 5.6. Female Endorsement Base Rates of Specific Sex-Role Behaviors at Three Levels of Competence

Masculine	High Competence (%)	Intermediate Competence (%)	Low Competence (%)	Probability
aggressive	25	31	23	
arrogant	0	6	11	
assertive	60	26	27	.01
autocratic	10	7	9	
conceited	5	5	17	.001
confident	55	48	25	.001
cynical	35	25	45	.01
deliberate	65	23	20	
dominant	35	23	20	
enterprising	45	33	24	
forceful	20	11	8	
foresighted	60	34	31	.05
frank	60	66	64	
handsome	10	2	3	
hard-headed	30	40	50	
industrious	80	43	33	.001
ingenious	30	15	13	
inventive	40	26	29	
masculine	0	1	4	
opportunistic	30	18	13	
outspoken	25	19	21	
self-confident	50	40	23	.01
sharp-witted	50	34	19	.01
shrewd	30	11	6	.01
strong	65	36	23	.01
tough	20	12	7	
vindictive	5	4	7	
stern	10	4	5	

Table 5.6 continued

Feminine	High Competence (%)	Intermediate Competence (%)	Low Competence (%)	Probability
appreciative	95	86	80	
considerate	100	89	81	.05
contented	50	50	21	.001
cooperative	85	82	81	
dependent	15	38	52	.01
emotional	55	79	82	.05
excitable	70	66	65	
fearful	5	17	36	.001
feminine	60	69	70	
fickle	15	25	24	
forgiving	60	75	74	
friendly	95	90	77	.001
frivolous	10	10	14	
helpful	95	72	72	
modest	60	48	58	
praising	45	35	34	
sensitive	90	85	89	
sentimental	65	79	70	
sincere	100	80	82	
submissive	10	21	36	.01
sympathetic	75	78	71	
talkative	55	50	39	
timid	20	19	34	.05
warm	60	73	59	.05
worrying	55	44	66	.01

intermediate and low competence groups were imposed, so alternative explanations for the apparent inconsistency are more appealing. Inspection of these base-rate functions offers at least two.

The endorsement rates for specific sex-role attributes reflect both linear and curvilinear functions when compared across competence levels. A linear function would be suggested when the rate increases or decreases significantly and regularly across levels; curvilinearity would be indicated when significant variations in endorsement rates are observed but regularity is not found. For an example of a significant linear progression among the masculine items, look at table 5.5; *aggressive* is selected increasingly by males as self-characteristic as low (28 percent), intermediate (37 percent), and high (53 percent) competence groups are considered. In contrast, the significantly variant endorsement rates for *arrogant* on the same table are curvilinear, with higher rates appearing at the extremes of low (18 percent) and high (17 percent) competence and the lowest rate found for the intermediate competence group (8 percent). If endorsement tables 5.5 and 5.6 are examined with linearity and curvilinearity in mind, a clear difference between masculine and feminine attributes is evident. Only 25 percent of the functions for significant masculine items are curvilinear, considering both sexes, whereas 45 percent of the comparable feminine items bear this functional characteristic. Thus endorsement of feminine characteristics by either sex is less likely to distinguish groups varying in competence, because a higher proportion of scale items bear a significant but erratic relation to competence levels.

The erratic contingency between feminine behavior and competence levels is also obvious within the eleven comparisons for which there was a significant differentiation of competence groups and a linear progression in base rates. Combining across sexes, eight linear functions indicated increasing prevalence of the feminine behavior as the competence of the group declined, but three functions indicated just the opposite. In other words, the significant feminine items included those with both positive and negative adaptive value. Inspection of significant masculine attributes on tables 5.5 and 5.6 identified nineteen as showing a linear progression of endorsement rate across competence levels. Every one of them reflected a positive adaptive value of the masculine attribute. Just as the presence of curvilinearity in the relation between rate of endorsement and competence level would tend to obscure any systematic link between Femininity Scale scores and personal competence, the presence of both positive and negative linear functions would contribute to the same effect. On the other hand, the sparse number of curvilinear functions and exclusively positive linear functions on masculine items would lead us to expect Masculinity Scale scores and competence to show a clear positive relation for both sexes.

There is a danger that the potential importance of these observations may be missed because of the language required for their description. Put in simpler terms, feminine behaviors are a more mysterious commodity as far as human competence is concerned. We were forewarned of this by some data I reported (Heilbrun, 1976) that were discussed in an earlier chapter. As was already described, subjects asked to simulate psychological health did not increase endorsement of feminine items, but the same subjects when instructed to portray psychological disturbance on the ACL provided Femininity Scale scores that plummeted to group averages never seen before or since. Without knowing it, these college students were telling us that feminine behaviors are curvilinearly related to psychological health; they make no systematic contribution by their presence but are a real problem if they are absent. More research is needed, as social scientists are fond of saying, to clear the mystery of femininity and human competence.

SEX ROLES AND SPECIFIC PSYCHOLOGICAL PROBLEMS

Thus far in our examination of the adaptive correlates of sex-role status we have been concerned with both the positive and negative features of masculinity and femininity. Our attention will now be directed to the types of psychological problems that are observed when someone showing any of the four sex-role outcomes requires professional assistance. This approach, in which we shall consider only negative correlates of sex-role status, rests on the assumption that no sex-role status provides immunity from personal problems. Furthermore, if such problems arise, they may show a different character depending on sex-role disposition.

An eleven-year sample (1967–77) of clients utilizing the mental health clinic on the Emory campus was collected for this analysis. To qualify for inclusion, the student client had to be seeking help for personal problems, as opposed to academic or vocational counseling. In addition, the ACL sex-role scores had to deviate at least a half-sigma (5 T-score points) from the college mean of 50 on each scale. This requirement avoided the assignment of any subject to a sex-role category when either the Masculinity or Femininity score was close to the cutting point, a major source of unreliability in this type of classification procedure. For present purposes, then, the following score combinations were used to define the sex-role groups:

- *androgynous:* at least 55 on the Masculinity and the Femininity Scales
- *masculine:* at least 55 on the Masculinity Scale and no more than 45 on the Femininity Scale
- *feminine:* at least 55 on the Femininity Scale and no more than 45 on the Masculinity Scale
- *undifferentiated:* no more than 45 on the Masculinity and Femininity Scales

The total sample included 145 male clients and 153 female clients, approximately 30 percent of the total number of clients seeking assistance for personal problems over the eleven-year period. Attrition resulted mostly from the exclusion of clients with sex-role scores falling within five points of the college mean, but also from the inevitable fact that some client records failed to contain ACLs or information required to judge the type of problems that were in evidence.

Information from which client problems were to be identified was abstracted from clinic records by two clinical psychology graduate students. Three sources of relevant information were used to judge major problem areas, although all three were not necessarily available in every record. First, upon application for service each client is asked to specify the problems for which help is being sought. Second, the initial interviewer completes a form calling for an early professional appraisal of client problems. Third, the staff member assigned as regular therapist discusses client problems in the summary report once the case is closed.

Once the information had been abstracted from the 298 files, I developed a procedure by which all major types of problems could be registered in what is (hopefully) a comprehensible and comprehensive way. The fact that more than one type of problem could be entered for each client and that some of the categories are related complicates statistical analysis, since the frequencies with which different problems occur are not totally independent of each other. The choice seemed to be between compromising our statistics by multiple entries for most clients or losing a great deal of information by trying to identify one primary problem for each client. The latter alternative would also have introduced considerably more subjectivity into the findings, since the files frequently failed to include enough information to allow us to rank order the importance of problems for a given client when more than one was described. As a result of this decision, a great deal of reliance on apparent differences will be required without the usual statistical safeguards.

Table 5.7 presents the most general collation of problem frequencies that has any relevance to the question at hand. These percentages address the question, Do college males and females show different types of personal problems independent of sex role? This table of base rates for the various categories of personal problems suggests that the special problems for the male included: (1) a sense of isolation and loneliness, (2) anxiety symptoms, (3) homosexual concerns, and (4) poor academic achievement. Problem categories more frequently represented in female clients included: (1) difficulties in developing,

Table 5.7. Base Rates for Psychological Problems in Maladjusted College Males and Females

Type of Psychological Problem	Males (N = 145) (%)	Females (N = 153) (%)
Interpersonal		
Difficulty forming/keeping/ resolving relationships	28	43
Special difficulty with heterosexual relationships	9	21
Poor communication	9	12
Need to control others	3	3
Overcompetitiveness	1	0
Abrasive style	1	1
Passive-aggressive	3	2
Imperception of others' needs	1	1

Table 5.7 continued

Type of Psychological Problem	Males (N = 145) (%)	Females (N = 153) (%)
Dependency	10	15
Helplessness/passivity/shyness	19	18
Isolation/loneliness	23	14
Lack of trust	4	6
Rigidity	4	1
Sex problems (heterosexual)	2	10
Intrapersonal		
Self-punitiveness		
Depression	24	40
Guilt	3	6
Suicidal Thoughts	1	3
Self-conceptual problems		
Low self-confidence	14	15
Low self-esteem	26	31
Identity confusion	2	5
Emotional problems		
Anxiety	29	19
Anger	14	14
Jealousy	1	1
Affective deficit	8	8
Cognitive Problems		
Indecision	2	3
Loss of concentration/control	9	2
Confused/bizarre thinking	3	5
Delusional	1	1
Self-control problems		
Overcontrol	1	1
Undercontrol	3	1
Deviant sexual orientation		
Homosexual	14	1
Other	1	0
Academic problems		
Poor achievement	16	7
Low motivation	7	3
Career problems		
Role conflict	1	2
Indecisiveness	20	20
Somatic problems		
Sleep disturbance	2	3
Eating disturbance	1	4
Weight loss/gain	1	3

maintaining, or terminating personal relationships; (2) special problems in heterosexual relationships (including sex problems); and (3) depression.

These observations lend credibility to the frequently voiced criticisms of stereotyped sex-role adoption; that is, the most salient problems for the male are those that seemingly would derive from the demand characteristics of masculinity, whereas the female problems can be linked to difficulties with femininity. The male suffers not only the price of feared deviation from culturally sanctioned masculinity (homosexual concerns and failure to achieve academically), but also the price of a deficit in relationship orientation (sense of isolation and loneliness). The uniquely female problem categories can just as readily be associated with stereotyped femininity. An emphasis on quality of relationships, implicit in an expressive orientation, is apparent in the concentration of problems involving personal relationships in general and heterosexual relationships in particular.

Yet in other ways the problem frequencies associated with gender presented in table 5.7 are interesting for what they do not show—evidence of the unique difficulties for the talented female created (according to feminists) by her subjugated and inferior status and restricted career opportunities relative to the male. College women did not present more problems suggesting concern over role subjugation (18 percent versus a male 19 percent for ''helplessness/passivity/shyness''; 14 percent versus a male 14 percent for ''anger''). Neither did they show special evidence of felt inferiority; some 15 percent and 31 percent displayed deficiencies in self-confidence and in self-esteem, but so did 14 percent and 26 percent of the college men. Finally, career problems in the form of role conflict (2 percent) and indecisiveness (20 percent) were certainly evident for the female, but little more so than for the male (1 percent and 20 percent). It remains a possibility that college females were more frequently and forecefully faced with these forms of discrimination based upon gender but simply did not seek professional help in commensurate numbers because they were inured to this reality or pessimistic about changing anything through professional help. We can only report what our data tell us; there was no apparent evidence of distress from sex-gender discrimination unique to the problems of college women seeking assistance between 1967 and 1977.

Base rates for psychological problems will be examined next at a greater level of specificity. Table 5.8 includes the percentage figures for males and females who fall high or low on masculinity or on femininity relative to college norms. These percentages address the question of whether either sex role considered alone plays a role in promoting or avoiding specific types of problems. Only those problems with at least a 10 percent base rate in college clients of either sex on table 5.7 will be considered from this point on.

First, let us examine the prevalence of specific psychological problems for these sex-role groupings within each sex. In the case of the male, high masculinity is generally associated with a lower base rate for problems than low masculinity. Clearest cases in point include fewer problems of (1) dependency, (2) helplessness/passivity/shyness, (3) isolation/loneliness, (4) depression, (5) low self-esteem, (6) anxiety, (7) poor achievement, and (8) indecisiveness. There were only two types of problems in which high masculine males demonstrated a higher base rate: (1) poor communication and (2) emotional deficit. Both seem to reflect the social unresponsiveness of the masculine character. The adaptive value of masculinity in the case of the male appears obvious even when we are examining only problem behaviors; these figures have to mean that when a masculine male seeks help his problems tend to be more restricted than is true of less masculine males. The same conclusion, that masculinity is an adaptive quality for males, was reached earlier in this chapter when groups differing in competence were compared. If any further affirmation of this is needed, table 5.8 reports three times as many male clients below the college norm on masculinity than above.

Femininity in the male offers a more balanced maladaptive picture, although the high-feminine male clients are identified by a larger number of problem areas than their low feminine counterparts. Low femininity in the male lends itself to (1) more difficulty forming/keeping/resolving relationships, (2) more problems involving anger, and (3) more indecisiveness about careers than high femininity. On the other hand, the high feminine males were found to have more problems of (1) isolation/loneliness, (2) depression, (3) low self-esteem, (4) anxiety, and (5) poor achievement. The more even adaptive balance also was suggested by the roughly equal numbers of high and low feminine male clients in the sample. The male data, in summary, suggest that level of masculinity is the more critical mediator of problem behaviors, with low masculinity being conducive to a broader array of problems. Level of femininity in the male seems to play a less important role as far as breadth of problem behaviors is concerned. Both high and low femininity are correlated with their own brand of problems, however.

Table 5.8.   Base Rates for Major Categories of Psychological Problems by Level of Masculinity and Femininity

	Sex Role							
	High Masculine		Low Masculine		High Feminine		Low Feminine	
	Males	Females	Males	Females	Males	Females	Males	Females
	(N=37)	(N=54)	(N=108)	(N=99)	(N=79)	(N=61)	(N=66)	(N=92)
Type of Psychological Problem	(%)		(%)		(%)		(%)	
Interpersonal								
Difficulty forming/keeping/ resolving relationships	24	54	30	37	20	38	38	47

Table 5.8 continued

Type of Psychological Problem	Sex Role							
	High Masculine		Low Masculine		High Feminine		Low Feminine	
	Males (N=37) (%)	Females (N=54) (%)	Males (N=108) (%)	Females (N=99) (%)	Males (N=79) (%)	Females (N=61) (%)	Males (N=66) (%)	Females (N=92) (%)
Special difficulty with heterosexual relationships	8	31	9	15	11	18	6	23
Poor communication	14	13	7	11	9	10	9	13
Dependency	0	15	14	15	10	18	11	13
Helplessness/passivity/ shyness	11	6	26	25	20	15	24	21
Isolation/loneliness	16	11	25	15	29	13	15	14
Sex problems (heterosexual)	5	9	1	10	1	8	3	11
Intrapersonal Self-punitiveness Depression	19	26	27	47	30	41	18	39
Self-conceptual problems Low self-confidence	11	13	16	16	16	21	12	11
Low self-esteem	16	26	29	33	35	30	14	32
Emotional problems Anxiety	5	15	25	21	30	25	8	15
Anger	11	22	16	9	10	8	20	17
Affective deficit	16	9	10	6	11	5	12	9
Deviant sexual orientation Homosexual	11	2	16	1	14	2	15	1
Academic problems Poor achievement	8	6	19	8	20	5	11	9
Career problems Indecisiveness	14	11	22	25	16	21	24	20

A parallel analysis of female base rates suggests that imbalance of problems by sex-role levels is less pronounced than was true for the male. Low masculine females were somewhat more problem-prone than high masculine females, with psychological difficulties involving (1) helplessness/passivity/shyness, (2) isolation/loneliness, (3) depression, (4) low self-esteem, and (5) career indecisiveness. Nevertheless, high masculine females presented their own array of problems: (1) difficulty forming/keeping/resolving relationships, (2) a special difficulty with heterosexual relationships, and (3) anger. Neither high nor low femininity appeared uniquely disadvantageous to the female. High femininity was associated with more frequent problems of low self-confidence and anxiety, and low femininity with higher prevalence of difficulties forming/keeping/ resolving relationships and problems with anger.

The final and most refined breakdown of the problem base rate data will be by sex-role type—androgynous, masculine, feminine, and undifferentiated. These figures (table 5.9) will allow us to go beyond the general conclusions regarding gender or even sex roles considered independently within gender to a more specific delineation of problem base rates considering the sex roles in combination. Unfortunately, the number of female clients who qualified as androgynous by our more stringent criteria of high/low status (only seven over an eleven-year period) was too small to be of much use except to further confirm the adaptive value of androgyny for women. There were not many androgynous males either, sixteen by actual count.

Table 5.9.   Base Rates for Psychological Problems by Type of Sex-Role Status

	Sex Role							
	Androgynous		Masculine		Feminine		Undifferentiated	
	Males	Females	Males	Females	Males	Females	Males	Females
	(N=16)	(N=7)	(N=21)	(N=47)	(N=63)	(N=54)	(N=45)	(N=45)
Type of Psychological Problem	(%)		(%)		(%)		(%)	
Interpersonal								
Difficulty forming/keeping/ resolving relationships	19	71	29	51	21	33	42	42
Special difficulty with heterosexual relationships	6	29	10	32	13	17	4	13
Poor communication	25	29	5	11	5	7	11	16
Dependency	0	14	0	15	13	19	16	11

Table 5.9 continued

Type of Psychological Problem	Sex Role							
	Androgynous		Masculine		Feminine		Undifferentiated	
	Males (N=16) (%)	Females (N=7)	Males (N=21) (%)	Females (N=47)	Males (N=63) (%)	Females (N=54)	Males (N=45) (%)	Females (N=45)
Helplessness/passivity/ shyness	19	0	5	6	21	17	33	36
Isolation/loneliness	25	14	10	11	30	13	17	18
Sex problems (heterosexual)	6	0	5	11	0	9	2	11
Intrapersonal Self-punitiveness Depression	31	0	10	30	30	46	22	49
Self-conceptual problems Low self-confidence	12	29	5	11	17	20	13	11
Low self-esteem	6	14	24	28	43	31	9	36
Emotional problems Anxiety	12	14	0	15	35	26	11	16
Anger	6	0	14	26	11	9	22	9
Affective deficit	12	14	19	9	11	4	9	9
Deviant sexual orientation Homosexual	6	0	14	2	16	2	16	0
Academic problems Poor achievement	6	14	10	4	24	4	11	13
Career problems Indecisiveness	12	0	14	13	17	24	29	27

High masculine males, whether androgynous or masculine in sex type, evidenced little in the way of problems unique to their sex type. Androgynous males more frequently demonstrated problems relating to poor communication (25 percent) than males of other sex types and masculine males an affective deficit (19 percent). Problems in males were found to be associated predominantly with the two sex types involving low masculinity. Feminine males were especially susceptible to low self-esteem (43 percent), anxiety (35 percent), and poor achievement (24 percent). Undifferentiated males presented problems in forming/keeping/resolving relationships (42 percent), helplessness/passivity/shyness (33 percent), anger (22 percent), and indecisiveness regarding careers (29 percent).

Masculine females presented the greatest number of problems unique to their sex type, including difficulties in forming/keeping/resolving relationships (51 percent), special difficulty with heterosexual relationships (32 percent), and problems handling anger (26 percent). Low self-confidence (20 percent) and anxiety (26 percent) were special difficulties of the feminine female, whereas undifferentiated status was especially conducive to helplessness/passivity/shyness (36 percent).

ADAPTIVE VALUE OF ANDROGYNY: EXPLANATIONS IN TERMS OF MIXTURE AND BLENDING

Four different procedures for considering the relations between sex-role behavior and personal competence have been reported in this chapter. The adaptive value of the sex roles was assessed in terms of self-esteem concerning instrumental and expressive aspects of student life, general sex-role comparisons between three groups of college students differing in level of personal competence, consideration of endorsement rates for specific sex-role behaviors by these three groups, and examination of problem base rates within a campus mental health agency for clients differing in gender and sex-role status. Despite the diverse approaches, a compelling constancy of results can be noted in the summary presented in table 5.10. Masculinity in general portends competence in both sexes. Femininity, considered independently of masculinity, shows no clear relation to competence. Androgyny emerges as conducive to personal effectiveness in both sexes, but the evidence is clearer for females.

Another conclusion emerging from the studies reported in this chapter was that since males have a generally higher baseline for androgyny than females, they stand to suffer more from a deficit in androgyny than to gain from an excess. Both the self-esteem and the competence criterion-group comparisons supported this contention. The opposite seemed to be true for the female, although the evidence was less compelling. The woman seems to have more to gain from heightened androgynous potential than to lose by its absence.

It is my purpose in this section to go beyond these empirically based observations regarding androgyny and to seek explanation for them by further

Table 5.10.   Summary of Major Findings Regarding Sex-Role Competence Relations

Approach	Major Results
Self-esteem	1. Masculinity positively related to overall competence for both sexes.
	2. Masculinity positively related to instrumental competence for females, and femininity positively related to expressive competence for males.
	3. Androgyny associated with instrumental/expressive competence for females using discrete typology and for both sexes using continuous index.
General comparisons of groups differing in competence	1. Masculinity positively related to competence for both sexes.
	2. Femininity unrelated to competence.
	3. Androgyny positively related to competence for both sexes, but more clearly related to high competence for females.
Endorsement base rates for specific sex-role behaviors	1. Masculine attribute endorsement generally demonstrates linear positive functions with competence level; the more competent the group, the more frequent the endorsement.
	2. Feminine attribute endorsement demonstrates an erratic set of relations with competence; many are curvilinear and others include both positive and negative linear functions.
Specific problem base rate	1. Low-masculine clients of both sexes, but especially males, demonstrate a broader array of personal problems than high-masculine clients.
	2. Difference in level of femininity is of less importance to problem range, especially in females.

analysis of the abundant data in hand. Two types of analyses will be considered. One concerns the numerical mixture of masculine and feminine behaviors identified by the subjects as comprising their sex-role repertoires, the ratio of male to female stereotyped dispositions. Since we know that this balance differs for men and women, it may be possible to identify why androgyny holds differing functional implications for competence by closer examination of the behavioral mix of masculine and feminine behaviors. The second mode of analysis will bear upon blending, the interweaving of instrumental and expressive orientations considered in an earlier chapter. The issue here will be whether androgyny is more conducive to personal effectiveness if the person blends the two orientations instead of maintaining both in more or less unadulterated form, as they are often depicted.

Analysis of the raw count of masculine and feminine behaviors endorsed on the ACL provided the basis for examining mixture as a possible contributor to competence. Each sex was separated into three levels of stereotyped sex-role behavior (low/intermediate/high masculinity for males and femininity for females) using the 1978 sample of Emory students as the index group. Table 5.11 includes the number of cross-sex-typed behaviors endorsed by low- intermediate,

Table 5.11. Number of Cross-Sex Behaviors Endorsed and Androgyny Scores by Levels of Sex-Typed Behaviors

	1950s–1960s			1970s			1978		
	Mean # Masculine	Mean # Feminine	Androgyny Score	Mean # Masculine	Mean # Feminine	Androgyny Score	Mean # Masculine	Mean # Feminine	Androgyny Score
Males									
High masculine (13 or more checked)	16.86	12.27	23.36	15.83	12.93	25.43	15.96	14.96	26.43
Intermediate masculine (8–12 checked)	10.03	11.11	17.57	9.93	12.27	18.05	9.75	11.33	17.75
Low masculine (7 or less checked)	4.11	9.02	7.70	4.77	11.07	9.23	5.31	10.27	10.82
Females									
High feminine (18 or more checked)	6.59	19.68	13.11	8.19	19.65	16.37	9.90	18.94	18.19
Intermediate feminine (14–17 checked)	5.94	15.55	11.53	5.57	15.62	11.01	6.87	16.08	13.74
Low feminine (13 or less checked)	4.39	9.34	7.52	4.57	9.52	7.95	5.76	10.18	11.09

and high sex-typed subjects along with the mean androgyny scores at each level. The same information is also provided for samples collected in earlier years, to place the results in a temporal perspective. The 1978 raw masculinity score ranges for males and femininity score ranges for females were used for trisection of these earlier samples.

As you can see, the decrease in androgyny from the most masculine to the least masculine males is accompanied by a diminishing ratio of masculine to feminine behaviors in every sample. The ratio of average masculine to feminine behaviors shifts downward from slightly more masculine than feminine in the high-masculine (high-androgyny) males to about one masculine to two feminine attributes for the low-masculine (low-androgyny) males. Thus, low androgyny in males may have especially salient maladaptive consequences, because it is likely to involve not only a deficit in masculine development but also a preponderant ratio of feminine to masculine attributes. The rapid dropoff in personal effectiveness under these circumstances is predictable because of both effects—the relative absence of masculine attributes, found to have positive adaptive value, and the preponderance of feminine qualities, found to have equivocal adaptive value.

A similar analysis of discrete masculine and feminine behaviors in females is also to be found in table 5.11. Females are broken down into three levels of femininity based on the 1978 college sample, with the same raw femininity score ranges being used to examine samples from previous years. The contrast between males and females in the balance of masculine and feminine behaviors is like night and day. Males who were highly masculine were also highly feminine, but the balance was toward more discrete masculine than feminine behaviors. As level of masculinity dropped male femininity remained relatively stable, so that the balance shifted to a preponderance of feminine behaviors. Females, in contrast, maintain a fairly constant ratio of feminine to masculine behaviors (between 2:1 and 3:1) no matter what level of stereotyped femininity is being considered. Since the figures on table 5.11 are means, they can be misleading, since an average score may not be representative of anyone in a particular group. However, an actual count of the 1978 sample of females found that about half actually demonstrated a balance of two to three feminine attributes to one masculine attribute. These were spread evenly over the three levels of femininity.

The constancy in proportions of feminine to masculine behaviors across levels of femininity for the females precludes an explanation of a curvilinear competence-androgyny function using reasoning similar to that offered for males. That is, there is no shift in proportion that would explain the significant rise in androgyny only for the most successful females with the general sample looking much like maladjusted females as far as level of androgyny was concerned (see table 5.3).

A different principle seems necessary to explain the androgyny-competence function in the female, and blending of sex-role orientations, discussed in the previous chapter, is the best candidate at the moment. Blending, the interweaving of masculine instrumentality and feminine expressiveness, appeared to be more characteristic of the female sex in our prior analyses. It also was found to be a correlate of the esteem shared by women for their instrumental/expressive competence. This allows for the possibility that androgyny in the college female is most likely to be coupled with high levels of all-around competence when she has blended the two orientations. Examination of the self-esteem data allows for a test of this possibility. A breakdown of the 105 females in the 1978 sample by median splits of continuous androgyny scores, instrumental blending ratings, and expressive blending ratings defined six groups, and average instrumental and expressive self-esteem scores were determined for each (table 5.12). The same procedure was followed for the 69 males, and table 5.12 also reports these results.

Table 5.12.   Instrumental and Expressive Self-Esteem as a Function of Level of Androgyny, Instrumental Blending, and Expressive Blending

	High Androgyny			Low Androgyny		
	Number of Blending Ratings above Median			Number of Blending Ratings above Median		
	Both	One	Neither	Both	One	Neither
Females	76.47	63.10	63.61	64.07	62.89	61.23
	(N = 15)	(N = 21)	(N = 18)	(N = 14)	(N = 19)	(N = 13)
Males	78.67	58.67	60.67	61.71	56.17	48.64
	(N = 9)	(N = 15)	(N = 9)	(N = 7)	(N = 18)	(N = 11)

Two aspects of the results are illuminating. First, examination of the numbers in each group make it clear that there is no relation between androgyny and blending. The androgynous subjects did not report any more blending of instrumental and expressive orientations than was true for the low androgynous subjects. However, if androgynous individuals, female or male, do engage in both forms of instrumental/expressive blending, they expressed extremely high self-esteem relative to their college peers. The self-esteem means of 76.47 and 78.67 for androgynous blenders are impressively higher than all other groups defined by our procedures, including those who endorsed both types of blending but were not androgynous (64.07 and 61.71). Statistical tests verified the differences between the means for androgynous blenders and the average scores for the other like-sex groups combined ($p < .01$).

Unfortunately, these blending results did not prove sufficient to explain the curvilinear relation that was found between competence level and androgyny in females. If blending and androgyny had proven to be positively correlated, a case could be made for predicting high competence in women only when the upper reaches of androgyny are reached so that extensive blending could be expected. As it stands, I have no ready explanation for the curvilinearity in the female competence-androgyny results.

REFERENCES

Bakan, D. *The duality of human existence*. Chicago: Rand McNally, 1966.

Bem, S. L. Sex role adaptability: One consequence of psychological androgyny. *Journal of Personality and Social Psychology*, 1975, **31**, 634–43.

Heilbrun, A. B. Measurement of masculine and feminine sex-role identities as independent dimensions. *Journal of Consulting and Clinical Psychology*, 1976, **44**, 183–90.

Jones, W. H., Chernovetz, E. O'C., & Hansson, R. O. The enigma of androgyny: Differential implications for males and females? *Journal of Consulting and Clinical Psychology*, 1978, **46**, 298–313.

Kelly, J. A., & Worell, J. New formulations of sex roles and androgyny: A critical review. *Journal of Consulting and Clinical Psychology*, 1977, **45**, 1101–15.

Parsons, T., & Bales, R. F. *Family, socialization, and interaction process*. Glencoe, Ill.: Free Press, 1955.

Spence, J. T., Helmreich, R., & Stapp, J. Ratings of self and peers on sex-role attributes and their relation to self-esteem and conceptions of masculinity and femininity. *Journal of Personality and Social Psychology*, 1975, **32**, 29–39.

Chapter 6

Lifestyle and Cultural Differences in Sex-Role Behavior

The topical distinction between the previous chapter and this one may seem arbitrary. In Chapter Five we examined the linkages between sex role and personal competence in the college student—the extent to which the individual had achieved or was making progress toward achieving the conventional goals of middle-class America. Educational attainment, assumption of responsible leadership roles, progress toward a career, mutually satisfying personal relationships, and pride in oneself pretty well sum it up.

In this chapter the spotlight will shift to the unconventional by middle-class American standards. Socialization practices offer standards of conduct to the young that orient them to the civil and moral laws of the community. Obedience to civil law and a sexual preference for members of the opposite sex would qualify as conventional alternatives, whereas criminal behavior and homosexuality, although far from uncommon, represent unconventional choices for the individual. The term *lifestyle* is appended to these choices for present purposes, since the breach of convention brings with it other choices and adjustments that have a broad influence on the day-to-day life of the individual. Both choices generate concerns about detection, gravitation toward those who condone the unconventional act, and self-directed efforts to change or defuse conventional values that conflict with chosen behaviors.

The rationale for studying the sex-role behavior of homosexuals and heterosexuals should require little elaboration. Whether the person directs his sexual interests toward those of the opposite or the same sex must be considered part of the stereotyped sex-role. The male role, defined in its most complete sense, entails the direction of sexual interest to women, and the female role subsumes the choice of men as objects of sexual interest. Popular belief would lead us to conclude that other sex-role behaviors would tend to deviate in line

114

with the homosexual's preference for sexual contact with the same sex. Homosexual males are expected to be generally feminine, because they share a sexual preference conventionally reserved for females. The female homosexual, having the sexual interests expected of a male, is expected to be masculine. Research evidence collected up to 1973 was consistent with these expectations. Male homosexuals were reported as more likely to have chosen their mothers rather than their fathers for their primary parental identification, presumably rendering them more feminine than their controls (Chang & Block, 1960; Stephan, 1973). More direct measurement of sex-role behavior also confirmed a greater femininity among homosexual males (Evans, 1971; Thompson, Schwartz, McCandless, & Edwards, 1973). The Thompson et al. study also reported a more masculine commitment among homosexual women than was true for heterosexuals. Since all of these investigations anteceded the change in sex-role measurement methodology to independent masculinity and femininity scales, they can offer no insight into the possible contribution of androgyny or undifferentiation to homosexual choice. We shall examine these possibilities in this chapter.

The basis for seeking some tie between sex role and criminal behavior may be more obvious to those trained in sociology and criminology than in psychology. Research and theory in criminology may attempt to explain crime, especially violent (against people) crime, in terms of "macho" subcultures and the ready resort to physical aggression following defiance of group code or challenge to personal honor (Wolfgang & Ferracuti, 1970). Aggressive crimes motivated by a code of honor could be viewed as an extension of the masculine role to the extent that physical aggression is stereotypically expected of men rather than women. The same conclusion that criminal behavior may be a masculine phenomenon can be reached by logical extension of what is meant by instrumental. An orientation that motivates the person to accomplish his ends without concern for other people provides a pretty good definition of criminal activity. Either way you choose to look at it, much criminal behavior appears to be an extension of the male role. The statistics regarding convicted criminals in the United States lend support to this conclusion, although the evidence is indirect. Male criminals far outnumber their female counterparts, so prevalence figures tell us that crime is a predominantly male if not a masculine activity. At least males have cornered the market on being caught and convicted of a crime.

Our examination of the sex-role correlates of crime will be somewhat more refined than simply seeking some overall difference between criminals and noncriminals. Although the specific acts will vary even within a single category of crime, it still may be possible to discover some common sex-role characteristic among those who have been convicted of a particular offense. Will the person who has murdered or seriously assaulted someone be hypermasculine? Will the rapist demonstrate the soft, effeminate qualities commonly found among men who cannot relate sexually to women, or will he be excessively masculine, playing the predator by taking what he wants without concern for the female victim? What about the nonviolent ''white-collar'' criminal? Does the more passive, impersonal character of his ''victimless'' crime signal a more feminine or less masculine identity?

The two types of unconventional lifestyles that have been discussed to this point have a pejorative ring to them no matter how objective one tries to be. Most middle-class Americans (the sort of people who provide nearly all of the data reported in this book) reject criminal behavior and homosexuality as a matter of value. Therefore, *unconventional* is essentially equivalent to *undesirable*. Cross-cultural research offers another way of examining sex-role behaviors among people whose styles of life presumably differ from each other. It also offers us the opportunity to make comparisons across social groupings with less concern about moral persuasions. The third sample of data, made available for this book by Peter Weller (1980), represents a study of two groups of middle-class Howard University college students, one having its national origins in the islands of the Caribbean and the other representing Americans matched for ethnic origin. This section bearing on cross-cultural comparison of sex-role behavior will also include an Emory study of regional differences in middle-class college students who come from the Middle Atlantic states and from the deep South. References to such a comparison as cross-cultural may appear naive, conjuring up such popular stereotypes as the assertive Easterner versus the noble and gracious Southerner. However, beliefs in such differences still exist and contribute to interpersonal attitudes on a campus such as Emory University where consequential regional diversity of this nature is found within the undergraduate student body.

SEX ROLE AND UNCONVENTIONAL LIFE STYLES

Sex Role and Homosexual Choice

If I may be allowed a scientific cliché, the value of any conclusions drawn from research is limited by the quality of the data from which they are drawn. In psychological research concerned with special groups, such as homosexuals and heterosexuals, quality is heavily dependent on the care with which the groups are defined and the methodology by which group membership is determined in keeping with these definitions. The data that shall be considered in this section were collected by Dr. Norman Thompson, who generously made them available for new sex-role analyses based upon the assumption of independent masculine and feminine dimensions (Heilbrun & Thompson, 1977). Homosexual subjects were chosen for his original study (Thompson, Schwartz, McCandless, & Edwards, 1973) with considerable concern for verification of primary sexual orientation both by the subject and by an acquaintance of the subject. Anonymity was maintained for all members of the homosexual community who volunteered to complete the questionnaires (including the ACL). Sexual orientation of the heterosexual subjects was verified in the same ways as with the homosexuals. While most of the subjects lived in the Atlanta area, about a third of them came from other Eastern states and from California. All were white and the four male/female homosexual and heterosexual groups were closely matched for average age (27 to 29 years) and education (sixteen to seventeen years). The Thompson samples are rather similar demographically to those collected in my own program of research over the years—white, middle-class, and college-educated. The major difference is in their ages. The Thompson subjects were about ten years older on the average and presumably settled into their sexual orientation with some greater degree of commitment.

The Thompson et al. findings with regard to sex-role behavior were published before independent masculinity and femininity scales became a methodological reality. Their ACL Masculinity-Femininity Scale data confirmed the popular belief that homosexuals departed from stereotyped behavioral roles generally, not just in their preferences for a sexual partner. Male homosexuals were more feminine than their heterosexual peers and female homosexuals were more masculine than heterosexual females. Other psychometrics included in the Thompson et al. battery were unsuccessful in identifying sex-role differences; neither semantic differential nor projective techniques distinguished between homosexuals and heterosexuals.

The Thompson data were reanalyzed following the development of separate ACL Masculinity and Femininity Scales. Heilbrun and Thompson (1977) reported the prevalence figures for sex-role outcome using the new fourfold typology. The classifications into high/low categories were based upon the average sex-role scores for college samples of males and females also included in this study. These figures, reproduced in table 6.1, were superficially in line with those reported previously by Thompson and his coworkers, but statistical analysis could confirm a sex-role difference only between female homosexuals and heterosexuals ($p < .01$). This difference was most clearly represented in the very high 60 percent figure for masculine females among those who preferred sex with other females. Although there were more feminine and fewer masculine homosexual males than were found among heterosexuals, this effect was weaker and could not be verified statistically by a common analysis of the four sex types.

It is not my intention to belabor the Heilbrun and Thompson findings much beyond this brief summary, since the results were largely expected except for the strength of the cross-sex-role effect in the case of female homosexuality and the failure to identify a statistically significant effect for males. Parametric analysis

Table 6.1. Sex-role Outcomes in Homosexual and Heterosexual Adults
(Percentage)

Sexual Preference	Androgynous	Masculine	Feminine	Undifferentiated
Homosexual				
Male (N = 127)	20	27	33	20
Female(N = 84)	20	60	7	13
Heterosexual				
Male (N = 123)	18	37	24	21
Female(N = 94)	19	33	15	28

and extreme group analysis reported in a general review article (Heilbrun, 1976) did establish significant cross-sex-role effects for homosexual males on both the Masculinity and Femininity Scales.

Rather, I would like to concentrate on the implications of the Thompson data for androgyny as a correlate of homosexual or heterosexual choice. The basis for doing so is certainly not evident in the results of the Heilbrun and Thompson study, since there was no hint whatsoever in the prevalence data (see table 6.1) that androgyny distinguished between homosexuals and heterosexuals among either males (20 percent versus 18 percent, respectively) or females (20 percent versus 19 percent, respectively). Recognition of additional ways of treating ACL sex-role data since the publication of this 1977 study encouraged further analysis. For one, the formulation of a generalized androgyny formula made it possible to focus upon androgynous potential in a different way than was the case using classification based upon independent cutting scores for masculinity and femininity. The extent to which all individuals approximate an androgynous sex role is a somewhat different question from that of the number who achieve clear androgynous status by some arbitrary criterion. The second realization was that by using raw score counts on the ACL Masculinity and Femininity Scales, some things might be brought to light that would otherwise be masked by standard score conversions from the norm tables. Cases in point were the sex difference in androgyny and in how the balance of masculine and feminine behaviors may relate to level of adjustment. Raw score analysis of sex-role behaviors in homosexuals and heterosexuals to clarify balance seemed in order.

Let us consider these reexaminations of the Thompson data in reverse order, by first considering the balance of masculine and feminine attributes within the sex-role repertoires of homosexuals and heterosexuals. Table 6.2 summarized the ratios of endorsed masculine to endorsed feminine behavior for these groups in about as simple form as possible—the extent to which the homosexual and heterosexual groups demonstrate the modal ratios of masculine to feminine behaviors observed in college males (1:1) and females (1:2). The first thing to be noticed within the heterosexual samples is that the gender difference in sex-role balance found within a college population of late adolescents is also apparent in these young adults of conventional sexual persuasion. A majority of the males (52 percent) presented an even balance of masculine and feminine behaviors, whereas a preponderance (82 percent) of females described themselves as having at least twice as many feminine as masculine qualities.

Table 6.2. Prevalence of Masculine: Feminine Behavior Ratios for Male and Female Homosexuals and Heterosexuals
(Percentages)

	Feminine Balance (1:2 or more)	Even Balance (1:1)	Masculine Balance (2:1 or less)
Homosexuals			
Male (N = 127)	54	38	8
Female (N = 84)	34	57	9
Heterosexuals			
Male (N = 123)	36	52	12
Female (N = 94)	82	18	0

NOTE: Ratios of masculine: feminine behaviors were rounded off to the nearest even ratio.

We see a shift in the female direction for homosexual males, and a shift in the male direction for homosexual females, in the ratio data of table 6.2. More male homosexuals display the 1:2 or greater ratio of masculine to feminine behaviors than is true for their heterosexual counterparts, although it is not an uncommon ratio in the latter group. The frequency patterns for the two male groups, reflecting this shift for homosexual males, is statistically significant ($p < .001$).

Now, what has this to do with androgyny in the homosexual? Logically, the shift toward balanced masculine and feminine repertoires for the homosexual female should lend itself to higher levels of androgyny than is true of the heterosexual female, unless the magnitude component (actual numbers of balanced masculine and feminine behaviors) is lacking. Using untransformed counts of sex-role behaviors, homosexual females could display either a high level of androgyny or, given an attenuation of both masculine and feminine characteristics, an undifferentiated sex-role development. Conversely, the shift away from even balance for male homosexuals could restrict the androgyny displayed by the group, although the effect should not be a substantial one. Application of the androgyny index to the raw scores on the ACL sex-role scales reveals that for once logic prevails, at least for females. We can observe in the mean androgyny scores (table 6.3) that female homosexuals display a far higher level of androgyny than female heterosexuals. Whether the male has chosen a homosexual or heterosexual lifestyle has no systematic bearing on androgynous potential. Analysis of variance applied to these four means revealed a significant sex × sexual-choice interaction ($p < .005$) that reflects statistically what was just said. Sexual choice makes a difference in the androgyny of women ($p < .001$), but not for men.

Table 6.3. Mean Androgyny Level for Homosexual and Heterosexual Adults

	Homosexual	Heterosexual
Males	16.50	16.39
Females	19.01	13.28

NOTE: Based upon the androgyny index applied to raw scores on the ACL Masculinity and Femininity Scales.

We have the first discordant note regarding the androgynous condition in these results. Whereas the evidence marshaled before pointed toward the advantages of androgyny (especially for the middle-class female) and no disadvantages, we now discover an association between androgyny and homosexuality in women. Whether one believes that this association points up the potential for problem behavior in androgynous women is both a matter of personal values and scientific inference. Values are important to the extent that homosexuality may be viewed by some as a healthy mode of sexual expression when practiced by consenting adults. Given such a view, the association between female androgyny and homosexuality could readily qualify as a courageous departure from restrictions of conventional social roles. On the other hand, most people presumably do not practice homosexuality nor do they find homosexuality to be an acceptable behavior in others. Accordingly, by majority values, the sex-role findings for homosexual women should cast a shadow of concern upon androgyny.

Some caution also is required in the interpretation of the female homosexual results, since demonstration that a statistical relation exists between androgyny and homosexuality in women does not prove any causal connection. These data do not prove that androgyny causes homosexual choice or, conversely, that homosexuality produces androgyny in women. I believe that the eventual understanding of an association between androgyny and homosexuality in women, once we come upon it, will be a little more complicated than either of these conclusions. In fact, I shall offer a tentative explanation for the androgyny of homosexual females in the next chapter, when parent identification and sex-role preference as factors in sex-role development are considered. This proposal will consider the evolution of homosexual choice in females out of the behavioral complex of a cross-sex identification with the father, strong masculinization, deficient potential for vicarious experience, and competitive drive.

Sex Role and Criminal Behavior

Anyone reading a newspaper today is keenly aware of the burgeoning crime rate, especially in our urban areas, and the special concerns about the upsurge in violent crimes directed towards people. What is not so obvious, considering the ubiquitousness of crime, is that it is not well understood. There is still little agreement even as to the most promising approach for eventual achievement of such understanding. There are those who seek to explain crime in terms of the extrinsic social conditions that shape criminal behavior. Others may favor constitutional deficiency. There will be some, including myself, who have attempted to explain criminal behavior in terms of personality factors, those regularities in behavior that set one person off from another as unique individuals. Human sex-role behaviors represent one category of such regularities and as such qualify as personality variables. Accordingly, the evidence presented in this section regarding sex-role differences among types of criminals falls within the personality research area. Since none of the approaches to understanding criminal behavior preclude the importance of the others, the long-range expectation would be that a comprehensive explanation would involve important contributions from each. The evidence at our disposal in this section is not likely to make a profound contribution toward this end. Its importance is more apparent in the sex-role domain and in continuing the lesson of the homosexual data: androgyny may not always be a blessing!

Sex-role data were collected from prisoners within the Georgia penal system. They were tested as part of a parole evaluation, with an average lag of about five years between their criminal act and the collection of sex-role information. These prisoners are not a representative sample from the state system or even from those referred for parole evaluation. The requirement of at least a sixth-grade reading proficiency in order to be given the California Psychological Inventory (Gough, 1965), from which sex-role scores were obtained, served to eliminate many prisoners from the study. What remained was a sample of 121 criminals with an average IQ of about 103 on a culture-free intelligence test. The sample was comprised of 77 percent white prisoners and 23 percent black prisoners.

The sex-role scales derived empirically for the California Psychological Inventory by Baucom (1976) were available for analysis in this study. The independent MSC and FMN scales were developed within a college population. Although their broader applicability to a general adult population might be assumed, it was considered valuable to gather additional data from such a population before proceeding to the prisoner analysis. Two purposes were to be served. One, as mentioned, was that some demonstration be made that sex-role distinctions drawn by these scales have relevance to the behaviors of adults in the community as well as to students on the University of North Carolina campus. The second purpose was to provide some standard for the sex-role scores

4

achieved by the criminals by comparison with the scores of adult noncriminals. No norms were provided by Baucom, and even if they had been made available the relevance of norms based on data collected from young college students to this prisoner sample is open to question. By making adult norms available for the MSC and FMN scales, the meaning derived from comparison of sex-roles between criminal types could be extended to a broader social context.

As I said in Chapter Three when the validity of the MSC and FMN scales was briefly discussed, the generosity of Drs. Harrison Gough and Wallace Hall of the Institute for Personality Assessment and Research at the University of California made 400 California Personality Inventory protocols available for our purposes. Half were collected from male adults and half from female adults living in communities surrounding the Berkeley campus. These control males were a good match for the criminal sample as far as average age is concerned (32 versus 31 years, respectively), although the predominantly middle-class controls were better educated on the average (fifteen years) than the prisoners (ten years). The fact that the ages were comparable and that about 22 percent of the control males did not attend college and 40 percent of those who did failed to complete a college degree suggests that this sample offers us a better comparison for our prisoners than would a college campus sample. The adult females were slightly younger than their male counterparts in terms of average age (29 years) and had an education level (fourteen years) that fell a year below that of the males. Of the females, 38 percent did not go beyond a high school education, but only 28 percent who attended college failed to obtain a degree.

The initial step in using the Baucom scales to explore sex-role differences among criminals was an examination of the scales' validity. You may recall that the items for each scale were selected by the differential endorsement rates of college males and females. In order to use these scales within an adult, middle-class sample for the purpose of evaluating sex-role orientation, it should be possible to show the same differential selection of scale item responses when adult males and females are compared. This was done in terms of the total scale scores achieved by the 200 males and 200 females in the Berkeley sample. The average raw score on the MSC scale was 38.34 for the men and 30.20 for the women. The significant disparity in means ($p < .002$) confirms the expected difference between the sexes on masculinity. Similarly, females achieved a higher average score on the FMN scale (32.80) than did males (26.68); the directional difference ($p < .001$) was consistent with expectations regarding overall level of femininity in the two sexes. While the precision of the Baucom scales remains to be demonstrated, they appear capable of eliciting differences in behavioral self-description between men and women on the campus and in the community.

The second stage of this study was concerned with the sex-role status of various types of criminals, with respect both to how they compare with one another and how they compare with noncriminal male adults. The latter comparison was made simply by developing male adult norms from the 200 protocols. These norms provide conversions of raw scores of MSC and FMN to T-scores with a mean of 50 and standard deviation of 10. By converting the prisoner scores with these normative tables, it can be immediately ascertained whether a given set of criminals is higher (> 50) or lower (< 50) than noncriminals on either masculinity or femininity. The fact that these conversion tables put the males' MSC and FMN raw scores onto the same standard scale will also allow us to more safely apply the generalized androgyny index to the prisoners' sex-role data. The greater range of raw scores on the MSC scale would have otherwise rendered such an application suspect.

The assignment of prisoners to specific criminal types was complicated by the fact that some were recidivists and had committed different crimes at different times and that others had been sentenced to their current imprisonment for more than one crime. To resolve this problem as best we could, only the most recent convictions were considered, and when this included more than one crime the prisoner was identified by his more serious crime. The order of seriousness (most to least) adopted for this purpose was as follows: murder, rape, manslaughter, assault, robbery, burglary/theft, and nonviolent "victimless" crimes (drug violations, forgery, fraud). Table 6.4 presents average sex-role scores for the various criminal groups.

Table 6.4. Average Sex-Role Scores for Various Criminal Types

	N	Masculinity	Femininity	Androgyny
Murder	23	49.04	47.65	85.30
Rape	19	56.32	53.53	102.00
Manslaughter	8	54.75	48.50	95.50
Assault	18	56.11	47.50	93.56
Robbery	18	51.56	46.61	88.56
Burglary/theft	26	55.58	44.46	87.54
Nonviolent	9	44.56	48.56	85.33

NOTE: The average score for masculinity and for femininity within an adult male noncriminal sample is 50 with a standard deviation of 10. The mean androgyny score for the adult noncriminal males was 89.44.

Analyses of variance demonstrated significant differences among the mean masculinity ($p < .001$) and androgyny ($p < .001$) scores represented in table 6.4. Considered overall, the results for masculinity and femininity may not hold many surprises. Male criminals in prison tend to be generally more masculine and less feminine than noncriminal males. The only obvious exceptions to this generalization are (1) the heterogeneous nonviolent prisoners, whose crimes tend not to be perpetrated upon a specific victim and who emerge as unmasculine, and (2) the rapist, to whom we shall now turn our attention.

The rapist is the only type of criminal who appears feminine relative to both other criminals and to adult noncriminal males. Since men convicted of rape also presented high masculine scores, the expectation would be that androgyny would be a prevalent psychological commodity in this group. That expectation was confirmed by the generalized index, on which a remarkably high level of androgyny was demonstrated by rapists. Their average score (102) was high by prisoners' standards but even more salient by general adult male standards. The latter observation can be demonstrated graphically by examining the numbers of rapists and other types of criminals who fall short of and exceed the median androgyny level displayed by the 200 noncriminal males. These proportions are reported in table 6.5. The rapists we studied included a disproportionate number of androgynous men (79 percent) by adult male standards.

Table 6.5. Number of Criminal Types Falling Below and Above the Androgyny Level of Noncriminal Males

Types of Crime	Below-Median Adult Male Level of Androgyny	Above-Median Adult Male Level of Androgyny
Murder	15	8
Rape	4	15
Manslaughter	3	5
Assault	8	10
Robbery	9	9
Burglary/theft	17	9
Nonviolent	6	3
Total	62	59

NOTE: Median $\geq$ 92

The finding that rapists emerge as androgynous on the Baucom sex-role scales invites interpretation at two levels. The more precarious comes in answer to the question of why men who commit rape should display androgyny. Caution is required for many reasons, but the most basic among these is that no causal relation is demonstrated by showing that the same men who commit rape also endorse behaviors suggesting a high level of androgyny: the two kinds of behaviors may simply coexist without being functionally linked. In fact, one might argue that a causal relation does exist but that it is the act of rape, the rapist's reaction to his own behavior, or the sequence of events that follow within the criminal justice system that produce androgyny in these men. This possibility cannot be refuted within the present data, although the fact remains that this makes no apparent sense at all. A more reasonable causal interpretation, it seems to me, is possible if the instrumental and expressive orientations of the sex-roles are considered. Rapists, like many of the criminals we studied, display above-average levels of masculinity, suggesting an instrumental orientation toward obtaining what they want without undue concern about how they achieve their ends. This certainly seems descriptive of the rapist. The unique thing about the rapists in the study, however, was their elevated level of femininity. The expressive orientation implied by their femininty would accentuate the priority of personal relationships. One contributing dynamic of rape, then, might be seen as a unique blending of the instrumental and expressive, a powerful and selfish demand for the satisfaction of personal aims within a heterosexual relationship. Not only do these goals reside within the most intimate adult relationship (between a man and a woman) but within what is conventionally considered the most intimate aspect of such a relationship—the sexual act. In his own warped way, the rapist introduces an excessively instrumental act into one of the most profound recesses of expressive concern.

It is not critical to the thesis of this section that the foregoing speculation about the rapist proves to be of value in understanding this criminal act or not. The androgyny results for men, like the homosexual data for women, are more important as an exception to the dictum that androgyny yields universal benefits to men and women. Neither the female homosexual nor the male rapist represents models of social effectiveness, yet each demonstrates a uniquely elevated androgynous potential. This is not the same as saying that androgyny *causes* homosexuality or sexual assault on women, although the possible antecedent contribution of dual sex-role development warrants study. Our data warn that, at the least, we should be asking, ''Androgyny and what else?'' before jumping to any conclusions about androgyny's value. In both studies reported in this section the ''something else''—perhaps coincidentally—appears to be related to the sexual act. Although there is an absence of proof that androgyny in male rapists or in lesbians caused their deviant sexual behavior, careful analysis of the sex-role research literature reveals a similar absence of proof that androgyny causes any positive outcome either.

CULTURAL DIFFERENCES IN SEX ROLES

Regional Differences in Sex-Role Behavior

Emory University, presumably like many Southern private schools, has evolved from a regional school having a geographically homogeneous undergraduate student body to a far more diversified campus attracting students on a national basis. At this time undergraduates are attracted principally from two regions in the United States. The largest number of students of both sexes still are from the South, mainly Georgia and Florida, but also to a lesser extent from Tennessee, the Carolinas, Alabama, Mississippi, and Louisiana. A substantial number of students represent the Mid-Atlantic region, including New York, New Jersey, Pennsylvania, and Maryland. As with the predominance of Georgia and Florida students within the Southern student body, New York and New Jersey residents constitute the majority within the Mid-Atlantic students for both sexes. It is the comparison of students from these two regions that concerned us in this study.

While no other choice for regional comparisons other than Southern versus Mid-Atlantic would be feasible considering current Emory enrollment, it stands as a propitious one. From my experience, a stereotype of the Easterner clearly exists, perhaps especially in the deep South, that still shows psychological vestiges, however remote, of the Civil War and Reconstruction. The Easterner stereotype, which I shall not document scientifically, most frequently connotes a frank, direct, and assertive manner that is frequently used to gain personal advantage in achieving interpersonal ends. The stereotypic Southerner, on the other hand, places far more emphasis on social amenities, with courtesy and pleasant personal transaction assuming central importance. In contrast to the assertiveness of the Easterner, the Southern stereotype conjures up a somewhat more passive image, dependent on convention and tradition but capable of firm behavior when the situation requires. The interesting thing about these stereotypes is how well they incorporate many of the instrumental/expressive distinctions between the two sex roles. Thus it was with some interest that our analyses focused on possible excesses in masculinity among students from the Mid-Atlantic states and the possibly more feminine character of the Southern student.

A sample of 192 students was used to consider regional differences in sex-role behavior, including 95 females and 97 males. All subjects were enrolled in Emory College during the fall term of 1979, and most were beginning freshmen. As might be expected, the average age of the students was slightly less than 19 years. Geographic location for each person was determined by the home address given as current within the 1979–80 student directory. This method of assigning the subjects to geographic regions within the United States does not involve the assumption that all were born or even raised within the regions represented. Assuming that geographic differences in sex-role behavior do exist, prior migration should most likely introduce confounding effects and make it more difficult to demonstrate such differences.

The original plan was to analyze the male and female data by total regions, thereby assuming each state encompassed within a region as having made a comparable contribution to the overall results. Preliminary inspection of the means for the male students encouraged such an assumption, but this did not turn out to be possible for females: there were remarkable differences in sex-role scores among the states, so analysis of the female data proceeded by a comparison of states rather than regions. Two steps were taken to avoid the problem that came with this decision of unreliability introduced by small-cell entries. States represented by less than four female students in our sample were eliminated from the study; states within a region represented by between four and eight students were combined if their average sex-role scores were clearly comparable. These procedures, brought about by sampling limitations, resulted in six state subsamples for the females. Three represented the Mid-Atlantic region (New York, New Jersey, and Pennsylvania/Maryland) and three the Southern area (Georgia, Florida, and Tennessee/North Carolina/South Carolina). Since the sex-role scores obtained by males from each region were homogeneous across states, the original plan to compare only by region was implemented.

Four sex-role scores offering cross-regional comparisons between college students—Masculinity and Femininity Scale scores taken from the ACL, and the derivative androgyny index based on both standard and raw scores—are made available in table 6.6. The results for males viewed statistically are rather easy to

Table 6.6. Masculinity, Femininity, and Androgyny in Students from Two Regions of the United States

Sex of Student and Region	Masculinity	Femininity	Androgyny Index	
			Standard Score	Raw Score
Males				
Mid-Atlantic (N = 43)	51.16	49.74	89.86	18.09
Southern (N = 54)	52.87	49.19	88.07	17.11
Females				
Mid-Atlantic				
New York (N = 19)	48.16	48.00	83.79	11.16
New Jersey (N = 12)	46.50	49.33	83.67	11.50
Pennsylvania/				
Maryland (N = 15)	48.87	53.00	88.80	11.07
Southern				
Georgia (N = 16)	44.19	48.50	84.65	8.75
Florida (N = 20)	54.55	50.05	92.70	15.40
Tennessee/				
North Carolina/				
South Carolina (N = 13)	57.31	51.38	100.77	20.62

discuss. There are no sex-role differences between Mid-Atlantic and Southern males. Both groups show average sex-role scores that appear to be about what would have been predicted from previous Emory samples—Masculinity and Femininity scores around 50, an androgyny index based upon these standard scores of about 88, and an androgyny index formulated from raw scores somewhere between 16 and 18. So much for male regional stereotypes, at least as far as they might be reflected in the sex-role behaviors of Emory students.

The female comparison by states suggested some very substantial differences in masculinity and androgyny that did not follow the regional lines layed out by stereotype. First, though, let us consider the results for females from the vantage point of similarities. Table 6.6's Femininity means for female students from each state hover about the norm of 50 and fail to differ from one another. Emory women were comparably feminine, no matter what their region or state of residence.

The masculine qualities of the female student were a different matter, since the masculinity scores varied significantly ($p < .005$) when compared by analysis of variance. Reference back to table 6.6, however, makes it clear that the variation was attributable to the Southern females. The Mid-Atlantic subgroups all displayed similar masculinity scale means, on the lower side of the campus norm. Southern females from Georgia were quite unmasculine by the same standard, in contrast to the above-average masculinity scores for the remaining Southern subgroups. The two extremes within the Southern sample enveloped the masculinity scores for the Mid-Atlantic subgroupings. As was the case for males, neither the masculinity nor femininity findings for females offered any encouragement for the stereotypes under consideration.

As we noted earlier in the book, systematic increases in female androgyny accompany increments in masculinity, since most females can be expected to incorporate a substantial number of feminine attributes in their personality makeup. In keeping with this dictum, the contingents of females varied extensively ($p < .005$) on both androgyny scores in predictable ways. The Georgia female demonstrated very low androgynous potential, all of the Mid-Atlantic females obtained average androgyny scores by campus standards, and the remainder of the Southern females presented surprisingly high scores.

Aside from disconfirming regional sex-role stereotypes on the Emory campus, the results of this study raise questions of meaning that I cannot readily answer. For example, why should there be such diversity of sex-role behavior among Southern females? Females from Georgia appeared to be more traditional in their sex-role orientation, especially as far as avoiding masculine behavior is concerned. Females from the bordering Southern states of Tennessee, North Carolina, South Carolina, and Florida took a page from the contemporary social literature extolling androgynous development. A safer observation, and one that will become more relevant following the description of the second study of cross-cultural sex-role differences, is that whatever the reason, sex-role variation was obtained for females but not for males.

Transnational Differences among Black College Students

The study that will now concern us (Weller, 1980) is of interest for several reasons. It provides further information on whether cultural variation is associated with systematic differences in sex-role behaviors. This time the comparison will be between college students from the United States and foreign students on the same campus (Howard University) who were visiting this country from island nations in the Caribbean area. A second ethnic feature of this study that sets it apart is that the comparison groups were black. This allows us to not only consider whether contemporary sex-role behavior in American middle-class black students differs from that of black students from the Caribbean area, but also, by reference to white norms, whether American blacks differ from American whites.

The PAQ (Spence, Helmreich, & Stapp, 1975; see description in Chapter Three) was the psychometric instrument used by Weller in his study of sex roles on the Howard University campus. Weller administered the PAQ to eighty students attending the university in 1978–79—twenty males and twenty females from several Caribbean island nations and the same number of males and females from this country. The sex-role scores generated by these groups (the first four columns of table 6.7) were compared by analysis of variance using nationality and sex as dichotomous variables. Considering only the PAQ scales of masculinity and femininity, the one significant effect ($p < .05$) turned out to be one of little intrinsic interest: the females achieved higher femininity scores than males.

The bipolar $M–F$ scale, made up of items that distinguished most clearly between the ideal stereotypes of masculinity and femininity in our middle-class culture, offered more interesting results. This scale not only produced the expected sex difference, with the higher scores of males indicating greater masculinity or less femininity ($p < .001$), but also an effect for nationality: American students appeared more masculine than Caribbean students ($p < .95$). Overriding this effect for nationality, however, was a significant interaction effect ($p < .01$). As is shown in table 6.7, black males contributed much the same $M–F$ score whether they were from the Caribbean area (18.85) or the United States (18.45), but black American females were far more masculine (less feminine?) (16.50) than the Caribbean females (12.50). Obviously, it was the female difference that produced the overall effect for nationality.

Analysis of androgyny scores (obtained by applying the index formula to the PAQ scales of masculinity and femininity) again identified an effect of nationality ($p < .05$). Black American students were more androgynous than

Table 6.7. Average Sex-Role Scores for Students from the Caribbean and the United States

Sex-Role Score	Caribbean Students (Black)		American Students (Black)		American Students[1] (White)	
	Males	Females	Males	Females	Males	Females
Masculinity	22.65	21.00	23.45	22.95	{ 22.28 { 21.08	{ 19.62 { 19.45
Femininity	23.55	25.80	23.50	25.85	{ 22.56 { 22.29	{ 24.36 { 24.37
Masculinity-Femininity	18.85	12.50	18.45	16.50	{ 16.87 { 16.50	{ 12.60 { 12.43
Androgyny	42.20	40.50	44.20	45.30		

[1]Two samples reported in Spence and Helmreich (1978).

black Caribbean students. The black American female emerged as the most androgynous in this comparison and was markedly higher on the index than her Caribbean counterpart, although the absence of a statistical interaction effect requires restraint in interpretation of this pattern. Fortunately, we can supplement Peter Weller's findings for black college students with those reported for white samples by Spence and Helmreich (1978). The last two columns on the right of table 6.7 show mean PAQ scores obtained on the University of Texas (Austin) campus, presumably from predominantly white college samples. Even without the use of statistics, the comparisons are informative. Sex-role development of black male and female college students in both national samples equals or exceeds that of white students on the masculine and feminine dimensions. When the bipolar M–F scale is considered, we can note the one clearly distinguishing feature of this interracial comparison: black American females stand out as uniquely masculine or unfeminine and the black Caribbean females look exactly like white American females—much less masculine or more feminine. This particular finding lends confidence to our prior observation that black American females in the Weller study were an androgynous group, since androgyny in women comes primarily through extraordinary acquisition of masculine attri-butes.

The conclusion to be drawn from the evidence on lifestyle or regional differences in sex-role pattern presented in this chapter will have little to do with the issues that might intrigue sociologists and anthropologists. The bodies of data that have been described were not systematically collected in such a way as to answer any definitive questions about functional linkages between region, culture, or race and sex-role behavior. Rather, the studies, viewed collectively, can best serve as additional warning against taking too much for granted regarding contemporary sex-role behavior. Results were rarely what we expected. Androgyny not only appeared in unexpected places, but it failed to show the sort of obvious bridge to personal effectiveness that its reputation would lead us to expect.

Another predominant theme of the studies described in this chapter on cultural differences in sex-role behavior is that females are more likely to demonstrate differences than is the case for males. It was homosexuality in the female and not the male that was found to be associated with androgyny. Regional United States differences in stereotypic sex-role outcomes as well as in androgyny emerged for the college female but not the male. Differences among black Americans and Caribbean nationals were more apparent for female college students than for males. The only study that found a salient sex-role effect for males lacked female criminals that might have served as a comparison; there is no female rapist in the eyes of the law. The fact that sex-role behavior for the female demonstrated more complex functional alignments seems fitting. These were all data of the 1970s, a decade in which things were supposed to be changing for women. From a scientific view, change appears to mean that matters are simply becoming more complicated.

REFERENCES

Baucom, D. H. Independent masculinity and femininity scales on the California Psychological Inventory. *Journal of Consulting and Clinical Psychology,* 1976, **44,** 876.

Chang, J., & Block, J. A study of identification in male homosexuals. *Journal of Consulting Psychology,* 1960, **24,** 307–10.

Evans, R.B. Adjective Check List scores of homosexual men. *Journal of Personality Assessment,* 1971, **35,** 344–49.

Gough, H. G. *Manual for the California Psychological Inventory.* Stanford, Calif.: Consulting Psychologists Press, 1965.

Heilbrun, A. B., & Thompson, N. L., Jr. Sex-role identity and male and female homosexuality. *Sex Roles: A Journal of Research,* 1977, **3,** 65–79.

Spence, J. L., & Helmreich, R. L. *Masculinity and femininity: Their psychological dimensions, correlates, and antecedents.* Austin: University of Texas Press, 1978.

Spence, J. L., Helmreich, R., & Stapp, J. Ratings of self and peers on sex-role attributes and their relation to self-esteem and conceptions of masculinity and femininity. *Journal of Personality and Social Psychology,* 1975, **32,** 29–39.

Stephan, W. D. Parental relationships and early social experiences of activist male homosexuals and male heterosexuals. *Journal of Abnormal Psychology,* 1973, **82,** 506–613.

Thompson, N. L., Jr., Schwartz, D. M., McCandless, B. R., & Edwards, D. A. Parent-child relationships and sexual identity in male and female homosexuals and heterosexuals. *Journal of Consulting and Clinical Psychology,* 1973, **41,** 120–27.

Weller, P. Personal communication 1980.

Wolfgang, M. E., & Ferracuti, F. The subculture of violence. In M. E. Wolfgang, E. Savitz, & N. Johnston (Eds.), *The sociology of crime and delinquency.* New York: Wiley, 1970.

Chapter 7

Parent Identification and Sex-Role Behavior of the Child

This chapter more than any other will illustrate the philosophy that has guided me in writing this monograph: deal with questions and issues concerning sex roles for which evidence from my research program can be brought to bear, and leave the rest to those who have the data. This offers a trade-off, by sacrificing the comprehensiveness of a classroom textbook that summarizes what everyone else has said and the sweep of popular rhetoric that boldly defies the necessity of evidence, in favor of systematic but narrow research findings. Sex roles have many antecedents; this chapter will concentrate on but one—the identification of children with their parents. Other influences on sex-role adoption are in no way minimized by this choice, and the reader should have no problem in finding an extensive research literature relating to other learning experiences in the family, peer group, or broader social context that affect sex-role development.

Parent identification as a learning process requires definition before we proceed. Since I have labored through the clarification of the term in an earlier publication (Heilbrun, 1973a), let me simply quote from the prior paper:

> Parent identification is a process of imitative learning which occurs over an extended period of time and results in behavioral similarities between the child and one or both parents. This source of learned behavior must be distinguished from learning occurring within the family context which involves direct tuition of the child by a parent or learning resulting from schedules of reinforcements, whether intentionally devised by the parent or not. Clear separation of behaviors learned in any of these three ways is exceedingly difficult, if not impossible, since a given behavior may be facilitated in the child by more than one of these learning conditions. For example, a boy may be exposed to an aggressive father as a model, a father who continually lectures his son on the virtue of "standing up for your rights" or "going after what you want" and who rewards his son for aggressive action and punishes him for passivity. Now if the boy turns out to be aggressive, should we attribute this behavior outcome to modeling, tuition, or the schedule of reinforcement?
>
> While I cannot offer any panacea for the identification researcher who must contend with this possible confounding between learning sources, I would warn against one tempting avenue of escape. Many would include within their definition of identification the stipulation that the

process is an unconscious one; somehow the imitative learning occurs beyond the awareness of the child. If this were so, we could use level of awareness as a rough criterion of learning source, for after all, the child should certainly be aware of what his parents have told him (direct tuition) and the behaviors which have been systematically reinforced. Be this as it may, I intuitively reject the assumption that imitation of a parent (or others, for that matter) occurs beyond the awareness of the child. I submit that both intrinsic and extrinsic rehearsal of behavior observed in a model may occur within the full awareness of the child, and furthermore, he is likely to be aware of his motivation to be like the other person. While imitation without awareness may occur, it is misleading, in my opinion, to offer it as a precondition for identification [p. 128].

One's viewpoint regarding parent identification would not be complete without a statement regarding the major source of reinforcement for this type of imitative learning. The earlier paper considered this question and extended the following conclusion:

It seems to me that what little evidence exists fails to indicate the importance of secondary (learned) reinforcement as instrumental to imitative learning. A secondary-reinforcement hypothesis would contend that the continued association between a potential parent model and primary reinforcement (e.g., feeding) results in the establishment of a secondary drive for the presence of the physical properties or behaviors of the model, which have assumed secondary reinforcing value. To behave like the model should, in theory, allow the child to secondarily reinforce himself, thereby stamping in these behaviors through reinforced rehearsal.

Bandura presented evidence in an earlier Nebraska Symposium (1962) which not only failed to support the importance of secondary reinforcement for imitation of a model (Bandura, Ross, & Ross, 1963a) but which clearly suggested the importance of vicarious reinforcement in mediating this effect in nursery-age children (Bandura, Ross, & Ross, 1963a; 1963b). Children tend to imitate models whom they observe to be successful in attaining their goals or see in a position of power to control a variety of resources which the child desires. People love winners and children are no exception, and we are left to assume that behaving like a winner is vicariously rewarding.

I propose that vicarious reinforcement is the primary type of reward involved in parent identification, with no assumption that all such modeling is reinforced. Other types of reinforcement may be more important to strengthening a response after the behavior has been incorporated into the child's repertoire through imitation [p. 129].

PROBLEMS IN THE MEASUREMENT OF PARENT IDENTIFICATION

Given a conceptual commitment to identification as an imitative learning process reinforced in the main by the vicarious rewards the child receives by behaving like a parent to whom the child attributes power and success, the next question might be how the researcher goes about the task of operationalizing such a view into a measure that will allow him to investigate this phenomenon. The answer, plain and simple, should be, "With great difficulty." In the first place,

Bronfenbrenner (1958) pointed out many years ago that research into identification always deals with outcome, typically the degree of similarity between a child and one or both parents. Behavioral similarity as outcome, according to Bronfenbrenner, could be the product of a number of influences besides the process of identification—genetic, parent reinforcement, or response to some common cultural pressure by both parent and child. Since measures of identification have traditionally failed to parcel out alternative influences, their research use must acknowledge the confounded nature of similarity scores. Identification as an imitation or modeling process can be used to account for only some indefinite fraction of score variance. Alternative interpretation of scores has never stopped us before in our use of psychological measures, nor has it created much consternation in identification measurement.

It would be possible, of course, to follow Bronfenbrenner's prescription for this dilemma of definition and interpret parent-child similarity measures quite strictly in just those terms—parent-child similarity. This approach settles for an ambiguous outcome term rather than a confounded index of the identification process. While this would represent an honest appraisal of the measure, it does nothing to unravel the confluence of possible meanings for the identification researcher. A better solution would be to establish the experimental conditions that are effective in determining imitative learning of adult model behavior by children in a laboratory (see Bandura, Ross, & Ross, 1963a; 1963b) and to see whether comparable relations can be demonstrated statistically with a psychological measure of actual parent identification. If this much can be done, the limits that can be expected of any single current measure of a complex human behavioral event may have been achieved.

A second limitation of parent identification measurement common to research prior to 1965 was the failure to consider even the most rudimentary differences between parent models beyond the fact that one is a woman and the other a man. This was a special problem because so much of the identification research was directly or indirectly concerned with the sex-role behavior of the child. The implicit assumption seemed to be that all mothers present feminine models and all fathers offer models of masculinity. There is a considerable gap between such an assumption and the true state of affairs. While women are generally more feminine than men and men more masculine than women, there is sex-role heterogeneity within both genders. This added sex-role information about parent models can be generated as part of the identification measure without excessive difficulty. The oversight among identification researchers was as unnecessary as the ignoring of multiple sources of parent-child similarity was inevitable. Our own identification research introduced parent model attributes as an independent variable in 1965 (Heilbrun & Fromme, 1965). This extended the potential of the program perceptibly, especially when filial sex-role behavior was under investigation.

Finally, the measurement of parent identification has been limited by the willingness of researchers to take parent-child similarity to mean too many things, sometimes at the expense of credibility. What we have in mind when we consider parent identification as a modeling process is the transmission of behavioral regularities from parent to child. In short, we are talking about personality attributes. When the research literature is considered, however, identification is defined in terms of similarity between almost any kind of psychometric responses given by or attributed to a parent or a child. For example, the instruments used to gauge parent-child similarity have included the Minnesota Multiphasic Personality Inventory (Sopchak, 1952), a venerable tool for measuring psychological disturbance but one of little value for investigating convergent personalities and the identification process.

The approach to parent identification measurement used in our research sought to solve the relevance problem by borrowing personality dimensions originally described by Henry Murray (1938) and subsequently adapted by Edwards for his Personal Preference Schedule (1957). These variables represent vital dimensions of normal social behavior, those that are commonly understood to be aspects of personality.

THE PARENT IDENTIFICATION MEASURE

The psychometric procedure devised to estimate parent identification in my program of research (Heilbrun, 1965a) was based on the assumption that the more similar the personality attributes of the child to those of a parent, the more the child has identified with (modeled after) that parent. There is no assumption made that similarity is contingent only on modeling. The specific operations chosen to estimate parent-child similarity represented an effort to improve upon some of the measurement limitations that have already received comment. The technique involves two sets of ratings that are administered without any instructional liaison between them, and preferably with some intervening task to further increase the subtlety of what is being measured. Procedures that had been previously in vogue were frequently more obvious in their intent and ran the risk of activating the subject's expectation that all boys should be like their fathers and all girls like their mothers, a tenuous assumption at best.

The first ratings obtained from the subjects are self-ratings on the ACL from which fifteen Murray-type manifest needs can be scored (Gough & Heilbrun, 1965). The manifest needs and their definitions taken from the ACL Manual are:
1. *Achievement:* To strive to be outstanding in pursuits of socially recognized significance.
2. *Dominance:* To seek and sustain leadership roles in groups or to be influential and controlling in individual relationships.

3. *Endurance:* To persist in any task undertaken.
4. *Order:* To place special emphasis on neatness, organization, and planning one's activities.
5. *Intraception:* To engage in attempts to understand one's own behavior or the behavior of others.
6. *Nurturance:* To engage in behaviors which extend material or emotional benefits to others.
7. *Affiliation:* To seek and sustain numerous personal friendships.
8. *Heterosexuality:* To seek the company of and derive emotional satisfactions from interactions with opposite-sex peers.
9. *Exhibition:* To behave in such a way as to elicit the immediate attention of others.
10. *Autonomy:* To act independently of others or of social values and expectations.
11. *Aggression:* To engage in behaviors that attack or hurt others.
12. *Change:* To seek novelty of experience and avoid routine.
13. *Succorance:* To solicit sympathy, affection, or emotional support from others.
14. *Abasement:* To express feelings of inferiority through self-criticism, guilt, or social impotence.
15. *Deference:* To seek and sustain subordinate roles in relationships with others.

Raw scores on each of these scales have been normed for college students, with average T-scores set at 50 and standard deviations at 10. These standard scoring procedures have the effect of allowing each scale to have equivalent weight in the identification scoring. It is important to keep in mind that the subject has no idea that these personality variables are to be measured.

The subject also provides a second set of ratings that focus on the behaviors of his or her parents. Descriptions of the behaviors commonly associated with the fifteen manifest needs are presented in paragraph form, and for each variable the subject is asked to identify the parent for whom the behaviors are more descriptive. The perceived similarity score is then calculated by combining the ACL scores with these parent descriptions. The absolute deviation of each ACL personality score from the norm of 50 is determined and assigned a positive or negative sign depending on the correspondence between the direction of deviation and whether that attribute is or is not more characteristic of the same-sex parental model. The cumulative algebraic raw score summed over the fifteen variables is determined and then entered into yet another normative table that compares the raw similarity score to other college students of the same sex.

Before proceeding, some examples may be in order, since the scoring procedure sounds more complicated than it really is. Take any one of the personality variables, let us say dominance, and consider the case of a male subject. There are four possible ways his score on the dominance scale of the ACL could be related to the dominance rating of his parents:

1. If the son is dominant (for example, has a score of 60 on the ACL) and his father is chosen as the more likely model for dominance of the two parents, a *plus* score is assigned to the 10-point deviation from 50. This is taken as evidence of behavioral similarity between the son and his same-sex parent.

2. If the son is dominant (for example, has a score of 60 on the ACL) and his mother is selected as the more likely model for dominance, a *minus* is assigned to the 10-point deviation from 50. The suggestion here is of behavioral similarity between the son and the cross-sex parent.

3. If the son is nondominant (for example, has a score of 40 on the ACL) and his father is rated as the more likely model for dominance, a *minus* is assigned to the 10-point deviation from 50. Behavioral similarity to the same-sex parent is contraindicated, and similarity to the less dominant cross-sex parent is suggested.

4. If the son is nondominant (for example, has a score of 40 on the ACL) and his mother is judged to be the more likely model for dominance, a *plus* is assigned to the 10-point deviation from 50. Dissimilarity to the cross-sex parent and similarity to the same-sex parent are inferred.

When this scoring procedure is followed for all fifteen personality variables, higher cumulative raw scores point to a heightened similarity to the same-sex parent (in this case, the father). A lower raw score would indicate the opposite, a closer alignment between the behavior of the son and that of the (cross-sex) mother. In practice, conversions from raw score to T-score are made within separate norm tables for college males and females. A T-score of 50 is the average degree of rated behavioral similarity between male subjects and their fathers or between female subjects and their mothers. I have found it convenient to interpret higher T-scores (above 50) as showing identification with the parent of the same sex and lower T-scores (below 50) as an indication of a cross-sex parent identification.

The second score that is derived within the identification scoring procedure represents the rated stereotyped or nonstereotyped character of parent model sex-role behavior for a given subject. Nine of the fifteen personality variables that are used to compare the mother and father were identified as differentially represented in the behavior of adult males and females and thus stereotyped (Heilbrun, 1964). Achievement, dominance, endurance, and autonomy were found to be male sex-typed, and deference, abasement, succorance, nurturance, and affiliation to be female sex-typed. The model score is given by the number of comparisons between the mother and father in which the parent selected as more aptly described by the behavior in question was in keeping with stereotype. Scores can range from 9 (the father described as the more achieving, dominant, enduring, and autonomous parent and the mother as the more deferent, abasing, succorant, nurturant, and affiliative parent) down to 0, where each of these is reversed. The model score represents a relative index that is most meaningful when applied to the parents as a couple. It allows the researcher to break down parents into those who appear to be stereotypic (that is, father more masculine and mother more feminine) and those who seem to represent nonstereotypic models (father more feminine and mother more masculine). Sample median-split procedures have usually been employed to create these parent model groups. This has resulted in cutting scores that define stereotypic models by scores of at least 6 or 7. I mention this to remind the reader that the difference in stereotypic and nonstereotypic parent models is a difference of degree and not of kind; a "nonstereotypic" pair may still show more stereotypic differences in sex-role behavior than nonstereotypic reversals.

EARLY RESEARCH INTO PARENT
IDENTIFICATION AND FILIAL BEHAVIOR

The studies included in this section were conceived prior to the conceptual revision of sex-role behavior in 1973 that compelled a view of masculinity and femininity as independent dimensions. The original bipolar Masculinity-Femininity Scale taken from the ACL as the measure of choice suffers from the same limitation as the other sex-role measures available at that time, by precluding the consideration of androgynous and undifferentiated subjects. Where possible the data will be reanalyzed using the independent Masculinity and Femininity Scales, but in some cases the data could not be retrieved in identifiable form from the files for this purpose.

Parent Identification and Adjustment of the Child. Three early studies conducted on the campus of the University of Iowa (Heilbrun, 1960; 1962a; 1962b) considered various indices of personal effectiveness for the college student and their relations to parent identification. Client status at a counseling center, being a college dropout, and psychometric indices of maladjustment were among the criteria. The results for males were consistent across studies; males who had failed to identify with their fathers (and presumably were less masculine) emerged most consistently within the maladjusted samples. No clear case could be made for the relation between identification and adjustment for the female, at least as far as statistical significance was concerned. Whatever trends were observed suggested that the choice of the mother as the daughter's primary identification model resulted in less effective behaviors.

It can be noted that the model score was not employed in the identification scoring procedures in these early studies. This was rectified in a subsequent large-scale investigation by Heilbrun and Fromme (1965) of the association between parent identification and level of adjustment. The 299 males and 324 females on the Iowa campus were broken down by extreme parent-model cutting scores (0–5 versus 8–9) and a trilevel partitioning of adjustment (normal samples/clients with vocational problems/clients with personal problems).

The first and third columns of table 7.1 portray clear relations between identification and adjustment for both sexes. Given stereotypic parent models, the primary identification of both the son and daughter with the masculine father is associated with normal adjustment. On the other hand, more serious maladjustment was correlated with the choice of the feminine mother as the primary identification object for both sexes. While this result came as no surprise for the males, it did raise intriguing questions regarding the role of parent identification in the development of the college female that retained our interest for many years, and to which we shall return later in this chapter. The other data columns of table 7.1 were important for what they did not show. They indicate that, given nonstereotypic parent models, there was no relation between parent identification and adjustment for either sex. Factors other than identification seem to assume importance when the parents have to some appreciable extent reversed expected sex roles, although at that time it was not at all clear what those factors were.

Table 7.1.   Mean Parent Identification Scores as a Function of Parent Sex-Role Stereotype and Level of Adjustment

Level of Adjustment	Sons		Daughters	
	Stereotypic/ Parent Models	Nonstereotypic/ Parent Models	Stereotypic/ Parent Models	Nonstereotypic/ Parent Models
Adjusted	53.9	48.3	48.4	53.7
Intermediate	49.3	49.1	51.0	49.2
Maladjusted	46.5	50.1	60.0	51.0

NOTE: Stereotypic models (scores 8–9) include a masculine father and feminine mother.
Nonstereotypic models (scores 0–5) include a feminine father and masculine mother.

Subsequent studies of identification that considered parent role models continued the trend of earlier results: clearly ordered and understandable correlates for males and quite the opposite for the female. The first of these (Heilbrun, 1969) examined vocational interest development in the college student, presumed to be an important contributor to effective career choice and, indirectly, to the adjustment of the young adult. Table 7.2 presents the average number of positive career interests as measured by the Strong Vocational Interest Blank (1959) within the parent-identification groupings. Both the male and female comparisons achieved statistical significance but offered quite distinct

Table 7.2.   Mean Number of Career Interests by Type of Primary Parent Identification

	Masculine Father	Feminine Father	Masculine Mother	Feminine Mother
Males	12.9	11.4	10.5	7.3
Females	3.4	4.6	4.9	2.7

NOTE: Based on the number of A and B+ scores from a total possible number of fifty-four occupations on the male form of the Strong Vocational Interest Blank (1959) and from the thirty-three occupations on the female form.

interpretations. Identification of the son with his masculine father was associated with the broadest development of career interests and a feminine-mother identification with the most circumscribed. To the extent that a range of interests is conducive to effective career choice, the male's choice of the stereotypic father over the stereotypic mother as a primary object of identification when presented with conventional parents should facilitate this culturally sanctioned goal. The variation among the female means suggested only that nonstereotypic models of identification were associated with a wider range of career interests. The meaning of this finding was not clear then nor is it now except as it signaled the more complicated nature of the identification process for the daughter.

The next study (Heilbrun, 1970) served to summarize a ponderous number of observations (some 600) of identification scores considered by adjustment level that had accumulated in my files. The findings were reported as percentages of subjects within each level of adjustment ("adjusted" = random college samples, "intermediate" = vocationally concerned clients, "maladjusted" = personally troubled clients). The most critical finding for males simply reaffirmed what was known already: the highest percentage within the adjusted group (33 percent) had identified with a masculine father, whereas the highest percentage of maladjusted males (38 percent) had shown a feminine-mother identification. Adjusted females demonstrated a masculine-father identification more often than any other pattern (32 percent), but it was identification with a masculine mother that emerged as the most prevalent pattern (36 percent) among maladjusted girls. It began to appear that it was not masculinity of the model per se that offered adjustive benefits to the female, but more the masculinity evidenced by the father. This prevalence finding was unexpected in light of conventional assumptions about the daughter's identification with her mother as the normal developmental experience. Then again, so was the earlier finding that *strong* identification with a feminine mother characterized the maladjusted college female. Both types of maternal identification had been unexpectedly indicted.

A quotation from the summary statements of this 1970 study will set the stage for where our program of parent identification/sex-role research was to head next. It also includes my first reference to differential sex-role blending in males and females, speculation that proved predictive of later evidence (reviewed in Chapter Four of this book).

> Perhaps the most promising direction that future inquiry might take would have to do with the sex-role reversal feature of this pattern [that identification with a masculine father was associated with favorable adjustment, and identification with a masculine mother with an unfavorable adjustment]. It is unlikely that a woman can present as adequate a masculine model as a biologically male father. It seems possible that masculinity in a woman is more blended with feminine qualities, whereas masculine men are likely to behave discretely in masculine or, under special conditions, in feminine ways. If so, the sex role reversed masculine mother will present a somewhat blurred model of masculine and feminine behaviors for either the son or the daughter to emulate. . . .
>
> The relationship between the biological-psychological sex of the parent chosen as the primary model for identification and subsequent competence of the daughter is a strange one. A masculine-father identification qualifies as the most facilitative of effectiveness for the girl, whereas a masculine-mother identification is seen to be the most likely correlate of ineffectiveness. Thus, while it is true that the girl is given greater leeway in adopting cross-sex behavior in our society than is accorded the boy, it appears to be equally true that the mother who has taken advantage of this permissiveness presents the poorest identification model for her daughter.
>
> Although other observations might be made from the graph data, perhaps enough has been said to stress the importance of the *pattern* of parental identification, meaning here the combination of both the biological and psychological sex of the identification model, for behavior development into the college years [Heilbrun, 1970, pp. 77–78].

THE FEMALE IDENTIFICATION PARADOX

The full yield of studies of parent identification in college-age youth within which we found puzzling results for the female accompanied by generally predictable findings for males has yet to be described. Not only was the daughter's primary identification with a stereotypically masculine father found to be a positive correlate of adjustment, but it was also associated with a surprising degree of femininity in the daughter. This paradoxical sex-role effect became the object of investigation after a lapse of several years following the originating study.

The Originating Study. The same year that the parent identification measurement procedures were first described (Heilbrun, 1965a), a second paper appeared describing research bearing on a theoretical issue concerning this process (Heilbrun, 1965b). Johnson (1963), taking her lead from Parsons and Bales' theory of family process (Parsons, 1958; Parsons and Bales, 1955), had proposed that the father contributed more to the sex-role development of both the son and daughter than did the mother. She proposed that sex-role development was functionally linked to a reciprocal-role relationship between parent and child, meaning the parent's elicitation and reinforcement of specific child behaviors within the parent-child relationship. Johnson proposed that the father, being more concerned with sex-role conformity by both the son and daughter, behaves in such a way as to elicit masculine behaviors in the son and feminine behaviors in the daughter, and then reinforces the appearance of these stereotyped behaviors. The mother was viewed as less inclined to establish reciprocal roles directed toward the child's sex-role development.

The 1965 study considered the same question of parental primacy in the child's sex-role development from the standpoint of modeling rather than reciprocal-role theory. I had assumed the importance of modeling in interpreting the data generated by our parent identification measurement procedures; parent-child similarity was viewed as evolving mainly from the child's imitation of parent model behavior. Modeling was not accorded much in the way of importance by Johnson, who proposed a type of shaping behavior on the part of the parent. The question, as we asked it, was, Which parent by serving as the primary identification model most facilitates stereotypic sex-role development in both sons and daughters? It remained a possibility that the same conclusion reached by Johnson within her reciprocal-role proposal would apply to identification as a modeling process.

The procedures involved the designation of 279 college subjects as identified primarily with one of four parent-model types based on our psychometric instruments: (1) masculine-father-identified, (2) feminine-father-identified, (3) masculine-mother-identified, or (4) feminine-mother-identified. Male and female subjects falling within each of these identification pattern groups were directly compared in their ACL self-descriptions, and the behavioral adjectives distinguishing the two sexes by chi-square analysis were submitted to psychologists to be judged for their instrumental, expressive, or indeterminate quality. The pattern found to be associated with the most extensive and clear-cut set of masculine features in the son and feminine features in the daughter was identification with the masculine father. The conclusion seemed to be that primary identification with a masculine father resulted in masculine sons but in feminine daughters.

This result was obviously more perplexing in the case of the daughter, so a supplementary analysis was run to be sure that the girls who identified with masculine fathers did not look feminine only because they were being compared with hypermasculine males. Females identified with masculine fathers were compared with females identified with feminine mothers to see whether the former group might look unfeminine by within-sex standards. They did not. Eight behaviors were differentially endorsed (15 out of 300 would be expected by chance); these signified some greater degree of passivity in the feminine-mother-identified girl relative to the masculine-father-identified girl but no other distinct feminine features. The scene was set for directly confronting the anomalous finding that a primary identification with a male model, and a relatively masculine one at that, seems to mediate a sex-role picture in the daughter approximating the feminine stereotype.

IDENTIFICATION AND VICARIOUS EXPERIENCE IN THE FEMALE

The key data from which an explanation for the identification paradox eventually evolved was collected eight years later in a study of 138 Emory students (Heilbrun, 1973a). The study involved two parts. A questionnaire session was offered first in which materials relevant to identification were administered, and later the subjects returned to the laboratory in small groups for a vicarious reinforcement experiment. I shall excerpt the description of the laboratory procedures from the earlier publication.

Upon arrival at the laboratory, the group was introduced to an experimental methodology devised to study the effects of vicarious reinforcement. The procedures, originally employed in an earlier experiment (Heilbrun, 1970b), were implemented by a female experimenter. Subjects were seated around a large table and given a perceptual-motor task modeled after the digit-symbol subtest of the Wechsler Adult Intelligence Scale (1955). For those not familiar with this task, the person is asked to fill in as many symbols as possible in 90 seconds within boxes associated with randomly ordered numbers. Number-symbol pairings are keyed for the subject at the top of the page. The experimenter scored digit-symbol performance for all subjects in the group immediately upon their completion of the task.

The next procedural step was to choose one of the subjects from the group and inform him that he was going to receive special training which we had reason to believe could help him perform on the digit-symbol task just completed. While the selection of the "trainee" was made to appear spontaneous by the experimenter, the subject to be selected had been chosen prior to the arrival of the group and was always a male. The trainee was seated at one end of the experimental room in a chair facing the rear wall. Mounted on the wall were five disks, each bearing a different-size angle. The trainee was told that he would be given experience in making difficult angular discriminations, and if he could do well in this regard, there should result an improvement in his ability to perform on the digit-symbol task. If he could not learn to make these difficult discriminations, the instructions continued, no improvement in digit-symbol performance could be expected.

The trainee was then introduced to an angle-discrimination procedure devised by James (1957) within which he was given 20 chances to match test angles with the same-size standard angle on the wall. No correct matching was possible, however, since each test angle fell $5°$ between two of the standard angles. This discrimination is so difficult that the subject almost invariably fails to detect the absence of an identical match, opening the way to imposing preselected schedules of reinforcement upon performance. In the positive (success) condition the trainee was put on a 14-correct-6-incorrect schedule, with the experimenter interposing positive statements about his performance after the tenth and twentieth choices. The negative (failure) condition involved a 6-correct–14-incorrect schedule and negative evaluative statements from the experimenter at the same two points. (The bona fide nature of this procedure was not questioned except in one group, and their data were excluded from the experimental part of the investigation.)

During the course of the angle disciminations, the remaining subjects were asked to sit in chairs, positioned so that they had a direct view of the trainee but could not see the standard angles. Thus, the observers were in a position to hear the reinforcement imposed upon the trainee and to view his responses; our interest was in determining the extent to which the individual was susceptible to experiencing that reinforcement vicariously.

Subjects were reasscmbled about the table as soon as the intervening reinforcement condition was completed and were administered an alternate form of the digit-symbol task. Prior to beginning, however, each subject was handed a slip of paper with the number correct from the first digit-symbol task printed upon it, and she was asked to write the number correct she thought she could achieve upon retest. The second digit-symbol task was then administered, which marked the end of the experiment.

Vicarious reinforcement was inferred when the subject's expectation of performance was influenced in a direction consistent with reinforcement imposed upon the male model. Given positive reinforcement of the trainee and the expectation that his success would facilitate digit-symbol performance, vicarious positive reinforcement would mediate the expectation of improved performance for the observer. Given negative reinforcement of the trainee and no expectation on his part of improved performance from the training, vicarious negative reinforcement would curtail the expectation of improved performance for the observer [Heilbrun, 1973a, pp. 172–74].

Analysis of the vicarious reinforcement data proceeded by determining the difference between initial performance score and anticipated performance for each subject, and cutting the distributions of difference scores for the positive and negative conditions at their respective medians. The mean parent identification and parent model scores were determined for the vicariously responsive and unresponsive groups (see table 7.3). Analysis of variance revealed a significant ($p < .025$) difference among the similarity scores but no effect for parent model score. Girls who were vicariously responsive to reinforcements delivered to a

Table 7.3.   Parent Identification and Model Scores for Females Vicariously Responsive and Unresponsive to Reinforcements Imposed on a Male Target

| Identification Variable | Vicarious Reinforcement Condition | | | |
| | Positive | | Negative | |
	Responsive (N = 26)	Unresponsive (N = 22)	Responsive (N = 19)	Unresponsive (N = 19)
Parent-Child Similarity[a]	49.03	55.09	47.68	53.16
Parent Model	5.81	6.23	7.00	5.89

[a]Higher scores suggest greater similarity to the mother; lower scores indicate greater similarity to the father.

male in their presence were more highly identified with their father than were those girls who appeared unresponsive.

The vicarious reinforcement study provided only a fraction of the data that were mustered in the 1973 report as support for the conclusion that parent identification was a very different process for the girl than the boy. The distinctions did not include anything so predictable as the choice of different (same-sex) primary identification models, as is traditionally assumed. The major contrast between the sexes was an obscure one: the parent identification of males entered into a totally reasonable network of relations with everything we studied, but in the case of the female any sense of consistency between the sex gender and sex role of the primary model and the correlates of identification was missing. The most blatant example of this was the paradoxical absence of masculinity in daughters identified with masculine fathers. The vicarious reinforcement experiment provided the basis for one of three hypotheses proposed as explanations for this paradox in the 1973 paper.

HYPOTHESES EXPLAINING THE IDENTIFICATION PARADOX

Male Sex-Gender Identification in the Daughter. Although the vocabulary of identification/sex-role development researchers was already swelled with conceptually overlapping terms, the 1973 article proposed yet another entry to the list as necessary to explain its findings. Sex-gender identification was proposed as a construct that built onto the traditional concept of sex-role preference. The two features of gender identification that were proposed were the person's preference for male or female sex-role behaviors and prerogatives (sex-role preference) *and* the capacity for vicarious experience of positive or negative reinforcements imposed upon models of that sex. The latter requisite sets gender identification apart from sex-role preference as traditionally conceived.

The sex-gender identification hypothesis would account for the paradoxical identification findings for females by assuming that the daughter's identification with the father is likely to be accompanied by a more general gender identification with males. The gender identification presumably would have its inception in the positive regard for the father that contributes to his attraction as an identification model.

We can assume, then, that many girls are in a position to gain vicarious satisfaction from observing the achievements (real or imagined) of boys and men. In short, they come to identify with maleness to the extent that they share the values of the group and vicariously experience the satisfactions which accompany group membership. The extent to which the girl's perceptions of her father contribute to her heightened evaluation of maleness will vary, of course, but it should be considerable. Our hypothesis would contend that the girl who identifies with her father is doing so both in a modeling sense and in a sex-gender identification sense because of his status as a male. Modeling should mediate some distinctions in behavior outcome, given masculine and feminine dispositions of the father. However, sex-gender identification involves the vicarious enjoyment of the rewards of maleness, not the imitation of behaviors by which these rewards are presumably achieved. The effect of this dual identification would be to divert some of the positive vicarious reinforcement necessary to imitative learning of specific behaviors of the father into the vicarious satisfactions of identifying with him as a male. This, in turn, should reduce the importance of the behavioral differences between male parent models, including their sex-role attributes, in mediating outcomes in daughters [Heilbrun, 1973a, pp. 187–88].

The paradoxical absence of a strong masculine orientation in the masculine-father-identified daughter (Heilbrun, 1965b) is explained according to this hypothesis by assuming that vicarious satisfaction for the girl may be generated as much by observing the achievements of her father as by performing the specific masculine behaviors through which these achievements are accomplished. This limits the imitation of masculine behaviors to some extent by diverting part of the reinforcement away from that normally associated with modeling.

Let me offer an example of how gender identification was thought to work in limiting masculine development in the daughter even though she selects the masculine father as a primary model. Assume the father was dominating in his personal transactions and that this was viewed by the daughter as a rewarded quality—one that accrued status, respect, and the attainment of personal goals. If she obtained vicarious satisfaction from observing or imagining this stereotypically masculine behavior in her father, there would be less incentive for her to incorporate dominating behaviors in her own repertoire so that she could emulate his effectiveness in obtaining social rewards. While this proposal would lead us to predict some attenuation in the strength of the behavior in question, it does not specify how much the development of the trait in the daughter will be restricted. Subsequent research offered some insight in this regard.

Our proposal that a male sex-gender identification in the daughter will influence the outcome of her identification with the father was investigated by Heilbrun, Kleemeier, and Piccola (1974). The psychological context for this study involved competitiveness, a traditionally male trait, and a situation in which vicarious responsiveness to male reinforcement could be expected to influence competitive behavior.

Eighty-six Emory College undergraduates (fifty-one females and thirty-five males) served as subjects in this study. This was a largely freshman class that I was teaching, and, like all Emory samples, was predominantly white and upper middle class. The procedures involved the self-administration of a number of questionnaires on the students' own time. These included the ACL, parent identification materials, the role consistency measure described in Chapter Four, and a questionnaire inquiring into contemporary versus traditional attitudes toward the female role (Fand, 1955). A fear-of-success measure (Horner, 1968) was group administered under the supervision of two graduate students at the beginning of the hour. The experimental manipulation followed and took the major part of the class time given over to this study.

Subjects were told by me that the study had to do with how perceptual-motor performance was affected by different conditions, and that in order to accomplish our goals some people had to be sent from the room. These rather vague instructions were followed by a request that all the males step outside the closed doors of the classroom and await further involvement in the study. An effort was made to make this request appear to the female subjects as a convenient way of dismissing "about half" of the class from the initial part of the study rather than as a prelude to a subsequent confrontation between the two sexes. After the males had left, the girls were given one form of the digit-symbol task that had been employed in the original vicarious reinforcement experiment (Heilbrun, 1973a). They were encouraged to work as quickly as possible in line with standard instructions for the task, but nothing else was said that might motivate them to compete with others in the room as far as scores were concerned. The digit-symbol tasks were scored for number correct by passing them to the next person in the row and then were returned to the subjects.

An instructional manipulation was then introduced. After the boys returned to the classroom, all subjects were prepared for the next administration of the digit-symbol task (with the girls given an alternate form to that used initially). Subjects were told that the task was taken from an intelligence test (which it was) as a way of increasing their ego involvement, and each subject was urged to be the "very best in the class." Besides these instructions intended to increase individual motivation to perform, the female subjects were told that we wanted "to see whether you girls with previous experience on the task can do better than the boys who have not had the experience." This part of the instructions, insinuating as it does that females might need the additional practice to do better than males on a task involving intelligence, qualifies at best as a sexist barb. However, it did set the stage for differentiating females who had made a male gender identification from those who had not.

Beyond the sexist implications of the final instruction, the female subjects were made aware that males had been put at a clear disadvantage in a competitive situation; they were being asked to overcome the female's prior experience on the competitive task. Keep in mind that vicarious experience of male reinforcement cut both ways in the original experiment. Vicarious responders among the females in both the positive and negative reinforcement conditions were more father-identified. The daughter who had made a male gender identification through parental identification with the father would be expected to show a vicarious sensitivity to both positive and negative consequences befalling him and other males. In this experiment, vicarious sensitivity would allow the girl to share the feeling of disadvantagement for male subjects just as girls in the earlier study seemed to share the disadvantagement of the male who failed in his "training experience." On the other hand, female subjects who were competitive, more sensitive to sexist overtones, and not placed in a quandary by vicarious sharing of the feelings of the disadvantaged males should respond to the second set of instructions with particularly vigorous performance.

Since this study focused on a substantial number of variables, it might prove helpful to the reader to elucidate what they were and how they were employed. Two independent variables were used to group the females according to potential differences in male gender identification. The parent-identification score was split at the college norm; scores at or above $T = 50$ defined a primary mother identification, and scores below this defined a primary father identification for the girl. General role consistency scores were split at the sample median into high and low groupings, since no norm table was available. Father identification was found to be a correlate of vicarious sensitivity to male reinforcement in the prior study (Heilbrun, 1973a), and thus a component of our definition of male-gender identification. Role consistency had been shown to relate positively to empathic sensitivity in college students (Edwards, 1965). Its inclusion allowed us to compare two types of father-identified females that were confounded in the 1973 investigation. Father-identified girls who also were more empathic (high-role-consistent) best fulfilled our specifications as male-gender-identified and should be more vulnerable to the experimental manipulation and male disadvantagement in the competition. Father-identified girls who were presumably less empathic (low-role-consistent) seemed especially suited to the competition, since their masculine competitiveness mediated by modeling after their fathers should not be tempered by vicarious concerns about male competitors.

The dependent variables fell into three categories and will be described as the results of this investigation are reported. Sex-role differences among the four parent-identification/role-consistency groups (table 7.4) were examined along masculinity-femininity lines (using the bipolar ACL M-F scale) and in terms of attitudes toward the woman's role in society. The attitude measure (Fand, 1955) considered a preference for maintaining traditional concepts of marriage, family, home, motherhood, selective employment, and deference to others' opinions or for revising role characteristics toward a contemporary view emphasizing personal achievement, autonomy, leadership, equal rights, freedom in marriage, and personal fulfillment outside of the home. Analysis of these sex-role variables set the pattern for almost all of the female results in this study; differences emerged between the two father-identified subsets but not between the two mother-identified groups. The father-identified/male-gender-identified women were modestly masculine (54.29) by female standards, as opposed to the extreme masculinity (63.40) of the father-identified women who were considered too

Table 7.4.   Parent Identification and Role Consistency as Related to Sex-Role Status and Attitudes Toward the Woman's Role

Identification-Consistency Groups	Mean Masculinity-Femininity[a]	Mean Female Role Preference[b]
Father-identified, high-role-consistent (N = 14)	54.29	7.09
Father-identified low-role consistent (N = 10)	63.40	20.10
Mother-identified, high-role-consistent (N = 12)	49.67	5.50
Mother-identified, low-role-consistent (N = 15)	48.73	6.40

[a]Higher scores (above 50) indicate masculinity, and lower scores (below 50) indicate femininity.
[b]The higher the score, the greater the preference for the contemporary version of the woman's role.

lacking in empathic skills to be susceptible to much vicarious experience (that is, had not made a male-gender identification). This difference achieved significance ($p < .05$). The latter group also coupled its extremely high masculinity with a markedly elevated woman's role score (20.10); by doing so these women expressed a strong preference for crossing over sex-role boundaries into what has been the traditional male domain. Women identified as more capable of achieving vicarious satisfactions from male accomplishment showed far less preference for such contemporary views of the woman's role (7.07), significantly less ($p < .025$) than their father-identified and less vicariously responsive peers.

Thus far the results are consistent with the gender-identification hypothesis. Daughters who identify with their fathers in particular but also with males in general need not display strong masculinity or be attitudinally disposed toward demonstration of male role prerogatives, since they can obtain vicarious reinforcement from males who do. Father-identified daughters without this vicarious potential are carried much further along into male role behavior.

Aspects of achievement motivation comprised the second category of dependent variables that were considered in this study. Need achievement was measured by an ACL scale (Heilbrun, 1959; 1962b; 1962c) representing the standard conception of a motive to attain socially recognized goals. The projective fear-of-success measure, initially described by Horner (1968) and popularized by a rash of studies in the 1970s, gets at the other side of the coin—the motive for the woman to avoid success for fear of some aversive consequence that would follow attainment of goals traditionally reserved for men. Table 7.5 points up the interesting fact that the need for success and the fear of success bear no apparent relation to each other in college females. Father-identified males generally demonstrated higher need achievement than those primarily identified with their mothers (p < .05). However, those father-identified girls who by our definition had not made a male-gender identification demonstrated a higher (p < .025) fear of success (.900) than those father-identified girls who had (.357). In other words, when the conditions surrounding the pursuit of goals are unspecified, achievement motivation in girls identified with the male parent looks much the same. When the conditions are specified for the female to include competition for goals in male-dominated fields (standing in medical school class and success, etc.), gender-identification differences within the father-identified group emerge.

Table 7.5. Parent Identification and Role Consistency as Related to Female Achievement Motivation Variables

Identification-Consistency Groups	Mean Need Achievement[a]	Mean Motive to Avoid Success[b]
Father-identified, high-role-consistent	53.36	.357
Father-identified, low-role-consistent	52.00	.900
Mother-identified, high-role-consistent	49.83	.250
Mother-identified, low-role-consistent	41.87	.467

[a] College mean = 50, with higher scores indicating greater need achievement.
[b] Score based on present-absent scoring of fear indicators in both projective stories (= 2), one of the two stories (= 1), or in neither story (= 0).

The third category of variables to be considered are performance measures taken from the digit-symbol tasks. Table 7.6 includes three such variables: (1) DS1 or initial digit-symbol performance prior to competition with males; (2) LOA − DS1 or difference between level of aspiration and prior performance after competition instructions but before performing again; (3) DS2 − DS1 or difference between performance when competing with males and performance when not competing.

Both the level-of-aspiration (middle column) and performance-change (right column) findings involved interaction effects (p < .05). Father-identified women who showed no evidence of a male-gender identification, and who were thought to be prime candidates for excessive competition with males, behaved according to form. They anticipated improving their performance by 6 points and far outstripped even their own expectations, improving their scores by over 13 points. Both scores far exceeded those of the other groups. Father-identified girls who should have been the most restricted by their identification with the males in the experiment also performed according to theory. They anticipated no real improvement the second time around (.69) and showed none (− .36).

Table 7.6.   Parent Identification and Role Consistency as Related to Female Competitive Performance Variables

Identification-Consistency Groups	Mean DS1	Mean LOA − DS1†	Mean DS2 − DS1††
Father-identified, high-role-consistent	71.50	.69	− .36
Father-identified, low-role-consistent	57.90	6.00	13.10
Mother-identified, high-role-consistent	63.58	3.55	4.83
Mother-identified, low-role-consistent	66.00	−2.80	5.73

†Plus scores indicate an expectation of improved performance in the competitional situation, and minus scores indicate an expectation of poorer performance.
††Plus scores indicate actual improved performance in the competitional situation, and minus scores indicate a decline in performance.

There was one complication in the performance data that was not anticipated but appears to make sense in light of the interpretation placed on the results. The DS1 column in table 7.6 makes it clear that the two father-identified groups did not respond in the same way to the initial digit-symbol task. There were no males present and no instructions to compete with others; subjects simply were told to "work as fast as you can" without specifying a comparison of performance with other subjects. Under these noncompetitive conditions, father/male gender-identified females performed exceptionally well (71.50) and father-identified females who were considered vicariously unresponsive to consequences befalling males demonstrated lackluster performance (57.90). These two means along with the intermediate means of the mother-identified groups produced yet another significant ($p < .005$) interaction effect. The discrepant performance of the father-identified women struck us as important, but, unfortunately, either of two explanations seemed equally viable. One would be that task achievement for the male-gender-identified subset is most facilitated when males are not involved as competitors, whereas such achievement is likely for those lacking a male-gender identification only when males are involved as competitors. The second explanation would propose that the male-gender-identified female may be especially responsive to situations in which she is asked to perform up to personal standards, but the father-identified but not gender-identified female may need structured competition with others (male or female) to generate a real effort. A follow-up study clearly was in order to sort out these alternatives. There was also a need to dispel the possibility that the father/male-gender-identified women had not improved nor expected to improve on the second task because their performance had approached an asymptote on the first task.

The second investigation of possible antecedent roles of parent and gender identification in females again explored competitional behavior (Heilbrun, Piccola, & Kleemeier, 1975). We set out to replicate the previous findings but included procedural refinements that might allow us to answer some of the lingering questions. Subjects were Emory College undergraduates and included 104 females as the object of study and 92 males to provide cross-sex competition. Demographic features of these subjects were highly similar to those described for the subjects of the prior study. Parent identification and role consistency measures were group administered, and each distribution of scores was split at the overall female median for assignment of women to experimental groups. The digit-symbol task of previous studies continued to be our choice as the performance measure.

The revised procedure is important to understanding the extent to which the unresolved questions of our 1974 study could be answered, so I shall quote fully from the published report.

> Subjects were administered the psychometric tests in small groups and in a set order. Prior to leaving the group testing session, subjects were assigned to one of two types of smaller laboratory groups. Some females were assigned to two-person or three-person competitional groups which included only girls, whereas other females were assigned to competitional groups including one or two other male subjects. Taken from the perspective of the female subject, the former represented the female competition condition ($N = 58$) and the latter represented the male competition condition ($N = 46$). The laboratory session was usually held within a week of the group testing session.
>
> Upon arrival at the laboratory, each subject was taken individually into the room while the remaining one or two subjects waited in the hall. The instructions for the digit-symbol task were presented by the female experimenter in a straightforward manner; while the subject was told to work quickly as possible, no special motivational admonishments were offered. After baseline performance had been obtained from each subject in the experimental group, they were called back together into the laboratory and presented with the competition instructions. Subjects were told that they were going to perform the same kind of task, but this time they were going to do it at the same time and in the same room. Additional instructions were given to facilitate competition including: (1) that this task was taken from an intelligence test, (2) that the experimenters wished each subject to maximize her performance and to outperform the other subjects, and (3) that a cash prize of $25.00 was to be awarded to the subject in the study who improved the most on this second trial.
>
> Prior to beginning the second digit-symbol task, the subjects were given their initial scores (number correct) on a slip of paper and asked to record the number that they thought they would correctly reproduce this time. Subjects were then administered the second digit-symbol task following which they were excused. Approximately half of the subjects performed initially on the first form followed by the second form, whereas the remainder of the subjects took the digit-symbol tasks in the opposite order [Heilbrun, Piccola, & Kleemeier, pp. 683–684].

These procedural changes from the 1974 study allow us to disentangle the role played by the gender of the competitors against whom the female subject is pitting her talents, on the one hand, and the extent to which the task is interpreted to be a competitive one, on the other. The instructions for the second task were unambiguous in calling for competition, and the conditions placed the female subjects in competitive situations in which the sex of the competitors was clearly defined.

The effects of these conditions upon expectancies and actual competitive performance for the same four female experimental groups that were under consideration in the previous study are summarized in table 7.7, except this time they are further separated by sex of the competitors. Analysis of level of aspiration revealed no significant effects in this follow-up study. The father/male-gender-identified females did not curtail their personal expectations of performance in anticipation of competing against males as they had in the first study. This might be explained by two changes in methodology. Males were not put at a disadvantage in the competition as they had been previously so that the gender-identified females no longer had a vicarious lid placed on their own performance. Furthermore, competitional instructions were bolstered, and this may have contributed to a more confident view of their own potential in competing with males.

When you examine what actually happened to the performance of father-identified women on the second task ($DS_2 - DS_1$), however, the previous results

Table 7.7. Parent Identification and Role Consistency as Related to Female Competitive Performance Variables (Follow-up Study)

				Sex Gender of the Competition				
		Male				Female		
Identification-Consistency Groups	N	Mean DS_1	Mean $LOA - DS_1$†	Mean $DS_2 - DS_1$††	N	Mean DS_1	Mean $LOA - DS_1$†	Mean $DS_2 - DS_1$††
Father-identified, high-role-consistent	14	71.21	7.79	.14	11	67.73	5.91	3.36
Father-identified, low-role-consistent	12	66.67	8.50	6.75	16	64.88	8.06	8.56
Mother-identified, high-role-consistent	9	63.00	7.56	4.11	18	68.67	6.44	4.83
Mother-identified, low-role-consistent	11	66.09	4.09	4.91	13	64.62	8.46	2.54

†Plus scores indicate an expectation of improved performance in the competitional situation.
††Plus scores indicate actual improved performance in the competitional situation.

are both replicated and extended. Father/male-gender-identified females, despite their optimistic aspirations, improved very little (.14) when they were competing with males. This curtailed performance against males was significantly less ($p <$ .05) than the average gain for all other female subjects combined (5.18). No comparable effect could be observed when the average gain score of the father/male-gender-identified group pitted against female competitors (3.36) was weighed against that of all remaining female subjects (4.63). Male-gender identification not only appeared to attenuate competition against males, but the effect seemed limited to male competition alone.

The competitiveness of the father-identified but less empathic female was replicated as well, but it was clear in this study that her competitiveness is aroused by both male and female competitors. Average gain scores against both male (6.75) and female (8.56) adversaries were similar for this group and, when combined (7.79), proved to be more substantial ($p <$ .025) than those obtained by the remainder of the females in the study (3.29). The contrast between the upsurge in performance of the less empathic, father-identified women when competing with anybody and the modest improvement of the father-identified, male-gender-identified females in particular (1.56) was especially striking ($p <$ .01).

Although the two competition studies offer some support for the importance of gender identification in females, the relevance of the findings to the original paradox is rather distant. The evidence had nothing to do with the siphoning of vicarious reinforcement from the modeling process when the daughter selects her father as the primary model. However, we can at least return to the paradox by inspecting the masculinity and femininity scores taken from the independent scales, something that was not possible in these pre-1976 studies. Will these studies show that the father/male-gender-identified females do not show either a high level of masculinity or a deficit in femininity? Rescoring of the ACL protocols from the 1973 originating study and the 1975 replication study (the 1974 ACLs had been returned to the subjects and were no longer available for rescoring) resulted in mean Masculinity and Femininity Scale scores of 50.60 and 47.90 in the former study and 49.44 and 53.40 in the latter for the father/male-gender-identified women. A score of 50 represents the college average for both scales, as the reader may recall, so these means depict this group of females as about average on both sex roles relative to their campus peers. The remaining father-identified females, who did not show evidence of a male-gender identification, continued to look more masculine (or less feminine) with the rescoring, as a father identification would lead one to expect. In the 1973 sample, the Masculinity and Femininity Scale means were 56.83 and 47.56; means of 51.96 and 46.78 were obtained for the 1975 females.

Investigation of the gender-identification hypothesis did not take the parent-model score into consideration as an independent variable, partly for logistical reasons (doubling the number of subjects required) and partly because the 1973 vicarious reinforcement study did not identify a significant effect for this score. However, a post hoc examination of model scores alleviated any concern that differences in the pattern of stereotyped sex-role behaviors displayed by the parents as models for identification should have been introduced as an independent variable in these studies. Logically speaking, this variable could have produced the sex-role differences discussed in the paragraph above only if the fathers of male-gender-identified girls were less masculine and more feminine than the fathers of the girls who did not share this gender identification even though they identified with the male parent. Table 7.8 summarizes the mean parent-model scores for the 1973, 1974, and 1975 studies. None of the comparisons of model scores within the three samples proved statistically significant, and certainly no trend can be detected toward the type of bias described above. In fact, the father/male-gender-identified female had the highest model score (and the most masculine/least feminine fathers) of all groups, averaging over samples.

Table 7.8. Mean Parent-Model Scores for the Parent-Identification and Gender-Identification Female Groups

| | Primary Parent Identification | | | |
| | Father | | Mother | |
Study	High-role-consistent	Low-role-consistent	High-role-consistent	Low-role-consistent
Heilbrun, 1973a	6.05	6.44	6.61	5.68
Heilbrun, Kleemeier, & Piccola, 1974	6.71	6.21	6.91	6.25
Heilbrun, Piccola, & Kleemeier, 1975	6.96	6.67	6.00	6.23

NOTE: Total possible parent-model score = 9, with higher scores indicating stereotypically more masculine fathers and more feminine mothers.

Other Proposals for Explaining the Female Identification Paradox. Two other hypotheses have been extended to explain the female identification paradox (Heilbrun, 1973a). One explained the attenuation of masculinity in the father-identified female by the versatility of the father as a model for his children; the name chosen at that time, the ''double standard'' hypothesis, may have been unfortunate in that it conveys surplus meaning. It was proposed that the father was capable of presenting a masculine model to his son within their interactions but of softening his qualities when interacting with his daughter, thereby presenting a more feminine model. This shift to the softer qualities of femininity was anticipated to be more or less restricted to the father-daughter relationship. Thus the sex-role characteristics of the father, as they are modeled in direct interaction with the daughter, might be expected to depart in a feminine direction from his more generalized masculinity.

The transmutation hypothesis represented the third attempt to explain the identification paradox for females. This proposal suggested that the modeling process differs for the son and daughter, at least as far as their perception of the paternal model is concerned. This hypothesis assumes that modeling behavior involves three stages: (1) an observational stage, during which the son and daughter view much the same behaviors on the part of the father; (2) a cognitive rehearsal stage, in which the observed behaviors are reviewed and in which the daughter systematically alters the qualities of the observed behaviors or selects from among the behaviors observed to provide a softer cognitive model that is more congenial to her needs; and (3) an action stage, in which the cognitive versions of paternal behavior are displayed in social transaction. Boys, then, are viewed within this hypothesis as more literal in their imitation of the father than are girls. It totally escaped my attention in 1973 that boys could have contributed to the sex difference in cognitive processing by distorting the degree of masculinity displayed by their fathers in the service of their needs just as daughters distorted the degree of femininity. That female thinking could be more readily influenced by their personal needs than male thinking does seem to qualify as a sexist view. At least, a very comprehensive review of sex differences in children fails to corroborate a difference in imitation, memory, or cognitive style that would encourage a unilateral view of cognitive distortion (Maccoby & Jacklin, 1974). Then, again, apperception of parent models in the identification process has not been studied directly, so the issue remains unresolvable at the present.

We are considering both hypotheses together in this section, because the kind of evidence that will be brought to bear is just as relevant to one as the other. If retrospective descriptions of the father by sons and daughters did differ, for example, there would be no way of telling whether this should be attributed to differences in actual behaviors or to differences that were created by the ways in which they cognitively processed the same observations. However, because of the finding that males present a consistently more androgynous sex-role picture than females (see Chapter Four), I now believe that the hypothesis that the male parent differentiates his behavior depending on the sex of his child has more merit. This view coincides with that expressed by Johnson (1963; 1975), who assigns the more differentiated parent role to the father in influencing sex-role development of both sons and daughters. However, her view assumes that the father's versatility is represented in the kinds of sex-role behavior that he elicits and reinforces within the father-child relationship, and not in the behavior he displays as a model.

Two kinds of evidence will be consulted as relevant to the proposal that fathers present distinct models to their sons and daughters, whether the differences are real or artificially induced by the needs of the child. One set of data was available at the time I proposed the hypotheses in the form of ratings by college students of paternal nurturant behaviors (Heilbrun, 1973a). These ratings were obtained on the Parent-Child Interaction Rating Scales (Heilbrun, 1964) from college subjects who were given five-point low-to-high options on eight paternal behaviors included within the nurturance construct: (1) felt affection, (2) physically expressed affection, (3) approval of the child, (4) sharing of experiences, (5) material giving, (6) encouragement, (7) trust, and (8) felt security within the relationship. Although this set of variables was rationally derived, the selection has been recently validated by factor analysis of parent child-rearing ratings provided by college students (Heilbrun, Bateman, Heilbrun, & Herson, in press). The eight variables clustered positively on a single homogeneous nurturance factor.

Table 7.9 presents the nurturance ratings of fathers as they were perceived by their daughters and their sons. The fathers were further subdivided by their masculinity or femininity, based on a parent model score split between 5 and 6. Fathers were described as generally more nurturant by their daughters than by their sons. Even more striking, however, was the fact that fathers conformed to stereotype with their sons but not with their daughters. Nurturance is a feminine quality, and feminine fathers were more nurturant than masculine fathers as viewed by their sons. This was not the case with the daughter; masculine fathers were rated by girls to be just as nurturant (and feminine in this sense) as feminine fathers. Fathers, whatever their sex-role identity, are described as equivalently

Table 7.9.   Mean Nurturance of Masculine and Feminine Fathers as Rated by Sons and Daughters

| Sample | Masculine Fathers | | Feminine Fathers | | |
	N	M	N	M	p
Male					
University of Iowa	38	25.2	18	28.4	<.05
University of California	46	25.1	18	28.4	<.05
Female					
University of Iowa	38	30.7	22	30.4	Not significant

warm and caring in relationships with their daughters. While these data tell us nothing about the identification of the daughter, they do suggest that the father will display a variety of feminine nurturant behaviors for her to model if she is so inclined.

A second set of data allowed us to examine differences in parent behavior contingent on the sex of the child within a somewhat broader behavioral context (Heilbrun & Landauer, 1977). The question of whether college-age daughters hold more feminine perceptions of their fathers than do college-age sons was answered without restricting the comparison to a single (albeit complex) feminine sex-role variable, nurturance. In fact, the question of differential perceptions of parents was investigated beyond the boundaries of sex-role behavior to establish the extent to which daughters and sons agree about characteristic parent behaviors in general. Thirty-six pairs of siblings attending Emory University were included in the study, representing eight pairs of brothers, eleven sister sets, and seventeen brother-sister combinations. Subjects in each sibling group were quite comparable in their demographic features to those described in this book for all prior research involving Emory students— white, middle-class, with an average age hovering around 19 years. The one demographic feature that is uniquely important to this study is the average difference in ages between sibling pairs. If opposite-sex sibs of substantially variant ages were asked to rate parental behaviors and differences were obtained, it would be difficult to dismiss widely variant offspring (and parent) age as the important source of the differences, rather than sex. Parents may relate differently to their children when they are babies, children, and adolescents; by the same token, parents may relate differently to the same-age child when the parents are young adults and when they are of middle age. As it turned out, the average differences in sibling ages for the three groups were quite similar, ranging between 1.5 and 2.1 years, and restricted enough to dismiss age of offspring and parents as a confounding variable. Birth order in the critical brother-sister group also could be ruled out as a source of bias in parental response. Sisters were born first in 46 percent of the cases, and brothers born first in 54 percent.

Sibling pairs were most frequently seen together, occasionally with a second pair. When circumstances did not allow for this, sibs were tested separately. The session consisted of two rating procedures. Subjects were given the ACL and asked to select their fathers' most characteristic behaviors by choosing 75 adjectives from among the 300 on the ACL. Following this, the same type of rating was obtained for the mother on a new ACL form.

Answering the question of whether daughters and sons perceive each parent differently required that we first establish a baseline for expected agreement. These stereotypes for fathers in general and mothers in general were generated by comparing about 500 different combinations of parent descriptions from unrelated subjects in the study. These comparisons told us about how much agreement would be expected in parental characteristics when two subjects are actually describing different fathers or different mothers. Average father-stereotype scores ranged between 35 and 37 for the three sib groups, and the stereotype scores for mothers fell between 31 and 33. Agreement scores between sibs when providing general descriptions of the same parent, reported in table 7.10 represent the extent to which agreement between sibs exceeded stereotype. The findings were the same no matter which parent was being considered. Brothers and sisters agree less with each other in selecting the characteristics of either parent compared to sets of brothers ($p < .005$) or sisters ($p < .025$). The lack of acquiescence between the son and daughter in describing the major characteristics of their father had been anticipated, fitting as it did the hypothesis that fathers differentiate their behaviors in keeping with the sex of the child. We were less prepared for the same effect in our analysis of the mother's rated behavior; the mother does differentiate her behavior, it would seem, at least with the late-adolescent son and daughter.

Table 7.10.   Agreement Regarding Parent Characteristics for Various Sibling Sex Combinations

Sex of Siblings	Father (Mean Agreements Beyond Stereotype)	Mother (Mean Agreements Beyond Stereotype)	Parents Parents Total
Brother-brother	11.88	10.50	22.38
Brother-sister	5.88	2.12	8.00
Sister-sister	8.64	9.00	17.64

The specific interest of our study was in the nature of the disagreement between brother and sister in describing their parents. To what extent can it be explained by their different views of the father's sex-role behaviors? Is the mother also viewed differently by the son and daughter as far as her sex-role behavior is concerned? The sex-role questions were considered by determining the number of masculine and feminine attributes assigned to each parent by sons and daughters using the behaviors included within the ACL sex-role scales as the criteria. The father, according to table 7.11, is described in different sex-role terms according to whether you ask the son or daughter. The son assigns more masculine than feminine attributes on the average, whereas the daughter identifies more feminine than masculine characteristics. (the interaction effect was significant at the 5 percent level.) The hypothesis proposing flexible sex-role behavior in the father governed by the sex of the child was supported.

In contrast to the differential perception of the father by the son and daughter, children of both sexes agreed about the sex-role attributes of the mother. Table

7.11 portrays identical descriptions of the mother's sex-role behavior by sons and daughters. Both describe her as much more feminine than masculine in the composition of her sex-role repertoire ($p < .001$). Male and female (college-age) children apparently elicit different behaviors from the mother, but for some reason this does not disturb the consistent sex-role picture of her held by both sons and daughters. This picture, by the way, is the same 1:2 ratio of masculine to feminine behaviors that was reported in an earlier chapter as characteristic of college females in general.

Table 7.11.   Masculine and Feminine Characteristics Assigned to Parents by Sons and Daughters

Sex of Parent and Child	Masculine		Feminine	
	N	M	N	M
Fathers				
Sons	33	10.29	33	7.71
Daughters	39	8.59	39	9.06
Mothers				
Sons	33	6.22	33	11.12
Daughters	39	6.33	39	11.24

A closer look at the specific sex-role behaviors attributed to fathers and mothers by our subjects sheds further light on the many questions that remain. Table 7.12 offers a summary of the ACL sex-role behaviors and the percentages of sons or daughters who listed each as a characteristic of the father and the mother. As might be expected, the column averages tell us the same thing as the previous analyses involving numbers of behaviors. Masculine behaviors were selected as characteristic of the father about 37 percent of the time by sons on the average and only 28 percent of the time by daughters taken on average. The percentage of sons selecting feminine attributes for the male parent (31 percent) was slightly lower than was true of daughters (33 percent).

Table 7.12.   Prevalence of Specific Sex-role Behaviors Attributed to Fathers and Mothers by Sons and Daughters

	Masculine Behaviors					Feminine Behaviors			
	F/S	F/D	M/S	M/D		F/S	F/D	M/S	M/D
aggressive	39	26	29	14	appreciative	61	60	61	54
arrogant	0	6	0	3	considerate	61	66	81	60
assertive	74	51	65	40	contented	32	37	32	29

Table 7.12 continued

	Masculine Behaviors					Feminine Behaviors			
	F/S	F/D	M/S	M/D		F/S	F/D	M/S	M/D
autocratic	19	3	6	3	cooperative	65	71	58	49
conceited	0	0	0	0	dependent	32	29	19	23
confident	84	74	52	43	emotional	23	11	81	71
cynical	0	6	6	3	excitable	35	14	45	40
deliberate	42	26	29	11	fearful	0	0	0	0
dominant	45	26	29	29	feminine	0	0	52	34
enterprising	61	29	19	29	fickle	0	0	10	14
forceful	55	29	39	23	forgiving	48	63	58	60
foresighted	45	34	45	26	friendly	81	74	84	69
frank	52	46	52	49	frivolous	0	0	3	3
handsome	39	37	0	6	helpful	65	69	58	57
hard-headed	26	17	29	23	modest	26	37	39	31
industrious	65	37	45	40	praising	16	34	39	34
ingenious	29	20	10	6	sensitive	29	49	55	57
inventive	35	23	19	23	sentimental	26	23	45	54
masculine	52	57	0	3	sincere	58	57	68	60
opportunistic	13	14	16	9	submissive	3	6	6	6
outspoken	32	9	35	23	sympathetic	29	34	65	54
self-confident	55	60	29	54	talkative	16	26	55	57
sharp-witted	29	40	23	14	timid	0	3	6	0
shrewd	32	14	19	9	warm	35	54	52	69
stern	32	37	6	14	worrying	23	11	45	57
strong	71	60	39	29					
tough	19	14	13	9					
vindictive	0	3	3	9					

NOTE: Prevalence figures represent percentages of sons or daughters who selected particular attributes as characteristic of the parent. F/S = fathers described by sons, F/D = fathers described by daughters, M/S = mothers described by sons, M/D = mothers described by daughters.

Table 7.13, listing the behaviors distinguishing the perceptions of the father by sons and daughters, represents a breakdown of the percentage figures of table 7.12 using a 10 percent differential as a convenient decision point. These lists indicate that the son's view of his father is permeated by his impressions of masculine forceful domination and control ("aggressive, assertive, autocratic, confident, dominant, forceful, outspoken, strong") and goal attainment ("deliberate, enterprising, foresighted, industrious, inventive, shrewd"). The sex-role behaviors that dominate the daughter's description of her father ("forgiving, modest, praising, sensitive, talkative, warm") are feminine qualities conducive to the positive relationship that she is likely to enjoy with him. This level of analysis probably takes us about as far as this type of data can in understanding why the primary identification of the son with his father is more likely to promote a masculine, instrumental sex-role identity than does a primary paternal identification by the daughter.

Table 7.13.   Characteristic Paternal Sex-Role Behaviors as Rated by Sons and Daughters

Sex-Role Behaviors More Frequently Identified by Sons		Sex-Role Behaviors More Frequently Identified by Daughters		Sex-Role Behaviors Identified Equally by Sons and Daughters	
Masculine	Feminine	Masculine	Feminine	Masculine	Feminine
aggressive	emotional	sharp-witted	forgiving	arrogant	appreciative
assertive	excitable		modest	conceited	considerate
autocratic	worrying		praising	cynical	contented
confident			sensitive	frank	cooperative
deliberate			talkative	handsome	dependent
dominant			warm	hard-headed	fearful
enterprising				ingenious	feminine
forceful				masculine	fickle
foresighted				opportunistic	friendly
industrious				self-confident	frivolous
inventive				stern	helpful
outspoken				tough	sentimental
shrewd				vindictive	sincere
strong					submissive
					sympathetic
					timid

NOTE: A difference of 10 percent or more was used to define more frequent attribution by the son or daughter; attribution rates that differed by less than 10 percent were defined as equal.

The counterpart data of table 7.14, representing the perceived sex-role behaviors of the mother, offer a far more balanced picture. There is better agreement about the mother's characteristics and even when disagreements occur, there is no clear tendency for either the son or daughter to shade their descriptions in either a masculine or feminine direction. The only modest exception to this statement can be found in the son's description of his mother in more masculine terms than is true of the daughter. I suspect, based on another program of research into maternal control of the son, (see Heilbrun, 1973b) that this is largely reactive. Mothers may have to exert more strenuous efforts with teenage sons in order to maintain parental control than with daughters. It is noteworthy in this regard that the masculine terms more frequently chosen to describe mothers by sons are heavily weighted in favor of this interpretation: "aggressive, assertive, deliberate, forceful, outspoken, strong."

Table 7.14. Characteristic Maternal Sex-Role Behaviors as Rated by Sons and Daughters

Sex-Role Behaviors More Frequently Identified by Sons		Sex-Role Behaviors More Frequently Identified by Daughters		Sex-Role Behaviors Identified Equally by Sons and Daughters	
Masculine	Feminine	Masculine	Feminine	Masculine	Feminine
aggressive	considerate	enterprising	warm	arrogant	appreciative
assertive	emotional	self-confident	worrying	autocratic	contented
deliberate	feminine			conceited	cooperative
forceful	friendly			confident	dependent
foresighted	sympathetic			cynical	excitable
outspoken				dominant	fearful
shrewd				frank	fickle
strong				handsome	forgiving
				hard-headed	frivolous
				industrious	helpful
				ingenious	modest
				inventive	praising
				masculine	sensitive
				opportunistic	sentimental
				sharp-witted	sincere
				stern	submissive
				tough	talkative
				vindictive	timid

NOTE: A difference of 10 percent or more was used to define more frequent attribution by the son or daughter; attribution rates that differed by less than 10 percent were defined as equal.

IMPLICATIONS OF THE FINDINGS

The research effort directed toward elucidating female identification can, I hope, contribute something to the understanding of sex-role behavior beyond our attempts to resolve an intriguing paradox. In this concluding section I will elaborate on a few possibilities that seem worth investigating because of their social significance.

Female homosexuals were found to be predominantly masculine in their sex-role status (Heilbrun & Thompson, 1977). To the extent that identification is to be used to explain the masculinization of this lesbian group, our findings within the paradox studies would suggest that a father identification without an accompanying male-gender identification was the common developmental pattern. This conclusion is based on two dispositions that would influence relationships with male peers. One would be a deficiency in vicarious (empathic) experience when males were concerned, and the other would be a hypercompetitiveness that is triggered by males as well as other females. Heterosexual experience should prove problematic when the female's ability to enjoy male sexual arousal vicariously is compromised and when she must perform in concert with a partner who usually represents a stimulus to competition. While these deterrents to female sexual gratification with males would not in themselves destine a woman to a homosexual choice, they certainly would narrow the alternatives so as to make sexual activity with other females more attractive. The possible implications of our identification research for the sexual behavior of females can be taken one step further. If homosexual choice could be mediated by the girl's pattern of parent/gender identification, why could less dramatic sexual adjustment outcomes, such as deficiencies in satisfaction within heterosexual relationships, not be a common derivative?

Encouragement for seeking a more subtle effect of female identifications in the curtailment of sexual interest in males rather than a full commitment to homosexuality can be found in data originally included in the Heilbrun and Thompson (1977) study of homosexuality. Scores of unselected college subjects on the Heterosexuality Scale of the ACL, reflecting the degree of interest shown in social/sexual relationships with the opposite sex, were considered in combination with the parent identification and role consistency measures. Looking at these data in terms of the parent identification/role consistency groupings employed in our research, the figures in table 7.15 represent the prevalence of college females in each group having high and low heterosexual interests. Given a primary identification with the father, male-gender-identified (high-role-consistent) women tended to score high on the scale of heterosexual interests and women without this gender preference tended to score low. It was the latter group for which a curtailment of heterosexuality was hypothesized. The mother-identification data, which provided a control analysis, failed to reveal any relation between the three variables.

Table 7.15. Number of College Females with High and Low Heterosexual Interests as a Function of Parent Identification and Role Consistency

Level of Heterosexuality	Father Identification		Mother Identification	
	High Role Consistency	Low Role Consistency	High Role Consistency	Low Role Consistency
High (above-median)	17	8	13	10
Low (below-median)	8	19	10	12
	$p < .01$		Not significant	

NOTE: Cutting scores for identification, consistency, and heterosexuality were 50, .480, and 51, respectively.

We did not determine in our studies whether the woman who identified with her father but not vicariously with males in general was responsive to other females; this was not tested. We did find that she was competitive with her own sex. Thus we have a more convincing argument for problems in heterosexual behavior than we do for satisfaction in homosexual behavior, which one might expect would involve vicarious responsiveness to females. This leads me to speculate that yet another deviant sexual choice, prostitution, could be even more directly linked to the identification variables. The instrumental and dispassionate use of sex for profit and disdain for the customer that are frequently encountered among prostitutes may represent derivatives of the masculine, nonempathic, competitive attributes of the father-identified female who is not vicariously responsive to either sex. Homosexuality and prostitution in females, then, may be distinguishable by the gender-identification variable. While both choices could be associated to some degree with a masculine identity based on a primary identification with the father, homosexuality should more likely involve a female-gender identification and prostitution no gender identification at all.

REFERENCES

Bandura, A. Social learning through imitation. In M. R. Jones (Ed.), *Nebraska symposium on motivation.* Lincoln: University of Nebraska Press, 1962.

Bandura, A., Ross, D., & Ross, S. A. A comparative test of the status envy, social power, and secondary reinforcement theories of identification learning. *Journal of Abnormal and Social Psychology,* 1963, **67,** 527–34. (a)

Bandura, A., Ross, D., & Ross, S. A. Vicarious reinforcement and imitation. *Journal of Abnormal and Social Psychology,* 1963, **67,** 601–7. (b)

Bronfenbrenner, U. The study of identification through interpersonal perception. In R. Tagiuri & L. Petrullo (Eds.), *Person perception and interpersonal behavior.* Stanford: Stanford University Press, 1958.

Edwards, A. L. *Manual for the Edwards Personal Preference Schedule.* New York: Psychological Corporation, 1957.

Edwards, N. L. The relationship between empathic ability and role consistency. Unpublished master's thesis, University of Iowa, 1965.

Fand, A. B. Sex role and self concept. Unpublished doctoral dissertation, Cornell University, 1955.

Gough, H. G., & Heilbrun, A. B. *Manual for the Adjective Check List and the Need Scales for the ACL.* Palo Alto, Calif.: Consulting Psychologists Press, 1965.

Heilbrun, A. B. Validation of a need scaling technique for the Adjective Check List. *Journal of Consulting Psychology,* 1959, **23,** 347–51.

Heilbrun, A. B. Personality differences between adjusted and maladjusted college students. *Journal of Applied Psychology,* 1960, **44,** 341–46.

Heilbrun, A. B. Parental identification and college adjustment. *Psychological Reports,* 1962, **10,** 853–54. (a)

Heilbrun, A. B. Prediction of first year college drop-out using ACL Need Scales. *Journal of Counseling Psychology,* 1962, **9,** 58–63. (b)

Heilbrun, A. B. Social desirability and the relative validities of achievement scales. *Journal of Consulting Psychology,* 1962, **26,** 383–86. (c)

Heilbrun, A. B. Parent model attributes, nurturant reinforcement, and consistency of behavior in adolescents. *Child Development,* 1964, **35,** 151–67.

Heilbrun, A. B. The measurement of identification. *Child Development,* 1965, **36,** 111–27. (a)

Heilbrun, A. B. An empirical test of the modeling theory of sex-role learning. *Child Development,* 1965, **36,** 789–99. (b)

Heilbrun, A. B. Parental identification and the patterning of vocational interests in college males and females. *Journal of Counseling Psychology,* 1969, **16,** 342–47.

Heilbrun, A. B. Identification and behavioral effectiveness during late adolescence. In E. D. Evans (Ed.), *Adolescents: Readings in behavior and development.* Hinsdale, Ill.: Dryden Press, 1970.

Heilbrun, A. B. Parent identification and filial sex-role behavior: The importance of biological context. In J. Cole (Ed.), *Nebraska symposium on motivation.* Lincoln: University of Nebraska Press, 1973. (a)

Heilbrun, A. B. *Aversive maternal control: A theory of schizophrenic development.* New York: Wiley, 1973. (b)

Heilbrun, A. B., Bateman, C. P., Heilbrun, K. L., & Herson, A. M. Retrospections of mother: The effect of time interval upon perception. *Journal of Genetic Psychology,* in press.

Heilbrun, A. B., & Fromme, D. K. Parental identification of late adolescents and level of adjustment: The importance of parent model attributes, ordinal position, and sex of the child. *Journal of Genetic Psychology,* 1965, **107,** 49–59.

Heilbrun, A. B., Kleemeier, C., & Piccola, G. Developmental and situational correlates of achievement behavior in college females. *Journal of Personality,* 1974, **42,** 420–36.

Heilbrun, A. B., & Landauer, S. P. Stereotypic and specific attributions of parental characteristics by late-adolescent siblings. *Child Development,* 1977, **48,** 1748–51.

Heilbrun, A. B., Piccola, G., & Kleemeier, C. Male sex-gender identification: A source of achievement deficit in college females. *Journal of Personality,* 1975, **43,** 678–92.

Heilbrun, A. B., & Thompson, N. L. Sex-role identity and male and female homosexuality. *Sex Roles: A Journal of Research,* 1977, **3,** 65–79.

Horner, M. S. Sex differences in achievement motivation and performance in competitive and noncompetitive situations. Unpublished doctoral dissertation, University of Michigan, 1968.

James, W. Internal versus external control of behavior as a basic variable in learning theory. Unpublished doctoral dissertation, Ohio State University, 1957.

Johnson, M. M. Sex-role learning in the nuclear family. *Child Development,* 1963, **34,** 319–33.

Johnson, M. M. Fathers, mothers, and sex typing. *Sociological Inquiry,* 1975, **45,** 15–26.

Maccoby, E. E., & Jacklin, C. N. *The psychology of sex differences.* Stanford: Stanford University Press, 1974.

Murray, H. A. *Explorations in personality: A clinical and experimental study of fifty men of college age.* New York: Oxford University Press, 1938.

Parsons, T. Social structure and the development of personality: Freud's contribution to the integration of psychology and sociology. *Psychiatry,* 1958, **21,** 321–40.

Parsons, T., & Bales, R. F. *Family, socialization, and interaction process.* Glencoe, Ill.: Free Press, 1955.

Sopchak, A. L. Parental "identification" and "tendency toward disorders" as measured by the Minnesota Multiphasic Personality Inventory. *Journal of Abnormal and Social Psychology,* 1952, **47,** 159–65.

Strong, E. K., Jr. *Manual for the Strong Vocational Interest Blank.* Palo Alto, Calif.: Consulting Psychologists Press, 1959.

Chapter 8

Some Reflections on Future Research and Social Applications

Writing a book such as this is a sobering experience. Two years ago when the work began I had in mind a treatise that was both sweeping and profound, as I suppose most authors do when they anticipate recording their views on a particular topic. I have accomplished neither objective, but I take consolation in knowing many reasons why this was not possible. The difference between the license for opinion that pervades most books and conferences on the roles of males and females in our society and the constraints on a book that depends fully on the data of research is vast. To further restrict oneself to evidence evolving from a single program of research accentuates the matter. Overshadowing all else, in my opinion, is the fact that our knowledge of the sex roles and their interrelations with other social variables is so limited at present as to defy generalized revelations *unless* all pretenses of scientific verification are relinquished.

Concentration upon my own research in this book did yield some advantages, as I had anticipated it would. Methodological consistency, systematic investigation of questions, and replication of results are luxuries not readily found when research emanating from many laboratories is considered. The data have been the source of several new insights about sex-role behavior; only time will tell whether these will prove useful additions to sex-role theory.

Two final objectives remain before the work of writing this book is completed. If research is going to contribute to the increasingly comprehensive theory of sex-role behavior that lies ahead, the sophistication of the questions to be asked and the methodologies by which the answers are to be found must keep pace. Certainly all social scientists who take a serious interest in sex-role behavior would share this sentiment. In the next section I will point out several directions that sex-role research may follow in the future that appear promising to me. As has been the case throughout the book, I will restrict myself to recommendations for which suggestive data can be mobilized. The final section of this chapter will be devoted to what little social commentary this book offers.

TRENDS IN FUTURE RESEARCH

Research into the Consequences of Sex-Role Status

The mind is making a comeback as a central construct in psychology. Shorn of the naive methodologies that characterized the early study of how people think, cognition has reemerged as a respectable area of investigation. More likely than not, cognitive functions will now be described in terms of information and how it is acquired, processed, and stored for later use by the individual. The human as computer is the popular and not totally inappropriate analogy, whether explicitly stated or not.

There are two ways that cognitive variables can be studied. They can be examined as an end in itself in an attempt to further expand functional knowledge of a host of cognitive variables—attention, perception, any number of processing variables (such as judgment, problem solving, or defensiveness), memory, and more. The second and more complicated way of studying cognition is to consider its role in the mediation of behavior. One of the unique things about humans is that thinking will occur sometime between a salient environmental cue and responsive activity. While the quantity and quality of cognition may vary drastically, no one should debate the fact that we are aware, that we interpret, and that our interpretations of environmental events may play a critical role in determining the response that occurs. Others before now have stressed the importance of considering cognitive mediation if we are going to progress toward a comprehensive understanding of human behavior (Bandura, 1978; Mischel, 1977). Scientific psychological inquiry soon may be ready to turn this corner.

What has this to do with sex-role research? Consider that individual sex-role attributes, viewed either as broad types (androgynous, masculine, feminine, undifferentiated) or in terms of the more specific behaviors comprising them, represent dispositions to respond in predictable ways given appropriate cues from the environment. This is the level at which our research into the consequences of sex-role status has been pitched up to this point. Someone whom we have identified as a masculine person (disposition) should, when faced with an infringement of his rights (environmental cue), respond assertively to correct the situation (in a masculine way). That our predictions frequently do not hold up can be understood in part by the fact that the person's interpretation of the situation plays a vital role in whether his ultimate behavior will correspond to prediction. Is the infringement actually interpreted by the individual as such? If it is, will an assertive response in this particular situation promise to gain more than it will lose? Given some way of anticipating how this particular individual would interpret this type of circumstance, the psychologist could do a better job of predicting response from knowledge of sex-role status.

Situational determinism can be carried too far in this scheme of things, to the point where no prediction from sex role is held to ever be possible without knowing how each specific individual will construe each specific situation. Sometimes sex-role dispositions will transcend situational differences. Furthermore, we never know exactly what an individual will think before a situation arises, as prediction would require. What psychological research must do is identify typical ways of thinking just as we have previously established typical modes of stereotypic social behavior. By putting the two together, we should be better able to anticipate sex-role behavior across situations. This approach should prove to be especially valuable for a fuller understanding of androgyny and undifferentiation. These sex roles by definition offer no clear basis for anticipating response to environmental cues, since masculine and feminine dispositions are balanced. Only the unverified assumption that the androgynous person will be blessed with the wisdom to make an adaptive choice between the two has allowed androgyny research and theory to ignore this logical dilemma. The data to be considered next are taken from a completed but not yet published study (Heilbrun, 1980) and represent a closer look at this assumption. This will hopefully provide a rudimentary example of what should become a new breed of sex-role research that considers cognitive variables potentially mediating between sex role and behavioral outcome.

The adaptive-choice assumption within androgyny theory holds that this sex-role status is advantageous to females and males alike, since it increases their behavioral potential in situations calling for stereotyped sex-role behaviors: when masculine behaviors are most appropriate, the androgynous person will behave in a masculine fashion, and when femininity is most timely, feminine behaviors will be drawn upon. There are problems with this line of reasoning. We can begin with the difficulties encountered in establishing what is or is not adaptive behavior. I have used terms such as *calling for, appropriate,* and *timely* to convey the idea that in a given situation one type of stereotypic sex-role behavior is likely to be more valuable (and thus more adaptive) than the other. I accept this basic premise on intuitive grounds, realizing at the same time that I have avoided any clear definition. The question is, appropriate for whom: the androgynous person? the object of social transaction? some supraordinate social unit, such as the family or community? The problem of defining adaptive behavior is not restricted to androgyny research and does not represent the central concern of our discussion. Accordingly, let us simply settle on a general understanding of adaptiveness for present purposes that embraces the idea of a response that maximizes the positive reinforcements available to the responder while at the same time benefiting or, at least, not disadvantaging others.

Even if it is granted that the presence of both masculine and feminine dispositions within the same individual opens the way to a more flexible demonstration of sex-role behaviors, it is apparently assumed by those who presuppose the value of androgyny that the individual will judiciously select the more adaptive choice from the expanded repertoire when given an option. This would not be difficult to accept if androgynous people were routinely graced with the motivation to analyze and an ability to diagnose social situations. However, what if the person were a dolt who rarely gave a second thought to why people behave as they do or what social situations mean or call for? Given androgyny and restricted intraception and social insight, we might have reason to expect consistent misapplication of stereotypic behaviors across situations. As a beginning, the adaptive-choice assumption needs to be examined to determine whether androgynous males and females demonstrate the requisite cognitive qualities for making judicious choices between masculine and feminine alternatives across situations.

The investigation actually included three bodies of data: (1) self-esteem comparisons for androgynous and other sex types to verify that androgyny is adaptive for the two sexes (discussed earlier in this book); (2) comparison of the level of intraception and social insight for androgynous subjects and other sex roles; and (3) consideration of personal defensiveness as a possible explanation for the results obtained in the first two bodies of data.

Sex-Role Status and Expressive and Instrumental Self-Esteem. Emory undergraduates were asked to consider how satisfied they were with three types of personal relationships: family, peers in general, and heterosexual in particular. These three ratings were combined to provide the person's self-evaluation of expressive competence. Similarly, rated success in meeting academic goals and in making progress toward a career were combined to serve as an instrumental self-esteem score. Since these self-esteem scores were discussed at some length earlier in the book, only a brief summary of these data will be provided here.

Scales ranged from 1 to 10, with higher scores representing greater satisfaction. Ratings of importance attributed to each area of accomplishment were also obtained; no importance was indicated by 0, some importance by 1, and great importance by 2. The self-esteem score for a given area was obtained by multiplying both scores, and could range by this system from 0 to 20. Expressive self-esteem, in turn, could range from 0 to 60, instrumental self-esteem from 0 to 40, and instrumental/expressive self-esteem from 0 to 100. The actual range of overall self-esteem ratings extended from 17 to 98.

The average ages for both the 69 males and 105 females fell between 18 and 19 years of age. The ACL was administered along with the rating scales to provide the sex-role estimates. The question being asked in straightforward: do androgynous individuals hold themselves in higher self-esteem with regard to expressive and instrumental activities than peers evidencing other sex roles? General instrumental/expressive self-esteem means are found in table 8.1.

Table 8.1. Mean Ratings of Instrumental-Expressive Self-Esteem for College Males and Females

Sex of Subject	Sex-Role Status							
	Androgynous		Masculine		Feminine		Undifferentiated	
	N	M	N	M	N	M	N	M
Males	16	61.69	19	60.05	18	61.44	16	54.06
Females	19	72.11	35	66.97	32	60.88	19	65.47

NOTE Potential range of scores from 0 to 100.

Analysis of variance for the male data revealed no differences among the four groups; androgyny in males was not associated with higher self-esteem. The female data were a different matter. A significant effect for masculinity ($p < .05$) was noted statistically, but also a suggestive ($p < .10$) interaction. Examination of the average ratings for females indicates that both effects can be attributed to the high self-esteem of androgynous females and the low self-esteem of the feminine group. Androgynous women expressed higher instrumental/expressive self-esteem than all other women combined ($p < .05$).

The conclusion emerging from the first part of this investigation was that androgynous college women view themselves as more capable than their peers in attaining goals and developing quality relationships in keeping with their own priorities, but that androgyny in college males does not offer a special advantage. Thus it should be possible to demonstrate, if common assumption is to be encouraged, that the female with androgynous sex-role potential is also especially endowed with those cognitive skills that would facilitate judicious display of masculine and feminine behaviors across situations with varying demand characteristics. The same expectation would not be held for androgynous males.

Sex-Role Status and Level of Intraception and Social Insight. Effective social behavior presumably depends to some extent on the person's ability to understand situational demands and to bring to bear available responses that will meet those demands in a mutually satisfying way. Androgynous sex-role status presumably fulfills the latter requirement—an expanded availability of responses to meet varying situational demands. We have been led to predict that for the androgynous female this expanded repertory is coupled with the level of cognitive skills that would be required to understand situational demands and to make the discriminations necessary for deploying appropriate stereotyped behaviors. No such case for the androgynous male could be made based on the self-esteem findings.

The potential for social understanding was considered in terms of two variables. Intraception represents the extent to which individuals reflect upon the meaning of their behavior or the behavior of others, the motives behind an action rather than the action itself. The Intraception Scale from the ACL (Gough & Heilbrun, 1965) was used to measure this variable. No validity evidence is available, so the personality characteristics included in the scale are listed in table 8.2 so that readers may decide for themselves whether the items adequately depict the correlates of intraception.

Table 8.2. Items Included on the Intraception Scale of the ACL

Plus Items	Minus Items
alert	fault-finding
calm	hard-hearted
clear-thinking	indifferent
considerate	intolerant
curious	opinionated
fair-minded	self-centered
foresighted	shallow
forgiving	
imaginative	
insightful	
intelligent	
logical	
mature	
methodical	
rational	
reasonable	
reflective	
sensitive	
serious	
sympathetic	
thoughtful	
tolerant	
understanding	

The second cognitive variable, social insight, represents the extent to which the individual can accurately diagnose social situations. The Chapin Test of Social Insight (Chapin, 1942) was used to estimate this ability. This test includes a series of social vignettes and multiple-choice solutions from among which the subject must select the most insightful commentary or wisest choice of action.

The purpose of this test, according to Chapin, is to measure the ability to recognize in any situation the psychological dynamics underlying a behavior and the solution necessary to resolve the situation and to bring it to a constructive solution. Gough (1965) has reviewed the validational evidence for the Chapin, which he considers to be impressive.

It is not difficult to conceive of intraception and social insight as being relatively independent of each other. For example, one could think long and hard about the meaning of behavior but do so without any real ability to recognize what is going on (high intraception/low social insight); similarly, one could be quite socially insightful but have little motivation to think about the underlying dynamics and nuances of meaning in most situations. Gough (1965) reports a median correlation of but .04 between the Chapin and his own Psychological-Mindedness Scale from the California Psychological Inventory (Gough, 1957), developed as a measure of the same variable described for the Intraception Scale. Looking ahead to our own data, the Chapin and Intraception Scale scores also correlated .04. Both statistics would lead to the conclusion that intraception and social insight vary independently of each other.

A typical Emory undergraduate sample of 48 males and 106 females was drawn for this study. The Chapin and the ACL were group-administered in a test battery, and a laboratory session followed within two weeks. (The laboratory data will be reported in the next section.) Our interest is in the intraception and Chapin scores for the four sex-role groups defined by the usual median-split procedures (table 8.3). Analysis of variance for the male data revealed significant effects for both intraception and social insight. In the former case, high-feminine males were higher in intraception than low-feminine males ($p < .05$), and, in the latter case, high-masculine males were more insightful than their low-masculine

Table 8.3. Intraception and Social Insight Scores by Sex-Role Status

Sex of Subject and Cognitive Variable	Androgynous		Masculine		Feminine		Undifferentiated	
	N	M	N	M	N	M	N	M
Males	10		15		13		10	
Intraception		57.00		50.60		55.23		48.90
Social insight		21.60		22.22		16.23		19.90
Intraception × social insight		3,050.40		2,760.07		2,367.31		2,459.00
Females	16		27		26		17	
Intraception		54.94		47.56		51.27		51.06
Social insight		19.62		21.15		19.58		20.76
Intraception × social insight		2,701.12		2,509.77		2,513.12		2,654.00

counterparts ($p < .02$). Androgynous males were the only sex type high on both variables, combining as they did the intraception of the high-feminine male and the social insight of the high-masculine male.

Since individual competence in social cognition has been proposed as dependent on the combination of intraception and social insight, a score reflecting this combination was derived by multiplying the two scores for each subject. To do this it was necessary to convert Chapin raw scores into standard T-scores with a mean of 50 and standard deviation of 10, the same as the Intraception Scale. This added step ensured that each score would have the same weight within the multiplicative function. Table 8.3 presents the mean social cognition (intraception × social insight) scores for the sex-role groups, and androgynous males emerged as the most competent. Analysis of variance of the male multiplicative scores identified level of masculinity as being the only reliable effect ($p < .05$), with higher masculinity being associated with higher scores. However, comparison of the mean social cognition score achieved by the androgynous males with that of the other males combined (2,546.47) resulted in a marginally significant ($p < .06$) difference. This left us with anomalous findings concerning the androgynous male. His cognitive potential for effective situational deployment of an extended repertoire of sex-role behaviors was greater than that of males demonstrating alternative sex roles, yet androgyny in males was not associated with higher self-ratings of attainment in valued instrumental and expressive activities.

The female data of table 8.3 offered as few significant effects as the male data offered many. There were no significant variations among the sex-role groups in level of intraception, social insight, or the product of intraception and insight. The only finding worthy of note was a significantly higher ($p < .05$) intraception score for androgynous females compared to the average for the remaining sex-role groups combined (49.79). Thus to the extent that both intraception and social insight are required for effective selection of social options by the androgynous person, these results appear as unpredictable in light of prior self-esteem findings as were those for the males. The androgynous female, uniquely high in her instrumental/expressive self-esteem, did not emerge as exceptional in her cognitive potential for effective deployment of sex-role behaviors across situations.

Sex-Role Status and Defensiveness. There are several ways that the inconsistencies between the two sets of data reported thus far could be treated. One would involve reminding ourselves that the self-esteem ratings may be so subjectively biased that their worth as indicators of actual competence is compromised. However, before we dismiss the self-appraisals as subjectively capricious, we should recall that something akin to the converse of the self-esteem findings was found when actual competence levels were compared. Androgynous females expressed high self-esteem; highly competent females displayed an exceptional level of androgyny. Males who were androgynous did not rate their own competency as exceeding that of other sex roles; similarly, highly competent males were not exceptionally androgynous relative to average campus males.

The inconsistencies between the first two bodies of data could be also rationalized by questioning whether social insight and intraception are important cognitive traits underlying effective response to varying situations. My own persuasion is that these variables have an almost incontestable bearing on how skillfully people engage in instrumental and expressive activities, although the measures we used are not as powerful as one would like.

The most intriguing explanation for the inconsistencies between androgyny, gender, cognitive potential for effective social behavior, and social competence is that some further unidentified moderator variable (besides the social cognition variables) is exerting influence. If this were so and the moderator were brought to light, some reasonable interpretation of the sex-linked results would then be possible. The third set of data, bearing on the subject's level of defensiveness, represented one candidate among many for the role of cognitive moderator. This variable was selected for investigation because of my vague conviction that defensiveness exerts a dominant influence on human social behavior. It also promised to serve a moderator role at either extreme. If a moderate level of defensiveness is considered optimal, either the vulnerability that attends having weak defenses against ego threat or the perceptual distortion associated with being hyperdefensive could limit social cognitive potential or compromise actual social competence. If no priori assumptions are made about an optimal level of defensiveness, very different and much more positive expectations could be generated at the extremes. Being nondefensive might be thought of as a virtue, allowing the individual the opportunity to respond to situations without "hang-ups." At the other extreme, strong defenses might be expected to facilitate the self-confidence and self-acceptance that are observed so frequently in successful people. Obviously, the theoretical rationale for defensiveness as a cognitive moderator was somewhat slack; sometimes as a researcher you have to get lucky.

Psychological defenses, as we have studied them, are considered to be cognitive behaviors that allow the individual to maintain a sense of personal worth. They include a number of ways of processing information about oneself so as to expand the positive implications or reduce the negative implications. The different approaches taken by people to defend themselves—and this seems to be a nearly universal human quality—are thought of as defensive styles in my work and as legitimate aspects of personality. The research conducted in my laboratory to date (Heilbrun, 1972; Heilbrun, 1977; Heilbrun, 1978a; Heilbrun & Schwartz, 1979; Heilbrun & Schwartz, in press) supports such a view. The interested reader is referred to the cited papers for more extended discussions of the three defensive styles studied thus far (projective, repressive, and rationalizing) and the standard laboratory paradigms that have been devised to sample the different ways people deal with evaluative information about themselves.

The forty-eight males and eighty-six female college subjects from whom the intraception/social insight data were collected also served as laboratory subjects in the study of personal defensiveness. They were required to consider the descriptiveness of sixty-six adjectives from the ACL for their own behavior; this number inadvertently included six masculine and nine feminine terms, slightly more than you would expect by chance only in the latter case. The laboratory paradigms structured the subject's processing of the ACL terms so that we could determine the extent to which individuals:

1. Denied negative attributes in themselves and assigned them to others (projective style of defense);
2. Forgot negative attributes that they previously admitted were self-characteristic (repressive style of defense);
3. Changed the desirability values assigned to behaviors so as to make them more positive or less negative when they are personal attributes and just the opposite when they are not (rationalizing style of defense).

Scores for these three defensive styles were converted into standard T-scores with the average for each set at 50 and standard deviation of 10. These scores show very low intercorrelations (ranging between $-.01$ and $+.34$), implying that people may combine these characteristic styles of defense in any number of ways, including utilizing all or none of them. Since our interest was in overall level of defensiveness rather than in specific styles, these scores were combined into a single defensiveness score for analysis. Table 8.4 records the averages for this combined score of the male and female sex-role groups. Standard analysis of variance comparisons revealed no significant effects for men and one effect for women: high-feminine women were more highly defended than low-feminine ($p < .05$). Our preplanned interest, however, was in the androgynous males and females. It was these groups that had provided the relational inconsistencies for which we were seeking explanation in a moderator variable. The male and female androgynous groups were the deviant groups as far as personal defensive-

Table 8.4. Mean Level of Defensiveness for Various Sex-Role Groups

Sex of Subject	Androgynous		Masculine		Feminine		Undifferentiated	
	N	M	N	M	N	M	N	M
Males	10	141.70	15	150.87	13	153.85	10	152.80
Females	16	159.56	27	149.37	26	150.35	17	145.06

ness was concerned, both with respect to the other sex roles and to each other. Androgynous males demonstrated a very low level of defensiveness (141.70) and androgynous females a very high level (159.56), and the difference in means achieved significance ($p < .05$).

The interpretation that I currently place on these results is that androgynous males, despite their exceptional cognitive potential for effective behavior relative to other men, are limited to some extent in realizing this potential by inadequate defenses that leave them vulnerable to dilemmas of self-worth. In contrast, androgynous females, without exceptional cognitive potential for effective behavior compared to other women, perform beyond prediction since they are so highly defended. The added confidence that accompanies the denial of limitations may be a major factor in the achievement of androgynous women. Whatever the meaning may be, defensiveness stands as a cognitive moderator that may help us understand why males and females show different relational patterns between androgyny, social cognition, and realization of their potential as effective human beings.

Research into the Antecedents of Sex-Role Status

The coverage of research into possible antecedents of sex-role behavior in this book has been restricted to one program of investigation into parent identification as a modeling process. The potential contribution of other psychological (learning), physiological, and sociological conditions to eventual sex-role status is obvious, as is the recommendation that such research be pursued. I will restrict myself in this section to suggestions for one avenue of parent identification research that may prove profitable, namely, finding behaviors other than sex role that are mediated by identification with particular parent models and then considering these variables in combination with sex-role status. A more comprehensive picture of the contribution made by parent identification to the sex-role development of the child should then be possible.

Parent Identification and Attentional Styles. The point already has been made that cognitive variables are receiving new emphasis as moderators of behavior— that the way people interpret and process information plays a role in their response to a particular situation. A study has been described that, consistent with this view, revealed how androgyny may hold different implications for the two sexes because of distinct cognitive patterns found in androgynous males and females. The question of how the distinct patterns developed was left unanswered.

The possibility that cognitive style may be influenced by parent identification was revealed by sifting through previously unanalyzed data from a study conducted several years ago. The findings, although unexpected, turned out to be quite provocative. See if you agree. Attentional styles represent characteristic ways of deploying attention that influence the type and amount of stimulation to which the individual is responsive. The stimulation is converted into information that is processed and that may intermediate between situational cues and overt behavior.

There are many ways that attention deployment can be broken down, but the two that stand out as most basic are the external/internal and broad/narrow dimensions. The former are differences in the extent to which the person commits his attention to his external surroundings, as opposed to directing his attention to internal cues such as thought and bodily sensation. While everyone is capable of doing both, depending on circumstances, attentional style theory would propose that there are some who regularly emphasize one form of attention deployment over the other. On the other hand, broad/narrow differences describe the amount of stimulation across which attention ranges without respect to whether the focus is external or internal. Again, humans are capable of extending or narrowing the range depending on situational demands, but it is assumed that certain people routinely seek a great deal of stimulation whereas others seek far less. The broad/narrow dimension has been alluded to in the literature as "scanning" (Silverman, 1964), and some readers may recognize the internal/external distinction as having much the same meaning as the original constructs of introversion (interest directed inward) and extraversion (interest directed outward).

The measures from which our present findings were belatedly retrieved included the parent identification questionnaires described in the previous chapter and the Test of Attentional and Interpersonal Style, developed by Dr. Robert Nideffer at the University of Rochester and kindly made available to me. Only the first seventy-five items of the Nideffer questionnaire dealing explicitly with attentional styles were used. The forty-six male and forty-nine female Emory College subjects were asked to rate the frequency of personal experiences related to attention, and the seventy-five items were scored on the following scales:

1. *Broad external focus*. A high score indicates that the individual views himself or herself as dealing effectively with complex, rapidly changing environmental situations. (Example: "I am good at quickly analyzing complex situations around me such as how a play is developing in football or which of four or five kids started a fight.")

2. *Overloaded with external stimuli*. A high score suggests that the person has a problem dealing with complex environmental situations, becoming confused and having difficulty in selecting appropriate stimuli to respond to. (Example: "With so much going on around me it's difficult for me to think about anything for any length of time.")

3. *Broad internal focus*. A high score indicates that the individual brings together material in the form of thoughts and feelings, and deals effectively with

a large amount of information. (Example: "It is easy for me to bring together ideas from a number of different areas.")

4. *Overloaded by internal stimuli.* A high score identifies the person who responds inappropriately to the environment because of an inability to block out or break away from irrelevant thoughts or feelings. (Example: "I get caught up in my thoughts and become oblivious to what is going on around me.")

5. *Narrow effective focus.* A high score suggests that the person can concentrate and narrow attention when necessary, and is able to keep irrelevant stimuli from interfering. (Examples: "When I read it is easy to block out everything but the book." "It is easy for me to forget about problems by watching a good movie or by listening to music.")

6. *Reduced attentional focus.* A high score indicates that the individual responds inappropriately because attention is narrowed so much that important information is missed. (Example: "I focus on one small part of what a person says and miss the total message.")

Although the styles of attention described by the Nideffer scales do not correspond precisely with those generated by the internal/external and broad/narrow dimensions, the similarities outweigh the differences. The purpose of exploring the data at hand is not to evaluate how well these two typologies overlap, however. Rather, we will consider post hoc the pattern differences in Nideffer attentional style scores to see what they may collectively suggest as far as our two dimensions of attention deployment are concerned. In fact, our central interest is in identifying possible linkages between parent identification and styles of attention, however conceptualized.

Subjects were separated into those primarily identified with the male parent and with the female parent based upon the college norm for the Identification Scale ($T = 50$). The average attentional style scores, broken down by parent identification and sex, are presented in table 8.5. Analysis of variance conducted for each attentional variable identified a sex difference (son versus daughter) on four of the six. Males, no matter what their identification, achieved higher scores on "Broad internal focus" ($p < .01$), "Narrow effective focus" ($p < .005$), and "Reduced attentional focus" ($p < .01$), with females scoring higher on "Overloaded with external stimuli" ($p < .001$). Generally speaking, the sex differences portray males as more internally oriented in their deployment of attention and more effective in broad scanning of internal stimuli than females. Males also described themselves as more effective in external deployment of attention when narrow scanning is called for. On the scales representing problems associated with attentional styles, females appear to be paying the price for being more externally deployed by a greater tendency to become overloaded with surrounding stimulation in complex situations. Males, for their part, described problems associated with their internal deployment when they respond inappropriately because external stimuli have been missed.

Table 8.5. Average Attentional Style Scores for Males and Females Primarily Identified with Their Mothers and Fathers

| | Primary Parent Identification | | | |
| | Mother | | Father | |
Attentional Style	Sons (N = 21)	Daughters (N = 21)	Sons (N = 25)	Daughters (N = 28)
Broad external focus	14.33	16.19	14.84	15.07
Overloaded with external stimuli	19.62	23.29	18.24	21.57
Broad internal focus	19.00	16.67	19.80	17.96
Overloaded by internal stimuli	14.33	15.05	13.52	15.40
Narrow effective focus	27.10	22.14	26.12	24.64
Reduced attentional focus	28.81	22.52	25.24	25.86

Parent identification enters the picture in this analysis because interaction effects on two scales called attention to the fact that the sex differences were produced only by mother-identified subjects. Mother-identified males (27.10) scored considerably above mother-identified females (22.14) in "Narrow effective focus" ($p < .001$), while the difference between the two father-identified groups on this scale was negligible. Similarly, mother-identified males had a significantly ($p < .001$) higher mean (28.81) on "Reduced attentional focus" than their female counterparts, while the two corresponding father-identified group means were almost identical. The son's identification with the mother is associated with an attentional style that predisposes him to narrowly scan his surroundings, to his advantage when focused attention is called for and to his disadvantage as far as missing information that is needed to respond appropriately to his environment.

Thinking of this narrow external scanning style as a characteristic of mother-identified males (and as a cognitive moderator), previously unassimilated data can be brought together to add to our knowledge of sex-role development. We can explain, for example, how femininity in the male can be expected to have both beneficial and detrimental effects. Some years ago, the degree of control and nurturance attributed to the mother was found to predict the maternal identification of the college male (Heilbrun & Hall, 1964). The combination of high control and high nurturance, defining social power in this study, was found to predict identification with the female parent compared to the other control-nurturance patterns. Four years later (Heilbrun & Waters, 1968) it was reported that male college achievers described their mothers in terms of the same combination of high control and high nurturance relative to their less achieving male peers. The present analysis of attentional styles provides a link between these two sets of results. Maternal identification in the son may facilitate his development into an introverted "thinker," but moreover one who can effectively focus his attention on the task at hand by excluding irrelevant and distracting stimuli, a rather good formula for achievement in college.

So much for the good news about a son's identification with the mother—there is ample correlational evidence (Heilbrun, 1960; Heilbrun & Fromme, 1965) that cross-sex identification in college males brings personal problems too. To the extent that modeling after the female parent mediates femininity, we should be prepared for more bad news. Femininity in males (measured by the Bem Social Role Inventory) was found to be correlated with some rather clear indications of social maladjustment by Jones, Chernovetz, and Hansson (1978). Comparing masculine, feminine, and androgynous males and females, feminine college males were most clearly identified as being neurotic, low in self-esteem, problem drinkers, and sensitive to criticism. A likelihood of unsatisfactory social relations also can be inferred from the social insight scores reported in table 8.3. The very low scores of feminine males suggest a deficiency in social judgment that bodes poorly for their effectiveness in dealing with others. Now we have been given a potential moderator of the feminine males' defective social judgement and ineffective social behavior: an attentional style that so restricts his attention to situational cues that he fails to pick up information necessary for appropriate response.

Parent Identification, Behavioral Differentiation, and Androgyny. One consequence of concentrating on sex roles as we have in this book is that one can easily lose sight of the fact that these are only part of the behaviors characteristic of the individual. Furthermore, as androgyny is considered, we need to remind ourselves that this sex-role status represents a more differentiated developmental end-product than any of the others, but that androgyny may be only part of a general differentiation of behavior. In other words, the androgynous person may not only have a broader array of sex-role behaviors at his disposal but may also be more versatile in his non-sex role responses. Available data permit me to consider two questions relating to this possibility. The first, of course, is whether androgynous people are more generally differentiated as well. The second question is whether the origins of differentiation are to be found in identification with particular types of parent models.

Data to be reviewed here were obtained by reanalyzing ACL protocols used in prior studies described in this book. Differentiation of behavior will be defined in terms of the number of adjectives endorsed as self-characteristic on the 300-item ACL, keeping in mind that this number may vary as many as 200 within a research sample. First we will consider whether subjects identified as more androgynous by the ACL also check more behaviors unrelated to sex role or whether differentiation tends to be restricted to sex-role behaviors. Splitting a recent sample of forty-eight males and eighty-six females at their common T-score androgyny index median of 90, the number of ACL attributes endorsed by the high and low androgynous groups was determined. The endorsed attributes, in turn, were divided into those included on the sex-role scales and those not. As would be expected, males defined as androgynous had checked more sex-role attributes (M = 31.61) than their nonandrogynous counterparts (M = 19.44). Females followed suit, with the androgynous group selecting more sex-type behaviors as personal characteristics (M = 24.35) than the nonandrogynous group (M = 17.65). Our interest is in the number of non–sex-typed attributes endorsed by the two groups, and here we find that androgynous males also selected more personal attributes unrelated to sex type as personal attributes (M = 106.87) than was true of nonandrogynous males (M = 79.40). The female androgynous group also selected more non–sex-typed responses (M = 84.43) as personal characteristics than did nonandrogynous females (M = 71.11). The greater differentiation of non–sex-typed behaviors for androgynous men and women achieved statistical significance ($p < .001$). The answer to the first question is clearly positive: androgyny is part of a more general differentiated repertoire of behavior.

The ACL is an ideal instrument to investigate differentiation, since it incorporates a large number of behaviors and gives the subject the option of endorsing some while rejecting others as self-descriptive, rather than soliciting ratings of degree. There is a problem of inference when we interpret that ACL endorsements in terms of differentiation, however. The alternative interpretation—that the number of behaviors checked as self-characteristic is a test-taking variable (fluency)—cannot be dismissed. One could reason that some subjects are better able to specify more behaviors on the ACL than others because their self-concept is more clearly articulated. As long as the androgyny score and the differentiation score come from the same ACL and are both vulnerable to alternative interpretation, this argument cannot be resolved. However, if androgyny level is inferred from an independent instrument that is not susceptible to differences in fluency, the distinction between behavioral differentiation and articulation on the ACL can be critically evaluated. We did this by taking another sample of 149 ACLs completed by a college sample of sixty-three males and eighty-six females who also rated themselves on independent ten-point rating scales for instrumental and expressive orientations. The androgyny index was applied to these ratings and the androgyny scores were separated at the common median (16) for the two sexes. The same subjects also were split into high and low differentiated groups based on their median number of endorsements on the ACL (102). Nonparametric analysis was then performed for the proportion of androgynous subjects who endorsed more (N = 42) and fewer (N = 27) behaviors on the ACL as opposed to nonandrogynous subjects who were on the high (N = 33) and low (N = 47) endorsement side. These proportions differed ($p < .02$), providing evidence that test-taking fluency is not the critical factor in the relation between androgyny and expanded behavioral repertoires.

The second question concerned the relation between parent identification and general differentiation of behavior. The major basis for optimism that a relation might exist was a very speculative one. The parent model score, reflecting how well the parents represent conventional sex-role behaviors relative to one another, allows us to distinguish the degree to which identification models conform to stereotype. Androgynous models should be found among the less conforming parents, although the possibility exists that the sex roles could be so completely reversed by a set of parents that each displayed a homogeneous set of traits stereotypically assigned to the opposite sex. This is highly unlikely, however. What the data actually show when the model score is used in our identification research is that the nonstereotypic parent models, defined by median-split procedures, show an average score of about 4.50. In other words, our average nonstereotypic set of parents shows an even balance of stereotyped and nonstereotyped traits, at least suggestive of androgyny.

About the only question that can be considered with the data on hand is whether college males and females identified with a less stereotypic (and perhaps more androgynous) parent model show a greater general differentiation of behavior. A computation of the average number of behaviors endorsed as characteristic by the subject, broken down by subject sex, sex of the parent serving as primary identification model, and conventional/nonconventional sex-role status of the primary model (table 8.6), answered the question in the affirmative for males only. Men primarily identified with unconventional models, whether mother or father, endorsed more adjectives on the ACL than those modeling after conventional parents ($p < .005$). This finding is consistent with the assumptions that nonconventional parents are more androgynous, more androgynous parents are more differentiated, and sons tend to model this expanded repertory. Neither the sex of the model nor the conventionality of the model showed an effect as far as female differentiation was concerned. This sex difference points to the apparent unimportance of modeling for female differentiation. Future research along these lines might consider features of identification unique to the female that would confound the logical relation found for males. The sex-role reversal of conventional fathers with the daughter is a case in point.

Table 8.6. Average Number of Behaviors Endorsed as Characteristic by Male and Female Subjects Identified with Conventional or Unconventional Parent Models

	Primary Parent Identification[a]							
	Conventional Model[b]				Unconventional Model			
	Father		Mother		Father		Mother	
Sex of Subject	N	M	N	M	N	M	N	M
Males	42	92.48	40	87.02	21	107.71	37	105.59
Females	61	100.70	49	102.06	35	102.17	48	97.54

[a]Based upon whether score exceeded the college norm of T = 50.
[b]Based upon whether score fell between 0-6 (unconventional range) or 7-9 (conventional range).

The Multifactorial Nature of the Sex Roles

Sex-role research was invigorated in the 1970s by accord among social scientists that masculinity and femininity should be considered as independent dimensions. The next step in conceptualization of the sex roles that should filter into our research is to recognize the multifactorial nature of one or both roles. In a sense we are perpetrating the same kind of either-or error in our thinking when we consider masculinity or femininity as a homogeneous commodity that was true when we thought of people as being either masculine or feminine. There may be several ways a person can be masculine, for example, and this fact is lost when we reduce masculinity to a single dimension measured by any of the popular scaling procedures. Components of a given sex role may enter into very different relations with antecedents, correlates, or effects, and sex-role theory will remain at a more rudimentary level until our measurement procedures allow us to investigate the components separately as well as in combination, as we do now.

Harrington and Anderson (1980) point out yet another problem facing researchers who do not squarely face the problem of factorial complexity of the sex roles. Inconsistency of results among researchers is in part due to the lack of factorial correspondence among our measuring instruments:

If psychological masculinity and femininity are factorially complex constructs . . ., and if different indices reflect those factors in different proportions, empirical results may vary substantially from index to index depending upon the degrees to which the various indices reflect the several factors . . . we believe the factorial complexity of these constructs and indices deserves substantially more attention than it has received to date [pp. 30–31].

Others also have noted the likely factorial complexity of masculinity and femininity as these are represented by current measurement devices (Bem, 1979; Berzins, Welling, & Wetter, 1978).

Factorial complexity of sex-role scales is not simply a matter for conjecture, since it has been studied extensively by factor analytic procedures. Considering the arbitrary nature of this statistical procedure, it is surprising how much consensus there has been among researchers as far as the component structure of the sex roles is concerned. The masculine sex role has been consistently found to break down into multiple factors including two independent major components, dominance (assertiveness) and autonomy (independence). These results have been reported whether the factor analysis was based on responses to the BSRI, the PAQ, the PRF-ANDRO, the ACL, or various combinations of these instruments (Berzins, Welling, & Wetter, 1978; Edwards, 1978; Edwards, Gaa, & Liberman, 1978; Gaudreau, 1977; Pearson, 1980; Pedhazur & Tetenbaum, 1979). Femininity, on the other hand, has most frequently been reported by the same studies as having but one major factor, nurturance (sensitivity).

This summary of factor analytic studies should not be taken to mean that other factors have not been identified by investigators within the responses to masculine and feminine items. There is, however, little agreement between studies regarding what these are and, furthermore, these factors have tended to be far more restricted and less important than the dominance, autonomy, and nurturance factors. As sex-role measures become more comprehensive, additional factors may come into clearer focus. Given the current consensus regarding factorial structure of the sex roles, let us consider data from various perspectives to see whether any importance can be attached to this distillation of the masculine and feminine roles.

Sex-Role Components and Level of Competence. In order to proceed with this examination of sex-role component structure in college samples varying in personal competence, I found it necessary to capitalize on the fact that Dominance, Autonomy, and Nurturance Scales have long been available on the ACL (see Gough & Heilbrun, 1965). In fact, dominance and autonomy are two of the masculine scales and nurturance one of the feminine scales included in the parent identification model scoring procedure (Heilbrun, 1964). The necessity for this was forced on me by the simple fact that factor components identified within the ACL sex-role scales would not include a sufficient number of items to be reliable. The three nominally identical scales available on the ACL show ten-week test-retest reliabilities ranging from .76 to .85.

The ACL items included within the Dominance, Autonomy, and Nurturance Scales are listed in table 8.7, with marker items actually found to cluster on the three factors in the published factor analyses further identified by italics. To be ideally representative of factors emerging from factor analysis, these scales should be uncorrelated. The ACL manual (Gough & Heilbrun, 1965) reports scale intercorrelations based on 800 subjects: while independence is not realized (dominance-autonomy, $r = .32$; dominance-nurturance, $r = .13$; autonomy-nurturance, $r = -.44$), the correlations among the scales are low enough to satisfy present purposes.

Table 8.7. Items Included within the ACL Dominance, Autonomy, and Nurturance Scales

Dominance Scale		Autonomy Scale		Nurturance Scale	
Positive Items	Negative Items	Positive Items	Negative Items	Positive Items	Negative Items
active	apathetic	adventurous	cautious	*affectionate*	aggressive
aggressive	dependent	aggressive	conventional	appreciative	aloof
alert	dreamy	aloof	cooperative	conscientious	arrogant
ambitious	easy-going	argumentative	dependable	considerate	autocratic
argumentative	effeminate	arrogant	dependent	cooperative	bitter
assertive	fearful	assertive	meek	dependable	cold
autocratic	inhibited	autocratic	moderate	forgiving	cool
bossy	irresponsible	confident	obliging	*friendly*	cruel
capable	lazy	cynical	self-denying	generous	cynical
confident	meek	dissatisfied	spineless	*gentle*	distrustful
demanding	mild	egotistical	submissive	good-natured	egotistical
dependable	reserved	fault-finding	suggestible	*helpful*	fault-finding
determined	retiring	frank	tactful	kind	greedy
dominant	self-pitying	hard-headed	timid	*loyal*	hard-hearted
energetic	*shy*	headstrong	tolerant	obliging	hostile
enterprising	silent	hostile		outgoing	impatient
forceful	spineless	*independent*		patient	indifferent
independent	*submissive*	indifferent		peaceable	intolerant
industrious	suggestible	*individualistic*		pleasant	nagging
initiative	*timid*	irresponsible		*sensitive*	quarrelsome
intelligent	unambitious	opinionated		sentimental	rude
opinionated	unassuming	outspoken		*sincere*	sarcastic
organized	weak	rebellious		sociable	self-centered
outgoing	withdrawn	self-centered		soft-hearted	self-seeking
outspoken		self-confident		*sympathetic*	selfish
persistent		tactless		*tactful*	snobbish
planful		unconventional		thoughtful	stingy
resourceful		undependable		tolerant	suspicious
responsible		uninhibited		trusting	tactless
self-confident				*understanding*	unfriendly
strong				unselfish	unkind
				warm	vindictive

The first set of research questions that available data allowed us to examine concerned the nature of the relations between the three sex-role factors and personal effectiveness (level of adjustment) for the two sexes. Although no clear expectations were in evidence, two possibilities existed, either of which would support the usefulness of sex-role component analysis. Sex differences have been as much the rule as the exception throughout this book, and were certainly a possibility in this analysis. An even more interesting possibility would be that one masculine component differed from the other in its relation to competence level. The ACLs of 547 college students were considered, broken down into the now familiar competence groupings by sex:

1. *Low:* clients seeking assistance for personal problems at the campus mental health agency (100 males and 67 females);
2. *Intermediate:* random samples of college students (144 males and 186 females);
3. *High:* students selected as generally outstanding by campus administrators and other students (30 males and 20 females).

Table 8.8 summarizes the average dominance, autonomy, and nurturance scores for these six groups. Dominance varied monotonically with level of adjustment for both sexes; higher dominance scores were obtained as level of effectiveness increased for both males ($p < .001$) and females ($p < .001$). The same relation for males and females can also be observed for autonomy across adjustment levels—or, better said, the same lack of relation. College groups showing wide discrepancies in competence were equally autonomous. These two findings considered together offer clear testimony to the potential importance of studying factorial structure in masculinity. Apparently one of the major factors, dominance, contributes positively to personal effectiveness for both sexes, whereas the other, autonomy, demonstrates no systematic contribution whatsoever for either sex. Rather than asking whether more masculine people make a better

Table 8.8. Dominance, Autonomy, and Nuturance Levels for Males and Females at Three Levels of Adjustment

Sex-Role	Low	Intermediate	High
Dominance			
Males	43.66	49.66	58.87
Females	39.48	50.65	59.90
Autonomy			
Males	51.53	51.69	53.50
Females	53.16	52.49	52.65
Nurturance			
Males	48.11	50.27	53.93
Females	41.73	48.58	47.80

NOTE: These group averages derive from independent male and female norm tables with college means set at $T = 50$ and a standard deviation of 10.

personal adjustment, as investigators have up to this point, these findings suggest that the question be rephrased, What *type* of masculine person is more likely to be successful? At first glance it would appear that the masculine type of person who achieved this sex-role status through a strong show of independence is not a good bet for success. Masculinity based on the display of dominance, quite possibly coupled with autonomy, bodes well for success.

The nurturance means on table 8.8 interject a different note. While the nurturance differences across adjustment levels were significant for both males ($p < .05$) and females ($p < .005$), a distinct pattern of differences was found for each sex. Males showed progressively higher nurturance scores as more competent college students were considered, but the female variation was curvilinear. Poorly adjusted females were low on nurturance, but the two better-adjusted groups did not differ from each other, with means falling slightly below the norm. The female pattern suggests that deficient nurturance contributes to personal ineffectiveness but that high levels do not contribute to effectiveness. Does femininity relate to personal competence? This question, rephrased, would become, What are the differing functional relations between the nurturance component of femininity and levels of competence for college males and females? The curvilinear function for the women calls to mind the dissimulation study reported earlier in the book in which both sexes, but especially women, when asked to look maladjusted on the ACL showed a precipitous drop in Femininity Scale scores. When asked to look as good as possible, the Femininity Scale scores remained around the norm. The same curvilinearity is apparent in our present competence level analysis and these earlier dissimulation findings.

Parent Identification and Sex-Role Components in Female Androgyny. If sex-role component analysis proves to be a valuable avenue for understanding human competence, as our preliminary findings suggest, the interest of investigators would certainly be directed toward developmental antecedents of the sex-role factors. We already know two things about androgynous females on the campus: (1) they are successful in their own eyes and as appraised by others, and (2) they do not evidence any particular parent identification pattern relative to the other sex roles (Heilbrun, 1978b). Despite the discouraging start in elucidating the developmental origins of androgynous competence in women, the possibility remained that a given type of parent identification may mediate different component patterns when it does occur even though it is no more likely to occur than any other. We examined this possibility and its implications for competence by looking to see whether components of masculinity may serve as moderators between parent identification patterns and the adaptive quality of androgyny for females.

The parent identification questionnaire materials of 174 college females were broken down by familiar median-split procedures into those demonstrating the four patterns of primary parent identification: masculine father, feminine father, masculine mother, and feminine mother. Level of androgyny was determined by the index formula applied to raw scores and split at its median as well. Table 8.9 includes the average dominance and autonomy scores for the eight groups resulting from these assignment procedures. Inspection of these figures isolates just one identification pattern associated with high and essentially equal levels of both masculine components in the daughter: the androgynous woman with the masculine father. The only pattern rivaling it is the androgynous woman who has chosen the masculine mother as the primary identification model. There was one glaring difference between the two patterns. While androgynous women identified with the masculine father and the masculine mother were both highly autonomous (60.14 and 57.88, respectively; $p < .05$), only the masculine-father-identified group could be described as highly dominant (58.00 and 51.00, respectively; $p < .005$). Since dominance was the masculine component positively related to competence, androgyny that follows identification of the

Table 8.9. Average Dominance and Autonomy Scale Scores for Females by Parent Identification Pattern

| Level of Androgyny and Masculine Sex-Role Component | Primary Parent Identification | | | | | | | |
| | Masculine Father | | Feminine Father | | Masculine Mother | | Feminine Mother | |
	N	M	N	M	N	M	N	M
High androgyny	36		18		20		15	
Dominance		58.00		48.67		51.00		44.53
Autonomy		60.14		51.33		57.80		49.67
Low Androgyny	25		11		29		30	
Dominance		50.92		48.55		49.07		41.67
Autonomy		53.20		51.55		49.51		44.00

woman with her masculine father should be more advantageous. No other pattern was associated with dominance of the daughter, although the masculine-mother pattern seemed conductive to a very independent androgynous female, not necessarily an advantage.

Table 8.9's figures do indicate a relation between the gender of the primary identification model and androgyny for the female that had not become apparent before the index was put into use. Identification with the father is more likely to be associated with higher androgyny than lower androgyny (54/36); a mother identification reverses this likelihood (35/59). The proportions differ ($p < .01$), so we can say with some confidence that a cross-sex identification is the more probable contributor to androgyny in the female as it was found to be in the male (Heilbrun, 1978b).

SOCIAL IMPLICATIONS

Readers need not prepare themselves for a review of every research finding reported in this book with extrapolated social significance for each. A few broad themes, some based on the data and some not, will suffice.

One striking feature of our research that emerged with monotonous regularity was the generally more androgynous character of men than women. Men are more feminine than women are masculine. As I remarked in passing early in the book, this should encourage some restraint on the part of those ''men's liberation'' advocates who pursue a course parallel to their ''women's liberation'' counterparts. There really is nothing compelling about an admonition to break out of stereotyped roles if men are not particularly restricted to begin with. It cannot be argued that our data do not apply because of their strictly middle-class origin; I strongly suspect that the effort to free men of their masculine shackles is equally a middle-class phenomenon. Both researchers and social evangelists who wish to realistically pursue the stereotypic plight of the male would find it profitable to shift their attention to the beleaguered lower social class of the inner city. The clearer androgynous character of men to women might very well disappear. The ''male libbers,'' for their part, should find it interesting to explain to the inner-city ghetto dweller why his interests are best served foregoing the ''macho'' role for the rewards of nurturance, sensitivity, and warmth.

Women appear to be more on track when they advocate an expansion of the traditional role assigned to their gender. In the first place, our findings substantiate the more general confinement of women to stereotype than was true for men. In order to achieve sex-role balance, females simply have further to go. Furthermore, androgyny is a desirable goal for women, at least for the young, middle-class women who have been extensively studied. This statement is based on the many empirical findings reported in this book and elsewhere and is not simply a slogan based on personal values, as is true of so many of the conclusions of sex-role books of the 1970s. Again, though, caution in generalization is in order. The more obvious caution derives from the fact that freedom from confinement to the female role is not advantageous or desirable for everyone. For every persuasive advocate of emancipation for women, such as Gloria Steinem, one finds an equally persuasive role conservationist such as Phyllis Schaffley.

Not so obvious, however, is the fact that "freedom from" is sometimes easier to see for most women than is "freedom to." It is not difficult to understand why a role comprised of scrubbing floors, cooking meals, cleaning bathroom fixtures, and changing soiled daipers would not be appealing, but let us not forget two things. First, these have little to do with femininity as we have studied it. They represent a selective listing of functional assignments to females and could be approached with either an instrumental or an expressive orientation. Second, the "freedom to" motif for women is most likely to be voiced by those whose competence is beyond question and for whom opportunities are boundless. One need look no further than the androgyny literature to make this point; those who burst upon the scene in the 1970s with influential ideas about androgyny were female college professors—Carolyn Heilbrun, Sandra Bem, Janet Spence, Jeanne Block, Anne Constantinople, and Judith Worell, to name just some. These brilliant women had already carved out successful careers for themselves and, more likely than not, represent the consummate androgynes. However, what about women without talent, special intelligence, driving ambition, or social opportunity? Certainly most women would be described by one or more of these deficits, as would most men. Are they to be convinced that the opportunity to achieve the status of a shop clerk, waitress, or field worker is their right? It is my opinion that the clearest functional property of the male role in our society, the job, has been seriously oversold. When the benefits of being a male are extolled, it is unlikely that the garbage collector or assembly-line worker will be selected as models. I wonder, when the veil of defensiveness is penetrated, just how many men find their work to be fulfilling except as a required source of income.

It boils down to the fact that the kind of careers from which women have been precluded by their sex—high-status positions in government, business, universities, service professions, and the church—are out of reach of most women anyway simply because they do not have the personal resources to qualify. An unadvertised fact, however, is that most men are unqualified as well. If the rebuttal to this is to be that it is just as important for women to gain the opportunity for a career at any level, I resubmit my opinion that the fulfillment of performing most work roles should not be taken for granted.

Another finding reported in this book that could have many social ramifications is that females tend to blend instrumental and expressive orientations more than males, whereas men sharing both orientations engage in reciprocal display more than women. Put another way, men are more likely to demonstrate instrumental and expressive acts in unadulterated form and women are more likely to mix the two within their actions. This is not necessarily what I expected to find; actually, I thought that women would blend expressive qualities more into their instrumental acts but that men would more likely use their expressive acts in an instrumental way. Since the blending evidence was not very powerful, there is a long way to go before being too firm in our conclusions, but let us take the evidence at hand and see where it takes us.

Given the potential for both instrumental and expressive behavior, should we expect blending or reciprocal display to be the most productive? The conservative answer is yet another question—productive for what? If productive is taken to mean something like the greatest social advantage to all concerned, I would vote for blending. Unadulterated instrumental behavior—gaining personal ends without concern for cost to others—holds little appeal to me and, I suspect, most others. Neither do I find the sacrificial quality of pure expressiveness to have much to commend it. If a person is to commit herself or himself to making others happy, there should be some reason for doing this that transcends the act. While someone who recommends the awarding of ''mother of the year'' or ''wife of the year'' accolades may be accused of being reactionary by contemporary standards, such awards at least represent some measure of goal achievement for women who are thrust into the position of maintaining the quality of family life. Perhaps the suggestion of economic compensation for maintaining such responsibilities within a family context, sometimes mentioned as part of the platform of female liberation, could contribute to this end. I leave the questions of who would pay and who would monitor the quality of these efforts to someone else.

The problems of unadulterated instrumental behavior go far beyond the reaches of the socially recognized competitive arena our research is likely to focus on; goal attainment at work, in the classroom, or on the sporting field at any cost is not the big issue. Political terrorism and many forms of street crime are becoming commonplace and have in common the principle that the end transcends the violence done to a victim. At the most general level, war presents the ultimate instrumental phenomenon, in which the soldier is encouraged to contribute to achieving a common goal by depersonalized destruction of an enemy. It seems little wonder that warfare, terrorism, and violent street crime have been the province of males, who, our research tells us, are more capable of the pure instrumental act.

It is one thing for men and women to believe what they will about the adult roles of the two sexes in contemporary society and to voice alternative views if so persuaded. It is quite another thing for advocates of role revision to prematurely promote child-rearing approaches that are presumed to achieve this developmental goal. The complexities of social engineering are far too great to specify with sufficient certainty how such role behaviors are to be shaped within the family. Let us sample just one of the problems that make prescription hazardous to the child. It is likely that parents will be told that in order to raise their child, boy or girl, free of the restrictions of stereotyped sex roles, parental behavior and teachings should reflect as few sexist behavioral distinctions as possible. I believe current phraseology would describe this approach as an attempt to teach children to be neither masculine nor feminine, but human, If totally successful, this parental philosophy would accomplish two things for the child: (1) it would remove the reward value for learning sex-typed behavior associated with conventional attitudes, and (2) it would avoid the pressures of conforming to social expectancies. The replacement for conventional expectations, such as they are, presumably would fall to some standard such as becoming a better person. While the adult parents may understand and be compelled by such lofty distinctions, something will be lost in translation for the child. Moreover, even more will be lost with the child's peer group, which contributes to sex-role development by its own brand of "boy-type" and "girl-type" behavioral expectations. The clear danger, to me, is that this child-rearing prescription, divorced from sex-typing, will produce undifferentiated rather than androgynous adults, since there will not be sufficient incentives to learn sex-typed behaviors of either type. Kelly and Worrell's (1977) review of the self-esteem literature places undifferentiated status in a very poor light, and the research reported from our own program tends to support this verdict.

It is fitting that this book should end on one of the notes with which it began. Sex roles are multifaceted, and we may talk at cross-purposes about them unless we keep our vocabulary straight. I tried to help in this regard by offering in Chapter One a list of similar-sounding terms that have different meanings to me. Differences were drawn between sex-role behaviors, sex-role functions, and sex-gender cues, and I would like to return to these distinctions in concluding my remarks. *Sex-role behaviors* represent personality attributes expected of one sex or the other by popular convention. These are what this book has been about. *Sex-role functions* include social tasks allocated to men and women, again by convention. Work and the military for males and homemaking and child rearing for females are among the more important tasks for which a division by gender has been maintained. Conventional functions can be fulfilled without any necessary implications for sex-role behavior; one person can work but do the job in a feminine way, whereas another person may maintain a home and be as masculine as the proverbial top sergeant. *Sex-gender cues,* referring to physical, motor, or grooming attributes that denote one's gender and the responses that these cues generate in others, play a central role as far as sex roles are concerned to the extent that they elicit the stereotypes of others and the prejudices that go with them. A woman may elicit prejudice simply because of her gender and without concern for her sex-role behavior or for the social function in question. For example, women who are blonde may be considered dumb whether they are keeping house or are on the job.

These three terms are recalled to your attention to again make the point that the major share of the contemporary struggle for social equality between the sexes has nothing to do with sex-role behavior at all. Feminist issues most often resolve into functional divisioning by sex and discrimination against women based upon gender alone. Similarly, the government-sanctioned countermeasures of redivisioning of functions by gender (equal opportunity) and discrimination against men in favor of women (affirmative action) are largely divorced from the sex-role distinctions we have studied. The extent to which sex-role considerations will become important as reallocation of functions continues and prejudices against both sexes wane is yet to be determined.

REFERENCES

Bandura, A. The self system in reciprocal determinism. *American Psychologist*, 1978, **33**, 344–58.

Bem, S. L. Theory and measurement of androgyny: A reply to the Pedhazur-Tetenbaum and Locksley-Colten critiques. *Journal of Personality and Social Psychology*, 1979, **37**, 1047–54.

Berzins, J. I., Welling, M. A., & Wetter, R. E. A new measure of psychological androgyny based on the Personality Research Form. *Journal of Consulting and Clinical Psychology*, 1978, **46**, 126–38.

Chapin, F. S. Preliminary standardization of a social insight scale. *American Sociological Review*, 1942, **7**, 214–25.

Edwards, K. J. Three dimensions of psychological androgyny and relationships to self-esteem. Paper presented at the annual meeting of the American Psychological Association, Toronto, Canada, August 1978.

Edwards, T. A., Gaa, J. P., & Liberman, D. A factor analysis of the BSRI and the PAQ. Paper presented at the annual meeting of the American Psychological Association, Toronto, Canada, August 1978.

Gaudreau, P. Factor analysis of the Bem Sex-Role Inventory. *Journal of Consulting and Clinical Psychology*, 1977, **45**, 299–302.

Gough, H. G. *Manual for the California Psychological Inventory*. Palo Alto, Calif.: Consulting Psychologists Press, 1957.

Gough, H. G. A validational study of the Chapin Social Insight Test. *Psychological Reports*, 1965, **17**, 355–68.

Gough, H. G., & Heilbrun, A. B. *Manual for the Adjective Check List and the ACL Need Scales.* Palo Alto, Calif.: Consulting Psychologists Press, 1965.

Harrington, D. M., & Anderson, S. M. Creativity, masculinity, femininity, and three models of psychological androgyny. Unpublished manuscript, 1980.

Heilbrun, A. B. Defensive projection in late adolescents: Implications for a developmental model of paranoid behavior. *Child Development*, 1972, **43**, 880–91.

Heilbrun, A. B. The influence of defensive styles upon the predictive validity of the TAT. *Journal of Personality Assessment*, 1977, **41**, 486–91.

Heilbrun, A. B. Projective and repressive styles of processing aversive information. *Journal of Consulting and Clinical Psychology*, 1978, **46**, 156–64. (a)

Heilbrun, A. B. An exploration of antecedents and attributes of androgynous and undifferentiated sex roles. *Journal of Genetic Psychology*, 1978, **132**, 97–107. (b)

Heilbrun, A. B. Androgyny, cognition, and personal competence. Unpublished manuscript, 1980.

Heilbrun, A. B., & Fromme, D. K. Parental identification of late adolescents and level of adjustment: The importance of parent model attributes, ordinal position, and sex of the child. *Journal of Genetic Psychology*, 1965, **107**, 49–59.

Heilbrun, A. B., & Hall, C. L. Resource mediation in childhood and identification. *Journal of Child Psychology and Psychiatry*, 1964, **5**, 139–49.

Heilbrun, A. B., & Schwartz, H. L. Defensive style and performance on objective personality measures. *Journal of Personality Assessment,* 1979, **43,** 517–25.

Heilbrun, A. B., & Schwartz, H. L. Low self-esteem and effective self-reinforcement in male chronic alcoholics: An explanation for a paradox. *Journal of Studies on Alcohol,* in press.

Heilbrun, A. B., & Waters, D. Underachievement as related to perceived maternal childrearing and academic conditions of reinforcement. *Child Development,* 1968, **39,** 913–21.

Jones, W. H., Chernovetz, M. E., & Hansson, R. O. The enigma of androgyny: Differential implications for males and females? *Journal of Consulting and Clinical Psychology,* 1978, **46,** 298–313.

Kelly, J. A., & Worrell, J. New formulations of sex roles and androgyny: A critical review. *Journal of Consulting and Clinical Psychology,* 1977, **45,** 1101–15.

Mischel, W. On the future of personality tests. *American Psychologist,* 1977, **32,** 246–54.

Pearson, J. C. A factor analytic stydy of the items in three selected sex-role instruments. *Psychological Reports,* 1980, **46,** 1119–26.

Pedhazur, E. J., & Tetenbaum, T. J. Bem Sex-Role Inventory: A theoretical and methodological critique. *Journal of Personality and Social Psychology,* 1979, **37,** 996–1016.

Silverman, J. Scanning-control mechanism and "cognitive filtering" in paranoid and nonparanoid schizophrenia. *Journal of Consulting Psychology,* 1964, **28,** 385–93.

Appendix A

Standard Behaviorial Terms Included in the Sex-Role Consistency Measures

Male Form	Female Form
Masculine items:	*Masculine items:*
aggressive	aggressive
assertive	assertive
confident	cynical
cynical	deliberate
deliberate	dominant
dominant	enterprising
forceful	frank
opportunistic	hard-headed
outspoken	self-confident
strong	strong
Feminine items:	*Feminine items:*
contented	considerate
cooperative	dependent
dependent	excitable
excitable	fearful
helpful	fickle
modest	helpful
praising	modest
sentimental	praising
sympathetic	submissive
worrying	worrying

Appendix B

Raw Score to T-Score Conversions:
Male College Norms

	Masculinity Scale					Femininity Scale			
Raw Score	77 or Fewer Items Checked	78-100 Items Checked	101-125 Items Checked	126 or More Items Checked	Raw Score	77 or Fewer Items Checked	78-100 Items Checked	101-125 Items Checked	126 or More Items Checked
28	125	108	95	76					
27	122	105	92	74					
26	118	102	90	72	26	104	140	87	74
25	115	99	87	71	25	101	133	84	72
24	112	96	84	69	24	99	127	81	70
23	109	93	82	67	23	96	121	78	68
22	106	91	79	65	22	93	114	75	66
21	103	88	76	63	21	90	108	72	64
20	100	85	74	61	20	87	101	69	62
19	97	82	71	59	19	84	95	66	60
18	94	79	69	57	18	81	88	62	58
17	90	76	66	56	17	79	82	59	56
16	87	74	63	54	16	76	76	56	54
15	84	71	61	52	15	73	69	53	52
14	81	68	58	50	14	70	63	50	50
13	78	65	55	48	13	67	56	47	48
12	75	62	53	46	12	64	50	44	46
11	72	59	50	44	11	61	44	41	44

Appendix B continued

	Masculinity Scale					Femininity Scale			
Raw Score	77 or Fewer Items Checked	78–100 Items Checked	101–125 Items Checked	126 or More Items Checked	Raw Score	77 or Fewer Items Checked	78–100 Items Checked	101–125 Items Checked	126 or More Items Checked
10	69	56	47	43	10	59	37	38	42
9	66	53	45	41	9	56	31	34	40
8	62	50	42	39	8	53	24	31	38
7	59	47	39	37	7	50	18	28	36
6	56	44	37	35	6	47	12	25	34
5	53	42	34	33	5	44	5	22	32
4	50	39	31	31	4	41	0	19	30
3	47	36	29	29	3	39		16	28
2	44	33	26	28	2	36		13	26
1	41	30	24	26	1	33		9	24
0	38	27	21	24	0	30		6	22

Appendix C

Raw Score to T-Score Conversions:
Female College Norms

Masculinity Scale

Raw Score	75 or Fewer Items Checked	76-99 Items Checked	100-123 Items Checked	124 or More Items Checked
28	184	123	116	88
27	179	120	113	86
26	174	117	110	83
25	168	113	107	81
24	163	110	103	79
23	158	107	100	77
22	152	104	97	75
21	147	101	94	73
20	141	98	91	71
19	136	94	88	69
18	131	91	85	67
17	125	88	81	65
16	120	85	78	63
15	115	82	75	60
14	109	79	72	58
13	104	75	69	56
12	98	72	66	54
11	93	69	63	52

Femininity Scale

Raw Score	75 or Fewer Items Checked	76-99 Items Checked	100-123 Items Checked	124 or More Items Checked
26	98	86	89	66
25	95	83	85	64
24	92	80	81	63
23	89	77	76	61
22	86	74	72	59
21	83	71	67	57
20	80	68	63	55
19	77	65	59	54
18	74	62	54	52
17	71	59	50	50
16	68	56	46	48
15	65	53	41	46
14	62	50	37	45
13	59	47	33	43
12	56	44	28	41
11	53	41	24	39

Appendix C continued

	Masculinity Scale					Femininity Scale			
Raw Score	75 or Fewer Items Checked	76-99 Items Checked	100-123 Items Checked	124 or More Items Checked	Raw Score	75 or Fewer Items Checked	76-99 Items Checked	100-123 Items Checked	124 or More Items Checked
10	88	66	59	50	10	50	38	19	37
9	82	63	56	48	9	47	35	15	36
8	77	60	53	46	8	41	32	11	34
7	72	56	50	44	7	41	29	6	32
6	66	53	47	42	6	38	26	2	30
5	61	50	44	40	5	35	23	0	28
4	55	47	41	37	4	32	20		27
3	50	44	37	35	3	29	17		25
2	45	40	34	33	2	26	14		23
1	39	37	31	31	1	23	12		21
0	34	34	28	29	0	20	9		19

Author Index

Anderson, S. M., 184

Bakan, D., 88
Bales, R. F., 43, 53, 88, 141
Bandura, A., 133, 134, 168
Bateman, C. P., 157
Baucom, D. H., 29, 41, 53, 57, 60, 68, 121
Bee, H., 35, 17, 55
Bem, S. L., 17, 30, 42, 49, 50, 53, 54, 65, 66, 68, 72, 76, 88, 181, 185
Berzins, J. I. 30, 185
Best, D. L., 7, 8, 9, 20, 21, 27
Block, J., 14, 26, 27, 29, 72, 115
Block, J. H., 22, 30, 31, 43, 68
Bowden, J. D., 66, 74
Bronfenbrenner, U., 134
Broverman, D. M., 17, 55
Broverman, I. K., 17, 55
Brown, D. G., 22, 67
Bruner, P. B., 15

Carlson, R., 30
Cartwright, R., 26
Caudill, M. S., 49, 77
Chang, J., 14, 115
Chapin, F. S., 172, 173, 174
Chernovetz, E. O'C., 87, 93, 181
Constantinople, A., 30, 38, 40, 52
Cosentino, F., 13, 61

Edwards, A. L., 135
Edwards, D. A., 14, 71, 115, 117
Edwards, K. J., 55, 185
Edwards, N. L., 148
Edwards, T. A., 55, 185
Erikson, E. H., 25, 26, 72
Evans, R. B., 14, 115

Fand, A. B., 14, 147, 148
Ferracuti, F., 115
Firestone, S., 67
Ford, W., 60
Fox, D. J., 31, 66
Friedman, A. F., 66, 74
Fromme, D. K., 134, 139, 181
Furman, W., 15

Gaa, J. P., 56, 185
Gaudreau, P., 185
Goodstein, L. D., 50
Gough, H. G., 5, 9, 10, 12, 17, 20, 21, 41, 51, 57, 60, 121, 122, 135, 172, 173, 185, 186
Grambs, J. D., ix, 31, 66
Green, R., 67
Greenberg, S., 31, 66

Hall, C. L., 180
Hall, W., 60, 122
Hansson, R. O., 87, 93, 181
Harrington, D. M., 184
Hathorn, S., 49, 77
Heilbrun, A. B., 5, 10, 13, 14, 15, 21, 26, 28, 29, 30, 33, 41, 44, 50, 51, 52, 53, 60, 61, 64, 66, 69, 71, 72, 73, 74, 76, 77, 84, 87, 99, 116, 117, 118, 132, 134, 135, 137, 138, 139, 141, 143, 144, 146, 147, 148, 149, 152, 155, 157, 158, 163, 164, 169, 172, 175, 180, 181, 185, 186, 188
Heilbrun, C., 30
Heilbrun, K. L., 157
Helmreich, R., 14, 17, 30, 31, 42, 43, 49, 52, 53, 55, 56, 65, 88, 129, 130
Herson, A. M., 157
Holzmuller, A., 15, 61
Horner, M. S., 147, 149

Jacklin, C. N., 156
James, W., 143
Johnson, M. M., 22, 141, 142, 157
Jones, W. H., 87, 93, 181

Kagan, J., 15
Kanner, A. D., 30
Kelly, J. A., 15, 30, 49, 65, 66, 74, 77, 86, 89, 93, 193
Kleemeier, C., 146, 152, 155
Kogan, N., 15

Lair, C. V., 26
Landauer, S. P., 158
Liberman, D., 56, 185
Lynn, D. B., 67

Maccoby, E. E., 156
Matteson, D. R., 31, 66
McCandless, B. R., 14, 23, 71, 115, 116
Meltzer, M. L., 26
Mischel, W., 40, 168
Murray, H. A., 61, 135

Nideffer, R., 178, 179

Oakley, A., 31, 66
O'Brien, C. G., 49, 77

Parker, G. V. C., 9, 10, 12, 13
Parsons, T., 43, 53, 88, 141
Pearson, J. C., 185
Pedhazur, E. J., 185
Piccola, G., 146, 152, 155
Pitman, D., 28, 33, 44, 72, 74, 76, 84
Pleck, J. H., 31, 66

Rosenkrantz, P. S., 17, 55
Ross, D., 133, 134
Ross, S. A., 133, 134
Ruffalo, C., 39

Sasek, J., 66, 74
Sawyer, J., 31, 66
Schaffley, P., 190
Schwartz, D. M., 14, 71, 115, 116
Schwartz, H., 69, 73, 77, 175
Sears, R. R., 13, 67
Siegel, S., 27
Silverman, J., 178
Sopchak, A. L., 135
Spence, J. T., 8, 14, 17, 30, 31, 42, 43, 49, 52, 53, 55, 56, 65, 88, 129, 130
Stapp, J., 14, 17, 30, 31, 42, 43, 49, 52, 53, 55, 56, 65, 88, 129, 130
Steinem, G., 190
Steinman, A., 31, 66
Stephan, W. D., 115
Strong, E. K., Jr., 15, 139, 140

Tetenbaum, T. J., 185
Thompson, N. L., Jr., 14, 23, 71, 115, 116, 117, 118, 163, 164

Van Buren, J. H., 55
Vogel, S. R., 17, 55

Waetjen, W. B., ix, 31, 66
Wakefield, J. A., Jr., 66, 74
Waters, D., 181
Weller, P., 116, 129
Welling, M. A., 30, 185
Wetter, R. E., 30, 185
Whitehurst, C. A., 66
Wiggins, J. S., 15, 61
Williams, J. E., 7, 8, 9, 20, 27
Wolfgang, M. E., 115
Worell, J., 30, 49, 65, 66, 74, 77, 86, 89, 93, 193

Yorburg, B., 66
Young, V., 15

Zabriskie, F. C., 55
Zimet, C. N., 8
Zimet, S. G., 8

Subject Index

Adjective Check List, and factor analysis of sex-role scales, 184-185
general description of, 5-6
Intraception Scale for, 171-172
parent identification scoring procedures for, 135-138
varying sex-role scaling procedures for, 9-13
Androgyny, and contribution of parent identification and behavioral differentiation, 181-184
and criminal behavior, 123-125
and defensiveness, 176-177
female parent identification and sex-role components in, 188-190
and homosexuality, 118-120
measured as a continuous index, 38, 44-45, 74
measured by four-fold typology, 43-44
and personal competence, 30-31, 64-66, 89-91, 108-113, 190-191
and rape, 123-125
and self-esteem, 94-95
sex differences in, 67-75
and sex-role blending, 76-78, 80-84, 112-113
and sex-role flexibility, 71-72
and social cognition, 174
transnational differences in, 129-130
Articulation versus fluency in self-description, 45-47, 182-183
Attentional styles, 177-181
Baucom MSC and FMN Scales, 41, 57-60, 68, 121-124
Bem Sex-Role Inventory, 16, 41, 49, 53-54, 68, 185
Chapin Test of Social Insight, 172-174
Criminal behavior and sex-role status, 121-125

Expressive behavior, definition of, 3
Fear of success, 149-150
Female identification paradox, and the "double-standard" hypothesis, 155-163
and the sex-gender identification hypothesis, 145-155
and the transmutation hypothesis, 156-163
Femininity, and age differences, 2
Femininity Scale, development of, 6-7, 60-62
and dissimulation, 21-22, 50-52
and expressive behavior, 6-8
and favorability of items, 20-21
relation to Masculinity Scale, 41-43
relations with other popular scales, 16
validity of, 13-16
Field independence, 15
Future trends in sex-role research, antecedent value of parent-identification correlates, 177-184
considering the multifactorial nature of sex roles, 184-190
contribution of cognitive mediators, 168-177
parent identification, behavior differentiation, and androgyny, 181-184
Homosexuality, and sex-gender identification, 163-165
and sex-role status, 67, 116-120
Independent versus common sex-role norms, 47-48, 74-75
Instrumental behavior, definition of, 3
Masculinity, and age differences, 25
and the favored-role myth, 19-22
and the inflexible-role myth, 22-29

Masculinity-Femininity Scale, validity of, 13-16
Masculinity Scale, development of, 6, 60-62
  and dissimulation, 21-22, 50-53
  and favorability of items, 20-21
  and instrumental behavior, 6
  relation to Femininity Scale, 41-43
  relations with other popular sex-role scales, 16
  validity of, 13-16
Parent model score, 137-138, 154-155
Parent identification, and attentional styles, 179-181
  and behavioral differentiation in androgyny, 181-184
  conceptual issues in, 132-133
  definition of, 132
  and the female identification paradox, 141-163
  and filial adjustment, 138-141
  measurement of, 133-138
  and sex-role components in female androgyny, 188-190
  and the successive-identification hypothesis, 68
  and vicarious experience, 143-155
Personal Attributes Questionnaire, 16, 49, 55-59, 65, 69, 129-130, 185
Personality Research Form—ANDRO, 16, 185
Prostitution and sex-gender identification, 165
Role conformity, and cultural sanctions, 22-23, 67
Role systems, 1-2
Sex-gender identification, definition of, 4

and fear of success, 149-150
and level of masculinity in daughters, 148-149, 154-155
and paradoxical father identification in the daughter, 145-155
Sex-gender identity, definition of, 4
Sex-gender preference, definition of, 4
Sex-role behaviors, definition of, 2-3, 4
  independence of, 29-31, 40-43
  measurement of consistency, 26-29, 72
  specific adaptive values of, 94-99
Sex-role blending, 76-84, 112-113, 191-192
Sex-role correlates, 2-3, 4
Sex-role functions, 3, 4
Sex-role identity, definition of, 4
Sex-role preference, definition of, 4
Sex-role stereotype, definition of, 4
  and Masculinity Scale and Femininity Scale composition, 8-9
Sex roles, and criminal behavior, 121-125
  and defensiveness, 174-177
  factor components of, 184-190
  and ratio of masculine to feminine attributes, 109-112
  and personal effectiveness, 91-94
  and psychological problems, 99-108
  racial differences in, 129-130
  regional differences in, 125-129
  and self-esteem, 87-90, 170-171
  and social cognition, 171-174
  and social desirability, 49-53
  transnational differences in, 129-131
Transsexualism and sex-role behavior, 67
Undifferentiation, 30
Women's role, attitudes toward, 14

About the Author

Alfred B. Heilbrun, Jr., is Professor of Psychology at Emory University, Atlanta. He was previously Assistant and then Associate Professor at the University of Iowa and Visiting Associate Professor at the University of California, Berkeley. Dr. Heilbrun received a Ph.D. degree in psychology at the University of Iowa. For many years he has maintained active research programs in the areas of sex roles and parent identification, parent-child antecedents to psychopathology, cognitive factors in alcoholism, criminal behavior, psychotherapy outcome and process, and, most recently, in cognitive styles as personality variables.

Pergamon General Psychology Series

Editors: Arnold P. Goldstein, Syracuse University
Leonard Krasner, SUNY, Stony Brook

Vol. 1. WOLPE—*The Practice of Behavior Therapy, Second Edition*
Vol. 2. MAGOON et al—*Mental Health Conselors at Work*
Vol. 3. McDANIEL—*Physical Disability and Human Behavior, Second Edition*
Vol. 4. KAPLAN et al—*The Structural Approach in Psychological Testing*
Vol. 5. LaFAUCI & RICHTER—*Team Teaching at the College Level*
Vol. 6. PEPINSKY et al—*People and Information*
Vol. 7. SIEGMAN & POPE—*Studies in Dyadic Communication*
Vol. 8. JOHNSON—*Existential Man: The Challenge of Psychotherapy*
Vol. 9. TAYLOR—*Climate for Creativity*
Vol. 10. RICKARD—*Behavioral Intervention in Human Problems*
Vol. 14. GOLDSTEIN—*Psychotherapeutic Attraction*
Vol. 15. HALPERN—*Survival: Black/White*
Vol. 16. SALZINGER & FELDMAN—*Studies in Verbal Behavior: An Empirical Approach*
Vol. 17. ADAMS & BOARDMAN—*Advances in Experimental Clinical Psychology*
Vol. 18. ZILLER—*The Social Self*
Vol. 19. LIBERMAN—*A Guide to Behavioral Analysis & Therapy*
Vol. 22. PEPINSKY & PATTON—*The Psychological Experiment: A Practical Accomplishment.*
Vol. 23. YOUNG—*New Sources of Self*
Vol. 24. WATSON—*Child Behavior Modification: A Manual for Teachers, Nurses, and Parents*
Vol. 25. NEWBOLD—*The Psychiatric Programming of People: Neo-Behavioral Orthomolecular Psychiatry*
Vol. 26. ROSSI—*Dreams and the Growth of Personality: Expanding Awareness in Psychotherapy*
Vol. 27. O'LEARY & O'LEARY—*Classroom Management: The Successful Use of Behavior Modification, Second Edition*
Vol. 28. FELDMAN—*College and Student: Selected Readings in the Social Psychology of Higher Education*
Vol. 29. ASHEM & POSER—*Adaptive Learning: Behavior Modification with Children*
Vol. 30. BURCK et al—*Counseling and Accountability: Methods and Critique*
Vol. 31. FREDERIKSEN et al—*Prediction of Organizational Behavior*
Vol. 32. CATTELL—*A New Morality from Science: Beyondism*
Vol. 33. WEINER—*Personality: The Human Potential*
Vol. 34. LIEBERT, NEALE & DAVIDSON—*The Early Window: Effects of Television on Children and Youth*
Vol. 35. COHEN et al—*Psych City: A Simulated Community*
Vol. 36. GRAZIANO—*Child Without Tomorrow*
Vol. 37. MORRIS—*Perspectives in Abnormal Behavior*

Vol. 38. BALLER—*Bed Wetting: Origins and Treatment*
Vol. 40. KAHN, CAMERON, & GIFFEN—*Psychological Methods in Evaluation and Counseling*
Vol. 41. SEGALL—*Human Behavior and Public Policy: A Political Psychology*
Vol. 42. FAIRWEATHER *et al*—*Creating Change in Mental Health Organizations*
Vol. 43. KATZ & ZLUTNICK—*Behavior Therapy and Health Care: Principles and Applications*
Vol. 44. EVANS & CLAIBORN—*Mental Health Issues and the Urban Poor*
Vol. 45. HILLNER—*Psychology of Learning: A Conceptual Approach*
Vol. 46. BARBER, SPANOS & CHAVES—*Hypnosis, Imagination and Human Potentialities*
Vol. 47. POPE—*The Mental Health Interview*
Vol. 48. PELTON—*The Psychology of Nonviolence*
Vol. 49. COLBY—*Artificial Paranoia—A Computer Simulation of Paranoid Processes*
Vol. 50. GELFAND & HARTMANN—*Child Behavior Analysis and Therapy*
Vol. 51. WOLPE—*Theme and Variations: A Behavior Therapy Casebook*
Vol. 52. KANFER & GOLDSTEIN—*Helping People Change: A Textbook of Methods, Second Edition*
Vol. 53. DANZIGER—*Interpersonal Communication*
Vol. 54. KATZ—*Towards the Elimination of Racism*
Vol. 55. GOLDSTEIN & STEIN—*Prescriptive Psychotherapies*
Vol. 56. HERSEN & BARLOW—*Single-Case Experimental Designs: Strategies for Studying Behavior Changes*
Vol. 57. MONAHAN—*Community Mental Health and the Criminal Justice System*
Vol. 58. WAHLER, HOUSE & STAMBAUGH—*Ecological Assessment of Child Behavior: A Clinical Package for Home, School, and Institutional Settings*
Vol. 59. MAGARO—*The Construction of Madness—Emerging Conceptions and Interventions into the Psychotic Process*
Vol. 60. MILLER—*Behavioral Treatments of Alcoholism*
Vol. 61. FOREYT—*Behavioral Treatments of Obesity*
Vol. 62. WANDERSMAN, POPPEN & RICKS—*Humanism and Behaviorism: Dialogue and Growth*
Vol. 63. NIETZEL, WINETT, MACDONALD & DAVIDSON—*Behavioral Approaches to Community Psychology*
Vol. 64. FISHER & GOCHROS—*Handbook of Behavior Therapy with Sexual Problems. Vol. I: General Procedures. Vol. II: Approaches to Specific Problems*
Vol. 65. HERSEN & BELLACK—*Behavioral Assessment: A Practical Handbook, Second Edition*
Vol. 66. LEFKOWITZ, ERON, WALDER & HUESMANN—*Growing Up To Be Violent: A Longitudinal Study of the Development of Aggression*
Vol. 67. BARBER—*Pitfalls in Human Research: Ten Pivotal Points*
Vol. 68. SILVERMAN—*The Human Subject in the Psychological Laboratory*

Vol. 69. FAIRWEATHER & TORNATZKY—*Experimental Methods for Social Policy Research*

Vol. 70. GURMAN & RAZIN—*Effective Psychotherapy: A Handbook of Research*

Vol. 71. MOSES & BYHAM—*Applying the Assessment Center Method*

Vol. 72. GOLDSTEIN—*Prescriptions for Child Mental Health and Education*

Vol. 73. KEAT—*Multimodal Therapy with Children*

Vol. 74. SHERMAN—*Personality: Inquiry & Application*

Vol. 75. GATCHEL & PRICE—*Clinical Applications of Biofeedback: Appraisal and Status*

Vol. 76. CATALANO—*Health, Behavior and the Community: An Ecological Perspective*

Vol. 77. NIETZEL—*Crime and Its Modification: A Social Learning Perspective*

Vol. 78. GOLDSTEIN, HOYER & MONTI—*Police and the Elderly*

Vol. 79. MIRON & GOLDSTEIN—*Hostage*

Vol. 80. GOLDSTEIN et al—*Police Crisis Intervention*

Vol. 81. UPPER & CAUTELA—*Covert Conditioning*

Vol. 82. MORELL—*Program Evaluation in Social Research*

Vol. 83. TEGER—*Too Much Invested to Quit*

Vol. 84. MONJAN & GASSNER—*Critical Issues in Competency-Based Education*

Vol. 85. KRASNER—*Environmental Design and Human Behavior*

Vol. 86. TAMIR—*Communication and the Aging Process*

Vol. 87. WEBSTER, KONSTANTAREAS, OXMAN & MACK—*Autism*

Vol. 88. TRIESCHMAN—*Spinal Cord Injuries*

Vol. 89. DUHL & BOER—*Making Whole: Health for a New Epoch*

Vol. 90. SARBIN & MANCUSO—*Schizophrenia: Medical Diagnosis or Moral Verdict?*

Vol. 91. RATHJEN & FOREYT—*Social Competence: Interventions for Children and Adults*

Vol. 92. VAN DE RIET, KORB & GORRELL—*Gestalt Therapy An Introduction*

Vol. 93. MARSELLA & PEDERSEN—*Cross-Cultural Counseling and Psychotherapy*

Vol. 94. BRISLIN—*Cross-Cultural Encounters: Face-to-Face Interaction*

Vol. 95. SCHWARTZ & JOHNSON—*Psychopathology of Childhood: A Clinical-Experimental Approach*

Vol. 96. HEILBRUN—Human Sex-Role Behavior

Vol. 97. DAVIDSON, KOCH, LEWIS, WRESINSKI—*Evaluation Strategies in Criminal Justice*

Vol. 98. GOLDSTEIN, CARR, DAVIDSON, WEHR—*In Response to Aggression: Methods of Control and Prosocial Alternatives*